AN UNLIKELY PRINCE

AN UNLIKELY PRINCE

The Life and Times of Machiavelli

Niccolò Capponi

Da Capo Press

A MEMBER OF THE PERSEUS BOOKS GROUP

Designed by Timm Bryson
Set in 11 point Arno Pro by the Perseus Books Group

Library of Congress Cataloging-in-Publication Data
Capponi, Niccolo.
    An unlikely prince : the life and the times of Niccolo Machiavelli / Niccolo Capponi.
        p. cm.
    Includes bibliographical references and index.
    ISBN 978-0-306-81756-4 (alk. paper)
    1. Machiavelli, Niccolò, 1469-1527. 2. Florence (Italy)—Politics and government—1421-1737. 3. Republicanism—Italy—Florence—History—16th century. I. Title.
    JC143.M4C28 2010
    320.1092—dc22
    [B]
                            2010003962

Published by Da Capo Press
A Member of the Perseus Books Group
www.dacapopress.com

Da Capo Press books are available at special discounts for bulk purchases in the U.S. by corporations, institutions, and other organizations. For more information, please contact the Special Markets Department at the Perseus Books Group, 2300 Chestnut Street, Suite 200, Philadelphia, PA 19103, or call (800) 810-4145, ext. 5000, or e-mail special.markets@perseusbooks.com.

10 9 8 7 6 5 4 3 2 1

CONTENTS

NOTES ON TERMINOLOGY

For the sake of clarity, throughout the book I have used the terms "Republic" and "Republican" to indicate the Florentine constitutional settlement and its followers after 1494. Technically, however, Florence had been a republic even before that date, and it continued to be one until 1737, even when the Medici became the city's institutional and hereditary rulers after 1532.

TIME

In the sixteenth century the Italians followed a system of telling time based not on the rotation of the earth but on the hours of daylight. For example, two o'clock in the morning would be the second hour after sunset. In addition, different dates were used to mark the start of the new year throughout the period. The calendar in Italy most commonly began on December 25 (commemorating the birth of Christ) or March 25 (commemorating Christ's incarnation), the latter being the Florentine usage until 1750. For practical reasons I have used the modern rendering throughout this book, with the year starting on January 1.

CURRENCY AND PRICES

The standard Florentine currency was the florin (*fiorino*), together with its subdivisions, dating back to the time of Charlemagne, of the *lira*, the *soldo*, and the *denaro* (1 lira = 20 soldi; 1 soldo = 12 denari). In Machiavelli's days the standard "broad florin" (*fiorino largo*) was worth 6 or 7 lire, the latter value becoming stable around 1515. The Venetian ducat, at the time the international coinage of reference, more or less equaled the fiorino largo. In addition, there existed the gold florin (*fiorino largo d'oro*), valued about 7½ lire in 1520 and, like the lira and the "sealed florin" (*fiorino di suggello*), used as a unit of account. The sealed florin was equal to 4 lire, and in a letter of 1505, Totto Machiavelli mentions that 3 sealed florins were worth 2 gold ducats.

On average during this period, a typical laborer earned about 8 soldi a day, and a skilled worker twice that sum. There were approximately 260 working days a year, and numerous holidays—Sundays aside—constantly interrupting the rhythms of labor. The cost of living varied according to the availability of certain goods; for instance, food prices soared in times of want and dropped in times of plenty. However, until chronic price inflation began to occur in around 1525, an adult needed roughly 1.5 to 2 soldi a day for food, while the yearly expenditures for all the necessities of life, food included, totaled around 65 lire per person.

Of course, some people spent well beyond that, and once Machiavelli admitted to squandering 14 soldi for a veal dinner for four at a friend's house—indeed, Niccolò had a pronounced tendency to live beyond his means. For many, extraordinary expenses always seemed to be lurking just around the corner, and when they did appear they could be crippling, particularly in the event, for example, of a prolonged illness. At the time of his wife's final infirmity, Machiavelli's friend and chancery colleague Biagio Buonaccorsi admitted to spending just under a florin a day for her medical care. The cost of giving a daughter away in marriage could also be considerable, and sending one to a nunnery could also be expensive. Even poor religious houses asked for a substantial monetary contribution, 100 lire not being uncommon. Perhaps the thirteenth-century poet Cecco Angiolieri was correct when he described florins to be "the best of kin."

PREFACE

Those who arrive in Florence by train may decide not to take a taxi but instead enjoy a leisurely stroll to their final destination. Coasting the gothic-style Dominican convent of Santa Maria Novella, one goes down the via Panzani, and then via Cerretani to the Duomo. Should the imaginary visitor then decide to go north, he will hit the old Medici palace on the via Larga (now via Cavour), and maybe drop in to admire the apotheosis of the once-powerful family fixed in the fresco cycle by Benozzo Gozzoli.

But usually people prefer to proceed along the crowded via Calzaioli, tarted up in the nineteenth century when most of Florence's ancient center fell under the pickax of Piedmontese goatherds, whose lack of artistic and historical sensibility makes barbarians of old look a rather civilized and cultivated lot. Even the piazza Signoria, at the end of the above-mentioned road, has been affected by such philistinism, a behemoth of a fake fifteenth-century edifice casting its shadow on the beautiful Medieval and Renaissance monuments in the square.

Matters only get worse on the via Porsantamaria, where the destructions of World War II have been underscored by the vandalism of the post-conflict rebuilding. Only the few old towers left remind us of the area's original flavor. The Ponte Vecchio at the end of the street is still standing, as the Wermacht troops—with impeccable, if distorted, military rationale—preferred instead to demolish the houses at both ends of the bridge in order to deny access to it. Yet, as tragic as the gutting of the Ponte would have been, it could have been rebuilt like the other bridges on the river Arno; but artistic treasures ten times as precious are now lost forever for the sake of its survival. "Florence recomposed herself with the same grace of a lady interrupted by a bomb while sipping tea," the poet Cristina Campo would write. But the dame's impassivity could not hide the scars the exploding shrapnel had left in her body.

Crossing the bridge and entering the via Guicciardini, one passes on the left the former monastery of Santa Felicita, home of one of the great masterpieces of all times: the *Deposition* by the maverick painter Jacopo Pontormo, still largely unaffected by the crowds of trippers unloaded by human fishbowls on wheels. A few yards ahead, a plaque on a house, seldom graced by the look of those passing by, tells us that there once lived one of the prophets of united Italy, the first to theorize its freedom by means of a citizen's army. Not surprisingly, the inscription bears the date 1869, when certain attitudes were quite fashionable in the whole of the Western world. One wonders if the object of the dedication would have shared such gushing rhetoric, but certainly not recognized the wall supporting it—the original house, like most of those in the via Guicciardini, being reduced to dust by German mines on August 4, 1944.

Like Florence, Niccolò Machiavelli—who once lived in the building—has in turn been demolished, rebuilt, altered, and repainted, suffering from the ravages of time and of humans. And, once more, akin to what has happened to the city, his dust has been turned into something scarcely recognizable.

In his book *The Military Revolution: Military Innovation and the Rise of the West*, historian Geoffrey Parker cites the case of an engineer who in 1722 wrote a treatise criticizing some 118 methods of fortification described by some seventy authors, providing then his own solution (the 119th). A similar fate appears to have befallen Machiavelli. Everyone who tackles him has to give a novel interpretation of his life and works, and over the centuries Niccolò has been turned into a tug-of-war for the most diverse analysis. From the very beginning Machiavelli became an enclosed hunting ground for critics, and it is thanks to them that he has turned into a character transcending time and physical boundaries: the first political scientist, the first modern philosopher, etcetera. By these standards he could also win the prize for first modern playwright, the first to prove with his personal history that theory is not the same as practice, and the first in fooling generations of commentators.

In the quest to find the "true" Machiavelli, a lot of writers have tried to make sense of the man and his works, and as a result Niccolò has become a sort of amoebic being: an Imperialist; a proto-libertarian; an atheist; a neo-pagan; a committed Christian, a freedom-loving Republican; a tutor to despots; a military genius; an armchair strategist; a realist; an idealist; and the shady founder of modern political science. Therefore it is rather heartwarming to discover that a lot of Machiavelli's contemporaries considered him something of a deluded crank and most of his ideas of little practical use. When people use the hackneyed and quite ridiculous term "modern" to describe Niccolò, they demonstrate not only a definite anachronistic approach to the subject, but also rather less wisdom than Machiavelli's own contemporaries.

In reality Niccolò was a complex figure, and trying to pin him down can have the same effect as eating a hot dog: You bite it on one end, and everything inside shoots out from the other. Moreover, any attempt to find some sort of consistency in his thought and actions has to take into consideration that he, like most of us, changed his ideas over time, or adapted them to fit certain circumstances. Also, one must remember that Machiavelli had in him all the traits typical of the Florentines of his day (and even of today): love of contradiction, provocation, and *bella figura*, with a pronounced jocular streak as seasoning.

Certainly, he appears to have possessed all of the above in an exaggerated form, and this eccentricity caused him at one time or other more than one problem. For one, only late in life did he learn how to behave "politically," after going through some very unpleasant experiences. Given all this, it is somewhat ironic that for the general public Niccolò's fame rests on *The Prince*, a work he wrote in a very precise moment of his life and for a very specific reason: to gain favor with the Medici rulers of Florence. Indeed, the book's negative reception would force him to try to find some pretty lame excuses for composing it in the first place.

For this reason I have developed something of a soft spot for Niccolò—not so much for the depth of his thinking, but rather for his personal, and very human, traits. Besides, I can relate to his sense of humor, as shocking as it may appear to those not born and bred in Florence. Indeed, the city itself is one of the protagonists of this book; not so much its art and culture, but instead that same peculiar spirit and attitude that pervaded—and still pervades—the place and that few outsiders appreciate or understand. During my lifetime I have not only met a number of Machiavelli, Francesco Guicciardini, Francesco Vettori, and other characters who appear in this work, but also witnessed the same civic behavior—or rather, lack thereof—described by Niccolò and his contemporaries.

Solitude and Machiavelli himself have been my companions while writing this book, Old Nick's grin being intermixed with my keyboard. In the time spent alone brooding over documents written or dictated by Niccolò, I have come to get a sense of his mind frame—as much as possible, of course, given what I mentioned before. As for secondary sources, I have gotten both pleasure and benefit from most of the vast literature on the subject, although some studies, well argued as they might be, have proven largely irrelevant. Actually, more than one erudite dissection of Machiavelli's writings gave me the distinct impression of the authors wondering adrift in some locality placed deeply within their own posterior orifices. And yet, the nature of this particular beast implies that any historical document, no matter how important, from an unknown individual will usually get relegated to a footnote, while an unpublished, undated, and anonymous *saluti e baci* ("greetings and kisses") by Machiavelli is gifted with a scholarly article.

Not that this is necessarily wrong, given the considerable documentary gaps existing in Niccolò's life. Every now and then researchers hit on an unknown piece of evidence, allowing us to make better sense of certain events, thoughts, or writings pertaining to Machiavelli. Sometimes the desire for new finds produces unfortunate results. A number of years ago a distinguished scholar published a book in which he claimed, on the basis of extensive archival research, that in the late 1480s and the best part of the 1490s Niccolò Machiavelli had busied himself as a banker in Rome. The work received some very positive reviews, until another distinguished scholar, with a display of both critical capacity and typical Florentine mischievousness, published an article proving that the Machiavelli in question happened to be not the more famous Niccolò, but instead his cousin and namesake.

Although preferring to rely on my own devices when researching and writing this book, there are a few people I wish to thank for their help. With Professor William Connell I've had many enjoyable and illuminating conversations; Professor Humfrey Butters first warned me about the traps I would most likely encounter on my path; Dr. Brooke Ettle constantly reminded me about looking at the forest, not the trees; the late, great Professor Gioacchino Gargallo di Castel Lentini displayed an uncanny knack for history; Dr. Mary Davidson, as always, has proven a veritable fountain of knowledge; Robert Pigeon of Da Capo Press showed patience and understanding; Renee Caputo, also of Da Capo Press, displayed a fortitude worthy of Job, in the face of my (many) last minute changes to the text; and Dr. Marco Manetti helped me to comprehend Machiavelli like no one else. Count Piero Guicciardini generously allowed me to see the papers of his ancestor Francesco. The staff of the Archivio di Stato di Firenze, the Biblioteca Riccardiana, and the Biblioteca Nazionale Centrale di Firenze provided constant help along the way.

My immense gratitude goes to my family, my daughters Francesca and Ludovica, and in a very special way to my wife, Maria, for her love and her knowledge of sixteenth-century Italian. Finally, I would like to remember my several-times great grandfather Niccolò Machiavelli, not just for his company, but also because, thanks to him (too long a story, however, to be included), my family received the right to have Mass said when and how it so desired—and I'm sure that the thought is making Old Nick, wherever his present abode, roll on the floor with laughter.

FLORENCE, MARCH 28, 2010

Italy in 1500

PROLOGUE

On the evening of December 10, 1513, a man could be seen walking on the road leading to a small country manor at Sant'Andrea
in Percussina, six miles from the city of Florence. One could clearly hear
the commotion coming from the nearby inn, where the former secretary
of the Florentine Republic, Niccolò Machiavelli, had loafed around for
hours playing cards and backgammon with some of the locals. He had
done the same practically every day, ever since he had voluntarily left
Florence the previous spring for the politically safer environment of
Sant'Andrea. Gambling with the country folk could be enjoyable, allowing him to keep his mind from his present woes even when, as often happened, the playing sessions ended in insult matches over as little as a
penny, and it was said that the inhabitants of San Casciano, three miles
away, could hear the shouting.

As he approached his home Machiavelli could see in the fading light
the distant silhouette of the great dome of Florence's cathedral—one of
the architectural masterpieces of all time. Little more than a year before,
he had been a powerful player in Florence's politics, the man who handled

some of the Republic's most important affairs with adroitness and skill. The return to power of the Medici family had brought his career to a crashing halt, and the goddess Fortune had turned her back on him. Ousted from his job and under suspicion by the new regime for his association with the old one, the once influential Niccolò had been implicated in an anti-Medici plot, arrested, and tortured.

The painful effects of the *strappado* still lingered in his mind, and he dared not return to Florence before things quieted down a bit. Once back in the city he inevitably would come into contact with his former colleagues in the Republican government—a potentially dangerous situation, since the Medici regime was always ready to link such social gatherings with plots against the ruling family. Luckily, and despite his forced exile in the country, he still managed to keep in touch with current Florentine events from the couriers and travelers who every day passed Sant'Andrea on their road south. At the right moment, he would return to Florence—but not before finishing a certain task, which he hoped would make him carry favor with the Medici.

He entered the house and went to his private chamber. The everyday clothes were dusty and dirty after a day passed walking through the fields and sitting on greasy tavern furniture: not the right garments for meeting certain people, those who every evening waited to receive him in a manner that befitted his status and intellect. Carefully donning his curial robes, Niccolò sat at his writing desk. He did not feel alone, for in that same room he perceived the presence of the great men of antiquity. He often imagined having conversations with them, listening carefully to their courteous replies to his many questions. They were a constant source of inspiration while he sat composing the work that he intended to dedicate to Giuliano de' Medici, Pope Leo X's brother. He glanced at the notes scattered all over the table before picking up his pen. The ancients had possessed unrivaled wisdom, but more recent authors could also be useful. Well, the great uncle of that friar certainly understood how states functioned—a pity that his relative had turned out to be so troublesome. The letters Niccolò had exchanged over the years with his friend Francesco Vettori could be distilled and added to the text, and he held high hopes of benefiting from Vettori's closeness with the Medici. As for personal experience, it could only add cache to the work, showing the chosen reader how wasteful it would be not to employ such a valuable person as the author.

He dipped the pen into the inkwell and started to fill in the blank sheets of paper. Now he needed just six more weeks to finish writing his book, *De Principatibus*, before presenting it to Florence's new rulers.

1

~

GRASPING, ENVIOUS, AND PROUD

Blind they are called of old and said aloud
Of these people: grasping, envious and proud
——DANTE ALIGHIERI
ON THE FLORENTINES

Niccolò Machiavelli entered this world on May 3, 1469, a scion of a distinguished, if not powerful, family and the first son of Ser Bernardo and Madonna Bartolomea de' Nelli. The Machiavelli, who claimed descent from the Lords of Montespertoli, derived their surname from an ancestor called Chiovello, "the nail," although in the early fourteenth century they were also known as Angiolini. Both the Angiolini and the original Machiavelli had a coat of arms sporting a simple blue cross on a white field, to which later would be added four nails—the *mali clavelli*, or the "evil nails" of Christ's passion.

From the beginning the Machiavelli had been involved in the running of Florence, producing a number of prominent politicians. Boninsegna Angiolini would be remembered by the novelist Franco Sacchetti not just as "a wise and famous citizen" but also for a humorous incident that Sacchetti used to make a point. Sacchetti tells the story of Boninsegna getting distracted by the vision of some comically painted figures on a wall during one of his public speeches, then goes on to admonish the reader about the importance of remaining focused on one's task. And indeed, there were activities that Florentines pursued with almost single-mindedness obsession, the primary one being increasing their personal and family status. Money making, marriages, and artistic patronage were all geared to the elevation of one's self or kin.

The main problem with the Machiavelli clan—notable characters notwithstanding—was its small size; worse, by the fifteenth century it had been relegated to the fringe of Florence's political inner circle. The close connection between large families and power was self-evident to all Florentines, since marriages meant alliances and, as a consequence, increased chances to enjoy political offices on a permanent basis. Having relatives in abundance could be an advantage in Florence, since it allowed the creation of a more extensive power network, but other factors also played an important role. Neighboring clans of the Machiavelli, such as the Guicciardini, the Ridolfi, or the Pitti, may not have been large, but their political weight belied the paucity in numbers. Wealth, personal connections, and the ability to jump on the right political bandwagon were not just cherished, but could also make the difference between a life of prestige or one spent in exile—if not an untimely death.

Unfortunately, a goodly portion of the Machiavelli had never been rich or powerful enough to marry into any family better than middle tier—our Niccolò's mother being a typical example of this, the Nelli boasting but few *priori delle arti* (priors, or members of the Signoria) in the course of their existence. Moreover, like all Florentine families of even modest standing, over the centuries the Machiavelli had repeatedly suffered from the vagaries of the city's political climate. Girolamo Machiavelli would eventually be remembered as a hero by the Florentine Republic of 1494 for his opposition to Cosimo de' Medici's power mongering, resulting in his exile and premature death (making him rather more memorable than the mid-fourteenth-century Ghiandone, exiled as a common criminal and condemned to death in absentia for corrupting a public notary). Another, and wealthier, branch of the family appears to have inclined toward the Medicean faction, enjoying as a result greater social status and political prominence. But although one Machiavelli was destined to be among those who eventually terminated the Florentine Republic for good in 1532, others would oppose the Medici and suffer the consequences of their actions. Personal beliefs played a part in the choice of political allegiance, but the latter also followed a consolidated Florentine family strategy: namely, never put all your kin in one party. In a world where survival was not simply a biological matter, being sure that some family member could side with a possible winner loomed large in the Florentine imaginary.

If lack of political savvy could in the worst-case scenario produce loss of life, freedom, country, and property, at best it usually meant an existence of obscurity, without "honor and gain" (*honore et utile*)—both highly prized and craved by every Florentine worth his salt. The first, in particular, was keenly, one could say frantically, sought: "life without honor is living like the dead," wrote Piero di Giovanni Capponi to his patron Lorenzo de' Medici. Such was the thirst for public office that some people, to obtain it, would not hesitate to cross the legitimate clientage boundaries. Piero Vespucci would remind the formidable Lucrezia Tornabuoni that he had received nothing from allowing his daughter-in-law, the celebrated Simonetta Cattaneo, to engage in a relationship with her son Giuliano de' Medici (that Piero uttered his protest from the jail where he had been sent for being implicated in the Pazzi Conspiracy, which had resulted in Giuliano's death, points also to the risks patrons faced when failing to deliver the goods). Niccolò Machiavelli himself would underscore the general attitude Florentines had toward official positions by having Messer Nicia—one of the characters of his play *The*

Mandrake (*La Mandragola*)—declare: "In this city any one of our peers who does not enjoy public office, is not given the time of day."

By putting such words into the mouth of a foolish and proud doctor of law, Niccolò was hitting very close to home. His father had been a lawyer, albeit a not very successful one; and while we cannot assume Messer Nicia to be an image of Ser Bernardo, the two did share some character traits. From his own *libro di ricordi* (commonplace book) Machiavelli's father appears a solid, somewhat unimaginative, and parsimonious individual, concerned as much about his money as his dignity and reputation. About the latter we have an amusing anecdote, containing much of the raunchiness to be found in his son's later plays. Ser Bernardo became very miffed to discover that a maidservant had become pregnant from one of his cousins, who engaged in the illicit relationship by entering his kinsman's house through a small window near the roof.

The thing that most angered Niccolò's father was that the impregnated girl did not come from the Mugello, where women had a rather loose reputation, but had been placed in his care by her parents, poor but dignified people from the Pistoia area.* Eventually the culprit remedied things by finding a suitable husband for the lass and providing her with the necessary dowry money; but to Bernardo the continuous fornication had resulted in his dishonor. One suspects it also made him the laughingstock of the whole neighborhood, for, as a Florentine proverb goes, "It is better to smell of shit, than of sucker" (*È meglio puzzar di merda che di bischero*).

Poverty is often substituted for gullibility in the above saying, and Niccolò Machiavelli would be acutely aware of his father's reduced financial circumstances, albeit in a relative sense. "I was born poor, and learnt to endure before enjoying," he would write later to his friend Francesco Vettori in a moment of adverse fortune. Of course, *Miseria e*

---

* Despite the fact that to this day Florentines maintain that only two things come from Pistoia: whores and thunderstorms, adding that the letters PT that appear on the vehicles from that city are short for *puttane e temporali*.

santità: metà della metà ("Penury and holiness: halve, and then halve again"), the Florentines would say, and while Ser Bernardo may not have been swimming in gold, he certainly enjoyed a more affluent lifestyle than what his son would like us to believe. From the *Catasto* (property tax records) of 1427 it emerges that Niccolò di Buoninsegna, Ser Bernardo's father, owned real estate worth 1,086 florins and taxable assets for 463 florins, ranking among the two hundred wealthiest citizens of his quarter.

Bernardo himself would declare in 1498 the ownership of a dwelling in Florence and a number of farmhouses with adjacent plots of land (*poderi*) in the countryside giving a yearly income of 110 "broad florins" (*fiorini larghi*). It would be wrong, however, to believe that this represented the actual wealth of that particular branch of the Machiavelli, tax-dodging and evasion being a normal practice in a city whose government frequently resorted to forced loans to compensate a chronic lack of liquidity. In *The Mandrake,* the above-mentioned Messer Nicia gives different statements about his affluence, explaining that should people know his real worth he could be hit with a colossal tax bill.

Our Niccolò would complain later in life that the income from his country property after taxes came to a mere 50 florins—equivalent more or less to the gross yearly earnings of a skilled worker. Nonetheless, we should be wary about accepting such words at face value, Machiavelli having the same griping habits of his fellow citizens, and in any case, at the time he was trying to get a tax rebate. Certainly, Ser Bernardo may have felt a pauper when comparing his own wealth with the 20,000 florins accumulated by his neighbor Piero Guicciardini, but then he had only himself to blame, since in a previous Catasto entry he had declared "not practicing any income-producing activity."

Yet, if not materially rich, Niccolò's father enjoyed a wealth of reputation among his peers as a legal thinker. Bartolomeo Scala, chancellor of the Florentine state in the 1480s, made him the protagonist of a dialogue on the nature of law. From the text we get an interesting portrait of Ser Bernardo as a man gifted with a formidable memory and a deep knowledge of Roman law, besides being a Plato scholar. This said, Scala presents his interlocutor as a conservative individual, utterly convinced of the unity and immutability of law, the chancellor instead maintaining that jurisprudence varies according to time, place, and circumstances. In the end, and despite all his citations of classical authors, Niccolò's father emerges as the vanquished of this erudite sparring match, but we can see very well where his son got his undue reliance on historical precedence.

Given that the elder Machiavelli was no fool and had some powerful friends in high places, one is left wondering why he never pursued a career in politics, or at least tried to obtain for himself some financially lucrative position. Equally puzzled contemporaries of Ser Bernardo could find no other explanation than an allegedly illegitimate birth to explain his failure to hold any sort of public office—bastards being debarred from enjoying automatic Florentine citizenship. This charge has long since been disproven, but the question of Ser Bernardo's retreat from the political sphere remains; although it is true that his chronic indebtedness and failure to pay his tax arrears did stop him from holding public office, he nevertheless had enough income to settle both of the above over time. Besides, had he been willing, these matters could have easily been solved, the Medici having built their following by paying people's taxes and debts.

Lacking evidence to the contrary, we can surmise that Niccolò's father had no interest in politics, and that maybe a rather plodding sense of legality did not allow for the exploitation of his personal connections. Indeed, from his *ricordi* the elder Machiavelli appears to have cared little about current events—unless they affected him directly. We hear from him about the war of 1478–1479 only because he agreed to house, in Florence, a female relative of one of his tenants, who wished to remove her from the possible unfriendly clutches of, in this case, friendly soldiery passing through the area of Sant'Andrea in Percussina. True to his rather parsimonious nature, Ser Bernardo insisted she should pay for her board, giving her a free bed in exchange for some domestic help.

Ser Bernardo, while aware of his own social position, did not recoil from dealing directly with social inferiors. When a butcher tried to short-change him over a sale of some lambs, Niccolò's father pursued the man relentlessly until he obtained his due. Like the episode of the pregnant housemaid, even this story has its comedic side, despite the constant sense of frustration recorded by the elder Machiavelli in his diary. We can imagine his chagrin as he waited for hours outside the butcher's shop for his debtor to appear, even going to the nearby barber for the sake of killing time. When he eventually managed to catch the meat seller, the two engaged in a verbal showdown, into which was drawn an unwitting yokel who served as an impromptu expert and suffered the indignity of being evicted from the butcher's shop on siding with Ser Bernardo. In the end the latter had to take recourse to external arbitration, at a cost, in order to get his money. When it came to cash, the elder Machiavelli had the determination of a mastiff's locked jaw.

To be fair, Ser Bernardo faced some outstanding and unavoidable expenses, such as his daughters' dowries and his sons' schooling. Despite a not lavish income, he would see that at least his male offspring got an adequate formal education. In the already-mentioned commonplace book, references to his children are scarce, but in 1476 he would record that Niccolò, then aged seven, was learning the rudiments of Latin grammar, first with a certain "maestro Matteo" and later the same year with "Ser Battista di Filippo da Poppi," both clergymen. In a subsequent entry dating from 1479, he would write about his eldest son learning the abacus, and finally, in 1481, we discover that the second son, Totto, had started school and Niccolò had been busy doing Latin translations under Ser Paolo Sasso da Ronciglione.

All this implied quite an expense. Ser Bernardo, for instance, paid the mathematics teacher the sum of 1 broad florin, a bit less than 1 percent of his yearly gross income. It would appear, however, that Niccolò, according to what he later told the historian Paolo Giovio, refined his Latin during his apprenticeship in the Florentine chancery under Marcello Virgilio Adriani, Bartolomeo Scala's successor as Florentine chancellor. The Machiavelli boys' education followed standard practice, as laid out by the humanist Leon Battista Alberti in his *I libri della famiglia*, stressing that, above all, Cicero, Livy, and Sallust should be studied, not so much for learning Roman history, but instead "to acquire with gentility that most perfect air of eloquence of the Latin language."

Not coming from an affluent family, Niccolò and Totto were schooled with other children, and not by private tutors. Their sisters, Primavera and Margherita, apparently did not receive the same scholarly upbringing, although this does not necessarily make Ser Bernardo a misogynist. In rich households boys and girls were educated in a similar fashion, although finding a tutor who would display appropriate behavior could be a major headache—one humanist complaining that many were violent individuals as well as pederasts, at the same time stressing the importance of parents as the first and foremost educators of their children.

Niccolò would imbibe quite a bit of knowledge from the family library, Ser Bernardo having an avid interest in books. His library sported editions of Livy and Macrobius, plus other works, most likely both literary and legal in nature. In addition, the elder Machiavelli borrowed from friends the writings of Aristotle, Pliny the Younger, Ptolemy, Justin, Flavius Blondus, not to mention a Bible. He would pass on to his eldest son this love for knowledge; sometime during his early manhood, Niccolò would even copy Lucretius' *De Rerum Natura* in his own hand. Indeed, Niccolò always considered himself first and foremost a man of letters rather than a political theorist. Later in life he would stress to his son Guido the importance of studying music and the humanities, "since they have given me the little honor that I may have." Earlier, in a sonnet to Giuliano de' Medici written while in jail, Niccolò had described himself as a poet, and in 1517 he griped to Lodovico Alamanni that the celebrated versifier Ludovico Ariosto had neglected to include his name among the poets mentioned in the *Orlando Furioso*, "leaving me behind as if I were some prick."

Yet, despite the knowledge he had acquired thanks to his father, Niccolò would resent the latter's stinginess to the point of chiding him about it in a sonnet, written sometime before 1500, in which he described himself as being reduced to skin and bones, while Ser Bernardo would buy "geese and ducks without eating them." In addition, the sums Ser Bernardo spent for the marriage of his daughter Primavera in 1483 to Giovanni di Francesco Vernacci were modest in comparison to what other people would fork out for a daughter's nuptials. Be that as it may, it was quite a financial burden for the elder Machiavelli.

It is possible that Niccolò resented the elder Machiavelli's preference for engaging in erudite discussion instead of seeking greater affluence for his family. This trait appears to have passed down the bloodline, at least every other generation, as may be gathered from a well-known anecdote having as protagonist canon Niccolò di Bernardo di Niccolò Machiavelli, our Niccolò's grandson. When a friar of Santa Croce complained that people were dumping bodies in the Machiavelli family tomb, canon Niccolò answered with bitter humor: "Well let them do it, for my father loved conversation so much that the more company he'll have the more pleased he shall be," leaving the poor friar speechless. The comment reeks of Florentine cynicism, given that the uninvited corpses were probably people of little means and even less culture. Canon Niccolò appears to have been a chip off the old block, for on more than one occasion his grandfather had demonstrated an uncanny ability to shock people with some callous remark or other, often to his own detriment.

Nastiness can be described as pervasive in Florence, and not just because, as the writer Giovanni Papini aptly put it, Florentines revel in other people's misfortunes. The root of such an attitude was a widespread sense of envy and mistrust. In 1421 Gino Capponi the Elder would encapsulate such feelings in his *ricordi*, written for his son Neri, a veritable list of bewares: Don't grant anyone any sort of influence, unless constrained by necessity; be cautious when dealing with your fellow citizens as much as with other polities; keep the ignorant, the licentious and the lowly under control, or pay the consequences. Needless to say, such a mentality cannot be described as conducive to harmonious collaboration, and at the end of the eighteenth century the grand duke of Tuscany, Peter Leopold of Habsburg-Lotringhen, would comment bitterly about the impossibility of accomplishing anything in Florence, since its citizens were always too busy squabbling among themselves. Furthermore, he added in exasperation, Florentines appeared incapable of acknowledging that anybody else could be right. Time and time again this destructive attitude would impede any sort of coordinated political effort that may have, at least in theory, benefited the Florentines.

In truth, Florence functioned (and the same is true today) only with a firm hand guiding it. The year Niccolò Machiavelli came into the world the ship of state was in effect run by a restricted oligarchy, led by a powerful branch of the Medici family, disguised behind the trappings of *soy disant* democratic institutions. Not that this leadership had gone uncontested over the years. In 1466, just three years before Niccolò's birth, a number of senior citizens, many of them former Medici allies or clients, had conspired to force a change of regime, and the attempt had failed only through a combination of bad luck, bad timing, and defections from the ranks of the plotters. As a result, the Medici not only tightened their grip on Florence but sought also to strengthen their family network outside the city walls. In June 1469, our Machiavelli but a month of age, Lorenzo di Piero de' Medici married Clarice Orsini, scion of a powerful and warlike Roman family, thus acquiring not just connections with the papal curia but also the possibility of tapping into a potential military force.

The 1466 conspirers had ostensibly been motivated by a desire to return to the constitutional settlement of pre-1434, the starting year of the Medici regime, characterized by a broader-based oligarchy. Over time, by an adroit exploitation of political and military emergencies, and by building a solid clientage thanks to the wealth provided by their bank, the Medici had managed to concentrate power into a smaller ruling elite. Before 1434, periodic general scrutinies had established an individual's political eligibility, and once approved, one's name was placed in the bags from which extractions were made for the fulfillment of various offices—drawing by lot being considered a safe way to stop demagogues from gaining power. In addition, there existed the *divieti*, debarring from any particular position anyone who may have filled it in recent times, the nearest kin of such a person, and citizens who were in debt, bankrupt, or in arrears with their taxes. In any case, tenure of any office was purposely short, between two and six months, not only to allow a quick turnover but also to prevent people from gaining too much power. To compensate for this lack of political continuity, semipermanent advisory boards—the *consulte e pratiche*—were created from time to time, and the names of those staffing them give us an idea about who really held power in Florence.

As prestigious as these advisory posts may have been, Florentines aspired to the *Tre Maggiori*, the three highest offices of the city: *Dodici Buonomini, Gonfalonieri di Compagnia,* and *Priori delle Arti.* There were twelve buonomini and sixteen gonfalonieri di compagnia, each making up one of the two colleges that advised the *Signoria.* In the Signoria, the most important collective magistracy of Florence and the one holding supreme executive power, there were eight priori delle arti and a *Gonfaloniere di Giustizia,* the head of the government. To guarantee the security of the state at the end of the fourteenth century, the office of the *Accoppiatori* was also created. These officials were charged with the task of filling the bags with the names of those who had passed the general scrutiny—an extra check to ensure that only safe names could hold office. New laws could only be approved by the two traditional, and socially broad, legislative councils.

However, in the political upheaval following the establishment of the Medici regime, the accoppiatori not only received the power to actually choose the names to be inserted into an electoral bag for the bimonthly sortition of the Signoria, but also the right to include or exclude citizens from the electoral process despite the results of the general scrutinies. To enact such a radical constitutional reform, the Medici clique used the time-tested system of calling a *parliament* (the general assembly of all male citizens with even minimal political rights) to approve the creation of a *balìa,* an extraordinary and temporary magistracy tasked with implementing those constitutional changes considered necessary. Later in the century, in order to tighten its control over the city, the ruling regime would force the creation of other *balìe*, who in turn established two leg-islative councils, the *Cento* (one hundred) and the *Settanta* (seventy), both staffed with Medici partisans. As a result, fewer and fewer people enjoyed the benefits of government. Although this arrangement was nei-ther water tight nor capable of satisfying everyone's ambitions—the plot of 1466 stemmed from the ranks of the Cento, while the Pazzi Conspiracy of 1478 included quite a few people whom the Medici had either snubbed or ignored—it still proved a pretty efficient power-mongering system.

Although we would search in vain among Ser Bernardo's *ricordi* for any comment about events related to Florentine history or politics, from his son's *Istorie Fiorentine* (*Florentine Histories*) we get an inkling of the incidents that could have helped to shape Niccolò's later way of thinking. He may well have witnessed Francesco de' Pazzi going to the scaffold in April 1478, looking intently at people and emitting no sound but a sigh. He almost certainly saw the corpse of Francesco's father, Jacopo de' Pazzi, being dragged through the streets of Florence and thrown into the river Arno by a crowd of Florentine youths (the same described in adoring and glowing words in *Romola* by George Eliot—who, one should re-member, had no family). We have no evidence that the young Niccolò participated directly in this desecration, but the image of Jacopo's cold body bouncing on the street's stones would make him reflect about what he called a "striking example of fortune's fickleness to see a man of such wealth and standing be brought so low with outmost misery, ruin and shame." Given that his kinsman Girolamo had suffered exile, imprison-ment, and premature death by backing the wrong political horse, Ser Bernardo had a good reason to keep away from the power game.

The rich and influential abounded in Machiavelli's neighborhood. Just outside his front door were the dwellings of the affluent Guicciar-dini, the main patrons of the local parish church—and high-class monastery—of Santa Felicita. Niccolò was older than the children of Piero Guicciardini, but in later years he would benefit greatly from his friendship with Luigi and, especially, the historian and politician Francesco. In Niccolò's lifetime they would expand their property on the street through the acquisition of some houses of the Benizzi, a small and declining family with close blood connections to the Machiavelli.

Up the via dei Bardi stood the impressive palazzo of Guglielmo Capponi, master of the Hospital of San Giacomo dell' Altopascio and a staunch Medici supporter. The mastership of Altopascio was a hereditary benefice of the Capponi, who had successfully revived the institution's sagging financial fortunes. Machiavelli would later indirectly pay homage in his *Clizia* to this example of entrepreneurship. Other members of the clannish and politically prominent Capponi resided near the Ponte Santa Trinita, including the ones known as *di banco*, due to the riches they had accumulated with banking. Nearby lived their once associates the Vettori, and Piero Vettori's son, Francesco, although five years younger than our Niccolò, would later on play a fundamental part in the latter's life. The fact that Piero Vettori, Piero Guicciardini, and Ser Bernardo Machiavelli had property in the same area of the Florentine countryside may have contributed to their children's familiarity despite age and social differences. On the via Maggio, to the back of the Machiavelli home, dwelled the Ridolfi, prominent in their Medicean allegiance to the point that one of them eventually married one of Lorenzo de' Medici's daughters. A bit down the same road were the houses of the Corsini, politically a middle-tier family—if somewhat more prominent than the Machiavelli—a member of which would play an important part in Niccolò's life.

There is some speculation that the children in Machiavelli's immediate neighborhood may have attended the same school under Ser Paolo Sasso, and quite a few members of the above-mentioned families would eventually emerge as Niccolò's epistolary or debating partners. In any case, they all enjoyed the same humanistic upbringing that allowed them to share a common culture and lingo. Schooling aside, physical vicinity must have meant that they saw quite a lot of each other even at an early age; besides, street games were universally practiced by young boys of all classes, and Machiavelli, although keen to hobnob with the rich and powerful, always retained an aloof liking for the lower members of society.

Apart from the occasional entry in his father's diary, we know little of Niccolò's youth and early manhood. Later, however, Niccolò would note "the great importance of good or bad opinion a child hears about something in his early years, since he will be somehow conditioned by this and regulate his behavior accordingly for the rest of his existence." The young Niccolò certainly heard much in the way of good opinion about books, not least from his father, and despite any differences that may have existed between them, that love for books did, indeed, have "great importance" for the rest of Niccolò Machiavelli's life, along with many of the social and cultural elements of the world in which he was brought up that can be traced as themes and motifs of his later work.

2

WORSE THAN A CRIME

It is worse than a crime, I say, it's a mistake.
—JOSEPH FOUCHÉ,
MINISTER OF POLICE UNDER
NAPOLEON, ON THE EXECUTION
OF THE DUC D'ENGHIEN.

On the morning of May 23, 1498, the roar of flames mixed with the crackling of burning flesh provided the Florentines with an unusual spectacle, as the gibbeted body of the visionary political and religious reformer Fra Girolamo Savonarola went up in a blaze. The friar's death marked the end of one of the most turbulent periods of Florence's history, three and a half years in which many had seen their world go topsy-turvy.

Fra Girolamo's impact on Florentine politics and society can scarcely be underestimated, and its effects, albeit after a fashion, have lasted to the present day. Originally from Ferrara, he first arrived in Florence in 1482 as the prior of the Dominican convent of St. Mark's, finding a city deeply immersed in a semi-pagan, humanistic culture that was riddled with vice. Savonarola, himself a humanist, tried to redress the situation through fiery sermons, announcing that terrible scourges were in store for the "new Rome." He met with little success; indeed, his grating voice and foreign accent seemed to fall on deaf ears. Reassigned to Bologna, he returned to Florence in 1490 to find a changed situation: The wealth glut of the 1480s had been overtaken by economic uncertainty.

Even the Medici bank, one of the mainstays of the family's power, was on the verge of collapse after years of bad management. In addition, more and more people were becoming dissatisfied with Lorenzo de' Medici's high-handed attitude. They resented the way he behaved as if he were lord of the city, concentrating all political decision-making in the hands of a small clique of followers. This time the friar's words fell on fertile ground as he inveighed against corruption and tyranny, much to Lorenzo's chagrin—not least because his family had richly endowed the convent in the past, and he considered St. Mark's to be nearly his own property. "A fox with a barren tail," as Lorenzo would tartly describe him, Savonarola nevertheless would attend the former on his deathbed in 1492, at a time when his preaching had assumed a more and more apocalyptic tone; a new Cyrus, he announced, was about to come and punish sinners with fire and sword.

This prophecy appeared to be fulfilled when the French king Charles VIII of Valois invaded Italy in September 1494 with the objective of conquering the kingdom of Naples and, in the course of a whirlwind campaign that stunned contemporaries, by the end of October reached Florence's border. In a vain attempt to ward off the threat of the French sacking Florence, the young Piero de' Medici, Lorenzo's successor, rushed to the king's camp—only to be forced to a humiliating treaty by surrendering a number of key fortresses and agreeing to pay a large indemnity. Piero had no legal authority to strike such a deal, worst of all one concluded without consulting the Florentine Signoria. On returning to Florence he found it in a state of open rebellion, everyone enraged about what was rightly considered a craven and abject surrender. Seeing the writing on the wall, he thought it prudent to quit the city, together with his brothers Giovanni and Giuliano, on November 9, leaving the populace to ransack the Medici palace.

Charles VIII entered Florence on the 17th, committing the military mistake of quartering his troops within the city walls. Although the Florentines by and large perceived the French as liberators, very soon tensions flared between the soldiery and the citizens: "Many became enemies of the French they had in their house," Machiavelli would later recall in the *Clizia*. On the diplomatic front matters were in a state of turmoil. Pisa, Florence's main port, had rebelled and given itself to the king, who was using it as a pawn in hard-nosed negotiations with the Florentine authorities. However, this and Charles's exorbitant monetary demands could not hide the fact that he feared being trapped in Florence; in any case, he wished to push on to Naples. After a heated exchange with some Florentine envoys he agreed to more modest requests, saying also that he would return Pisa to Florence at the end of his campaign and leave the city before the end of the month. He would later renege on that promise.

In the meantime, Florence's political and constitutional landscape was being turned upside-down. Following the departure of the Medici, a parliament had nominated a balìa for reforming the constitution. The rather limited changes that were presented—in essence a return to the pre-1434 constitution by abolishing the Cento, the Settanta, and all other Medicean additions—provoked an uproar, many perceiving these proposals as simply an attempt of the former oligarchs to retain their power. The widespread opposition forced the balìa to consider a more incisive transformation, which resulted in the abolition of not only the Medicean legislative bodies but also a number of other ancient institutions, as well as the creation of the very inclusive Gran Consiglio (Great Council).

For Florence, the changes were both revolutionary and dramatic, not just because the new body had the power to elect the city's magistrates and the ultimate say in all legislative matters, but also due to its composition; anyone whose father, grandfather, or great grandfather had been *seduto* (taken office) or even *veduto* (had his name extracted from the electoral bag, but then being debarred from office due to some *divieto* or other) for the Tre Maggiori had the hereditary right to sit—a total of about 3,000 people. However, since the end of the fourteenth century six of the eight priors, and always the gonfaloniere di giustizia, had stemmed from one of Florence's seven major guilds, the fourteen minor guilds providing but two. In addition, there had been families who in the course of the fifteenth century had constantly enjoyed the city's highest offices, while others not belonging to Florence's inner circle— even those whose members belonged to a major guild—had been chosen but occasionally.

Now people of middling rank found themselves on a more equal footing with their political betters, the establishment of the Great Council effectively creating a broad-based aristocracy. The awareness shared by all the council's members of being permanently in power meant that the assembly could not be browbeaten or blackmailed into submission except with the utmost difficulty, and then only under very extraordinary circumstances. Prominent families that had grown used to monopolizing governmental power soon found out, to their dismay, that the tune had changed. Nevertheless, at the beginning the Great Council appeared to satisfy everyone, since it combined the idea of *governo largo* (i.e., a more inclusive regime) with aristocratic elements.

The inspiring sources of the new constitution were Venice and Girolamo Savonarola. In the course of the fifteenth century, Venice had become the model of a functioning republic, and not just for Florence. Humanists such as Poggio Bracciolini saw it as the perfect example of an aristocratic regime, yet this very thing made it suspect to those Florentines who had an ingrained distrust of anything that smacked of patricianism. And yet, the way the Medici had managed to manipulate the city's politics had clearly shown the old constitution's limits. Venice's system, with its well-tuned checks and balances, appeared as good a way as any to avoid the emergence of another de facto lordship, and the creation of the Council of the Eighty (the Ottanta), loosely based on the Venetian senate, was a further step in this direction. However, Venice had developed its own constitution through trial and error over a period of centuries, and in any case, the power given to the Eighty was rather more limited than the one enjoyed by the Venetian senate. The main problem lay in the different character traits of the citizens of the two republics, as succinctly encapsulated in a proverb from the time: "The Venetians are good barrel staves, and the Florentines bad ones." The Venetian constitution implied a strong sense of political unity and collaboration, something the Florentines seemed unable to master.

Savonarola's part in the adoption of the city's constitution has been a matter of debate, but given the influence he wielded at the time, his endorsement of Florence's new political structure carried considerable weight. He saw the post-Medicean settlement as being part of Florence's spiritual and moral renewal, and religion certainly became a constant component of Florentine politics. Up to the flight of Piero de' Medici, Savonarola had limited himself to preaching about repentance and church reform, prophesying the arrival of a chastisement for the whole of Italy. The French invasion seemed to be the fulfillment of such predictions, and this, combined with his support for the new constitution, gave the friar much credence among the populace at large—especially since his personal appeal to Charles VIII had avoided much loss of life and property. After the Medici left he changed the tune of his message from apocalyptic to glorious: Fulminating the *realpolitik* tenet often expressed by Cosimo de' Medici, "One does not govern states by saying the rosary," he now saw Florence not just as the new Rome but also the new Jerusalem, chosen by God to implement the Christian regeneration of Italy so that the city could then reap the material benefits of its conversion. Given the severe economic crisis that Florence had been experiencing since 1492, this sort of message contained a very strong appeal indeed.

Machiavelli attended a few of Savonarola's sermons, but, unlike some of his fellow citizens, he took a rather dim view of the friar's rhetoric. In a long letter to Ricciardo Becchi, a priest and Florentine orator in Rome, written on March 9, 1498, Niccolò provided a summary of two such homilies. Savonarola had come under fire (and soon would end up in the latter) from the pope—whose licentious lifestyle he had been denouncing—and his political enemies in the city. Lashing back at both from the pulpit, the friar called them tyrants—only to change his tune once he found out that the Signoria had written to the pontiff on his behalf. Machiavelli's caustic comment would be, "Thus he follows the times and colors his untruths* accordingly."

Niccolò had gone to hear Savonarola on Becchi's request, and, with some malice, he emphasized to his clerical correspondent how the friar, commenting on a passage from Exodus, had berated the Egyptians and their priests. But the wording of Machiavelli's letter could also be read as referring to the clergy in general—given also that he described the pope in such a way "as could be said of the most evil person ever." One may speculate that Niccolò wished to ingratiate himself with Becchi—no follower of Savonarola—but it is quite possible that the political events since 1494 had contributed to his critical assessment of the friar.

For three years Savonarola had tried to impose his agenda on the city. Together with his devoted followers, dubbed *frateschi* (of the friar) or *piagnoni* (weepers) by their adversaries, and by whipping up the zeal of the notoriously riotous Florentine youths, he organized processions as well as "bonfires of the vanities": the public burning of all objects, from paintings to female ornaments, deemed dangerous to people's morals. Savonarola's partisans in the Great Council convinced the assembly and the Signoria to approve—not without strong opposition—the friar's political agenda, including the establishment of a public loan bank (the *Monte di Pietà*), a general amnesty for all Medicean followers, an alliance with France, and the reconquest of Pisa.

Some people expressed doubts about the treaty with Charles VIII, since the king had failed to give Pisa back to Florence, but the Florentine merchants and bankers in France, fearful of negative repercussions for their businesses, were more than happy to back the frateschi on this mat-

---

* I have translated *bugie* as "untruths," not "lies," because the latter in English has a much stronger connotation than in the Florentine usage. In Florence a *bugiardo* can simply be someone who tells tall tales.

ter. In order to discourage the use of the death penalty as a political weapon, the Gran Consiglio Maggiore also approved a law granting the right of appeal to the general assembly in the case of capital sentences. Its application would shortly be put to a test.

Opposition to Savonarola and his followers soon emerged, and not just on religious grounds. Charles VIII entered Naples at the end of February 1495, but his success caused Venice, the pope, Milan, Spain, and the emperor to form an alliance, called the League of Venice (or the Holy League). Fearful of being trapped in southern Italy, Charles retreated north, leaving a strong contingent to guard his new conquests. The league's troops confronted the French at Fornovo on July 6, 1495, and although Charles managed to extricate himself with his army largely intact (the biggest loss being, probably, his love letters, read and gleefully published by their captors), it became clear that the Valois hold on Naples was tenuous, to say the least.

Despite initial successes in the field, the French were ultimately driven from the kingdom of Naples in mid-1496, leaving their Florentine allies to fend for themselves. Charles VIII had initially declined to hand Pisa back, and when eventually he changed his mind his restitution orders were disobeyed. Now, Florence's refusal to join the League of Venice provided some of its members with a chance to pose as defenders of Pisa's freedom. Venice and Milan withdrew their military support for the Pisans in 1498, but Florence's incompetence in the field would mean another eleven years of war before the city could be recaptured—in the course of which Machiavelli would come very much into his own.

Florence's lack of military success weakened Savonarola's position and increased the disaffection that many had started to express toward the political settlement he so strongly supported. The creation of the Great Council had displeased many of those who saw their political predominance threatened, and opposition to the institution would characterize many old and important families—who more and more were described as *ottimati*, aristocrats, as opposed to *popolani*, middle classes.

Still, it would be misleading to see the division between ottimati and popolani in purely social terms, as necessity, personal issues, and beliefs created some very peculiar bedfellows. Some aristocrats, such as Paoloantonio Soderini, Francesco Valori, and Giovanbattista Ridolfi, were popolani because of staunch frateschi; yet not all of Savonarola's followers favored his idea of governo largo. Likewise, some families or individuals of popolano extraction sided with their social betters due to personal or neighborhood ties or simply for their own peculiar motives. The friar's opponents, the *arrabbiati*—the rabids—also recruited from a wide social spectrum, and to complicate matters further, some frateschi and arrabbiati would gang together to support the French alliance, or maybe, seeing the unwieldiness and factionalism of the Great Council, even to plot the return of the Medici.

The summer of 1497 saw the uncovering of such a conspiracy and the arrest of five leading citizens, the most prominent being Bernardo del Nero, who had served as gonfaloniere di giustizia the previous spring. Del Nero appears to have always favored a *governo stretto* in the style of Piero's father, but initially had thought of Lorenzo and Giovanni di Pierfrancesco de' Medici, cousins of their exiled kinsmen, as leaders of the regime. Piero de' Medici, in the meantime, had not been idle, and with the backing of Venice and Milan he made a number of attempts to regain control of Florence, encouraged also by the political rift within the city.

The previous April Piero had arrived in Siena and from there led a small army to the gates of Florence, hoping to provoke an uprising in his favor. Nothing had come of it, his partisans inside the walls considering it prudent to keep their heads down, but nonetheless the exiled Medici continued to be informed by his allies about the happenings within the city as they awaited the right moment to aid Piero's return. Bernardo del Nero had been privy to the exchanges between Piero and his cousin Lorenzo Tornabuoni, as emerged after the latter was arrested in August together with Giannozzo Pucci, Niccolò Ridolfi, and Giovanni Cambi. A *pratica* of about two hundred citizens was convened to discuss their fate and decided on the death penalty, despite the misgivings of many, and the sentence was confirmed by the Otto di Guardia, the criminal court.

The relatives of the condemned appealed the judgment to the Great Council, a right they had according to law, therefore putting the government in an awkward spot. The Signoria was split, some saying that the laws should be observed and others instead maintaining that, given the peril these men posed to the Republic, their rights should be waived. In the end, the extreme frateschi, led by Francesco Valori—who had a personal grudge against del Nero—won the day by threatening the Signoria's members with physical harm. The majority of the government voted for death, and that same night the five were beheaded.

Francesco Guicciardini, whose father had been one of the *signoria* at the time, would comment later that the refusal to grant the culprits statutory rights damaged the city's reputation. Machiavelli, however, maintained that Savonarola suffered the most loss of repute, since many believed that the friar had pushed for execution no matter what, thus violating the appeal legislation that he himself had helped to introduce. The extent of Savonarola's intervention in the matter is still disputed, but nonetheless, public opinion believed him to be responsible for the conspirers' judicial murder. In any case, his followers had shown themselves unable to rise above petty partisanship, "and so the city remained under a dark shadow and filled with vengeful spirit," Machiavelli would comment some time later. As the beginning of a new age of liberty and justice, it could not have been worse.

Savonarola himself would not last long. His attacks against Pope Alexander VI allegedly got him excommunicated, and he was prohibited from preaching. The friar maintained these censures to be invalid, but, pressured by the government, he agreed to stop delivering sermons. More than anything, his prophetic messages were losing their appeal against a growing impatience toward the holier-than-thou attitude of his followers. A number of young men of good family openly defied Savonarola by ganging together in a band known as the Compagnacci—the bad companions.* They not only led a debauched lifestyle but also became

---

* It should be noted that the suffix *accio* or *accie* (pl. *acci*, *accie*), which in Italian has a very negative meaning, in Florence is often used in an endearing manner: For example, *un ragazzaccio*, "a bad boy," can simply denote someone particularly lively. This use of negatives in a positive way speaks volumes of the Florentine twisted mindset.

troublemakers, harassing religious processions, for instance. Far from being against religion, however, the Compagnacci displayed a typically Florentine iconoclastic attitude that Machiavelli would also prove to exemplify. More important, the impunity they enjoyed for their actions marked a change in the city's political attitude, to the point that a staunch *fratesco*, Paoloantonio Soderini—following a well-established Florentine tradition of covering one's backside—would make his son Tommaso join the Compagnacci "so that he could be on good terms with them should matters change for the worse." Soderini would prove himself singularly prescient.

Violating all prohibitions, Savonarola resumed his preaching during the 1498 Lenten season, attracting Machiavelli's scorn. He was not alone in his criticism. Some people were even going as far as calling the friar a tyrant; others waited for the right chance to bring him down. Savonarola's fall would, paradoxically, come in a moment of victory. Since he and his followers maintained that those who preached the truth would be allowed, by God's grace, to pass through flames unscathed, a Franciscan friar from Santa Croce, an enemy of Savonarola, challenged them to an ordeal by fire. On the appointed day Franciscans and Dominicans gathered in today's Piazza della Signoria, but those from Santa Croce immediately started quibbling about what sort of clothes should be worn during the test, with some claiming that robes could be used by Savonarola's followers to hide evidence of "some sorcery or other."

Then, having found out that the Dominican representative intended to enter the flames carrying a consecrated host, the Franciscans refused to go forth, stating that the burning of the blessed sacrament would be tantamount to a sacrilege. Savonarola quickly announced his victory from the pulpit, but the matter of the host had alienated many of his followers and emboldened his enemies. On the evening of April 8, a mob, led by the Compagnacci, assaulted the convent of San Marco, and in the ensuing fight the guards of the Signoria who had been sent to restore order arrested Savonarola and two of his friars. That same night Francesco Valori saw his house ransacked and his wife murdered, before himself falling to the blades of his enemies. Paoloantonio Soderini managed to escape the same fate, owing to his son's connections with the Compagnacci, once more proving discretion to be the better part of valor.

In the days that followed, the Great Council fired all the frateschi holding governmental positions, replacing them with arrabbiati, and then proceeded to create a committee of twenty citizens to judge Savonarola and his associates. In defiance of their ecclesiastical status, the friars were tortured in order to make them confess, real or imaginary crimes, while Alexander VI pressed the Florentines to send Savonarola to Rome for trial. Fearful that a canonical proceeding would permit Savonarola to escape their clutches, his enemies rebuffed the pope's request. Eventually, a compromise was reached, allowing the friars to be tried in front of two specially appointed papal delegates. Swiftly condemned to death on the evening of May 23, the convicted were hanged and burned the next day. "Thank God, now we may sodomize," would exclaim one of the arrabbiati with visceral satisfaction on entering the government palace after the execution. Once again, despite all attempts to the contrary, the foundations of the Florentine Republic were cemented with division and factionalism.

Francesco Guicciardini would recognize Savonarola's merits, adding, however, the cynical note that if he had been a good person, then he had been a great prophet; but if he had been a bad individual, one had to call him a very great man indeed, as he had managed to bamboozle everyone without being caught. Machiavelli himself, despite the criticism of Savonarola that he had expressed in the letter to Becchi, would later state that "of such a man one can not speak but with reverence"; he added that he would nonetheless consider the friar deluded in his prophetic vision. Indeed, by being "ambitious and partisan," he had brought ruin to himself and nearly to Florence itself.

Niccolò also considered the friar "cunning," but not a hypocrite, unlike "frate Alberto" (the one who suggested that Alexander VI call Savonarola to Rome and then throw him in jail), or the crafty, unctuous, and miscreant Fra Timoteo in *The Mandrake*, of whom one of the characters in the play states: "It is sad to see those who should set the example behave in such a way." Interestingly, the nearest Machiavelli ever came to uttering the statement "The end justifies the means" can be found in another of Fra Timoteo's utterances: "It is the end that we must consider in all matters." Given Niccolò's negative portrait of Timoteo, we may well question the commonly held belief about Machiavelli endorsing in full an amoral approach to politics.

A lot of ink has been spilled about Machiavelli's attitude toward religion, his texts being subject to a variety of interpretations. Of his anti-clericalism there is little doubt, but then again, he shared that trait with most of his fellow citizens. The short-story collections of Giovanni Boccaccio and Franco Sacchetti are filled with anecdotes about immoral ecclesiastics, and at the beginning of the fifteenth century Gino Capponi would warn his son: "Never get enmeshed with priests, for they are scum of the earth; nor with the Church and its business, except for the sacraments and divine offices." He would also add that a divided church was useful to Florence and its liberty; since it damaged the soul one should not abet such a situation, however, "but let nature do its business." Francesco Guicciardini would later state that he always wished for the destruction of the church's temporal power, and that, if not for the benefits he had received working for two pontiffs, he "would have loved Martin Luther more than myself; not to free myself from the laws induced by the Christian religions as it is normally interpreted, but to see this bunch of scoundrels put in their proper place: that is either without vices, or devoid of authority."

Machiavelli would echo such a sentiment in a number of his writings; however, he was far from unique in his feelings. It should be remembered that until 1870 the papacy governed a large swath of Italy, and thus many Italians saw the church as simply another princely power, albeit a peculiar one, and to be treated as such. Sharing a border as it did with the papal territories, Florence felt this problem more acutely than other areas of Italy, and the attempts of a number of popes to influence, condition, or

even subvert the city's political life would be a constant source of resentment up to the eighteenth century. Indeed, anticlerical sentiments remain a constant feature of the city's life to this day, even among the
metropolitan clergy.*

Again, to understand Machiavelli's religious feelings, one should once
more look at the particular environment in which he lived. Niccolò's
somewhat grudgingly positive judgment about Savonarola stemmed
from the fact that the Florentines had followed him even though they
did not "appear either ignorant or unrefined." Savonarola understood
this. His sermons were filled with references to themes dear to the humanists, such as the dignity of man, reconciliation, and the desire for an
existence without the encumbrances of guilt and sin. He also delivered
a positive message about creation, and he regarded human reason as the
highest authority, though he believed it worked along with divine reve-
lation. More important, he managed to posit an eschatological role for
Florence, grafting it to the city's political mythology. Unfortunately, he
did not take into account one factor: namely, the Florentines themselves,
who were always polemical, corrosive, and wary of anything they felt
could constitute an imposition on their lives.

Not that Florentines were nonbelievers; religion instead played a fundamental part in their daily lives like everyone else's of the era. Public
and private devotions, the cult of relics and miraculous images, religious
processions, and celebration of the sacraments were normal happenings,
yet Florentines had, and still have, a rather skeptical attitude toward religion that tallied with their dislike of being told what to do. Besides,
the realities of life often clashed with a truly Christian worldview, and
pious Florentines would not recoil from impious ruthlessness if circumstances should warrant it. When Giorgio Ginori, a Medici henchman,

---

* Once, at the time of a general election, a canon of Florence's cathedral—a
man of great science, piety, and common sense—told me: "I hope the
Communists don't win." He paused and then, with a wry grin, added:
"Otherwise the priests will be the first to strike a deal with them." Slapping his
hand on his mouth, he chuckled: "Whoops, what did I just say?!"

and incidentally a friar of the Military Order of St. John of Jerusalem, was sent to Prato to suppress an anti-Medicean plot in that town, he proceeded to hang a few people for their sins and without trial. To one of them who on the scaffold asked for time to say a prayer, Ginori answered, as he pushed him to his death, "Go down, you'll pray later."

Though Florentines shared this sort of attitude with other Italians, the city's humanistic milieu, stressing the importance of ancient texts, had encouraged a religious syncretism of sorts. After all, people believed the pagan mage and philosopher Hermes Trismegistus to be as old as Moses, and in a world where antiquity and authority went hand in hand, his writings carried the equivalent weight of the Bible. By the same criteria, the works of Virgil, Cicero, and other ancient Roman authors could be seen as carrying a weight equivalent to the Gospels. Machiavelli, imbued with classical culture, had this sort of attitude in abundance, and it should be remembered that he had transcribed Lucretius's atomist poem *De Rerum Natura*.

In many ways Niccolò can be considered a Renaissance skeptic, his friend Luigi Guicciardini, brother of Francesco, describing him as "a man who with difficulty believes what should be believed, and even what should be laughed at." However, his relaxed attitude toward traditional religion was shared by many, including philosophers, ecclesiastics, and even pontiffs: "Since God has given it to us, let's enjoy the Papacy," Leo X would tell his brother Giuliano de' Medici on the morrow of the former's elevation to the papacy. In addition, Machiavelli's love for ancient Rome would bring him to make an articulated comparison between the Roman set of beliefs and Christianity:

> The ancient religion prized only those men propelled to the achievement of earthly glory, such as military and political leadership. Our religion esteems people who lead a life of humility and contemplation rather than action. It considers humbleness, lowliness, and the disregard of worldly things as the supreme good, while the other emphasized greatness of spirit, bodily resilience,

and all those things that strengthen men to the utmost. And if our religion demands fortitude, it does so that you may face suffering rather than react against it. Thus, this way of life appears to have made the world weak and placed it at the mercy of wicked men, who control it utterly, seeing that humans as a whole are more inclined to suffer beatings than to avenge them for the sake of earning Paradise. And this effeminizing of the world and disarming of the Heavens for sure is the work of those cowardly individuals *who have interpreted our religion by following sloth rather than virtue.* For should they consider that our beliefs allow us to exalt and defend one's country, they would realize how much it desires that we love, honor, and be prepared to defend it. (Emphasis added.)

In the original Italian, this passage is ambiguous—since on one side it describes Christianity as being spineless, and yet Niccolò then emphasizes its virility—and in any case, Machiavelli cannot be described as versed in theology. Moreover, when penning this passage, in the *Discourses,* he had his own personal experiences to meditate upon, not to mention the need to cater to the attitudes of his classical-minded friends of the Rucellai gardens; besides, by emphasizing *ozio* (passivity) and *virtù* (civic virtue) as the Romans intended them, he demonstrated not so much an anti-Christian sentiment as a desire for a more muscular form of Christianity. In any case, he held to the belief that free will—although not necessarily in a Christian sense—could be a sufficient antidote to the fickleness of Fortune.

Machiavelli had been born and raised a Christian, but his ingrained skepticism often brought him to disregard the church's tenets. On one occasion his friend Francesco Vettori would be forced to remind him to attend Mass on feast days. As we shall see, Machiavelli did not limit this lackadaisical behavior toward religious practices; nevertheless he sometimes displayed a certain uneasiness toward those who did not abide by the church's rules. Even taking into account the fact that in many of his writings religion is seen as bound to civic duty in the tradition of the ancient Romans, his passage of the *Istorie Fiorentine*, where he talks about the 1471 visit to Florence of the duke of Milan, Galeazzo Maria Sforza, goes beyond such classical examples:

> We saw then something never before seen in this city. It being Lent, when the church commands us to fast without eating flesh, that [the Milanese] court, showing no respect for God or the church, went on consuming meat. Many spectacles were put on to honor [the Duke], including one in the Church of Santo Spirito representing the descent of the Holy Ghost on the apostles. But because of all the fires that are usually lit on such occasions, the building went up in flames, and many believed it to be a sign of God's wrath toward us.

Although we may suspect that Machiavelli intended to impress his ecclesiastical superiors (after all, he was writing the Histories for Pope Clement VII), we can also surmise that, with all his cynicism, anticlericalism, and profanities, he possessed a rather traditional view of what constituted appropriate behavior in certain circumstances: Eating meat during Lent was simply not done. The passage in his satirical *Capitoli per una Compagnia di Piacere* prescribing the crime of *Laesae Majestatis* for the members of a made-up confraternity, who, "while attending Mass do not constantly look around, or place themselves where they can't be seen," shows a pronounced uneasiness toward the many whitewashed sepulchers walking around Florence—possibly including the members of one of the religious brotherhoods to which Machiavelli belonged. Likewise, when it came to family values, he could be as conservative as any other Florentine, despite, as we shall see, a strong taste for philandering. To his son Guido he would stress the importance of domestic principles: "Live in harmony and spend as little as possible," he would write, concluding the letter with "Christ watch you."

Christ watch you! As much as this closing may have been a convention of the time in letter writing, it simply does not match up with our vision of an iconoclastic Machiavelli who, according to Giovio and others, died "godless." Alamanno Salviati, who disliked Niccolò intensely, once wrote to him: "I don't say you have no faith, but rather you have little left." Machiavelli's grandson Giuliano de' Ricci would state that "in all his writings Niccolò showed a pronounced unrestraint, not only when attacking lay people or ecclesiastics, but also by reducing everything to natural or fortuitous causes." But then, Ricci was living in a very different religious and intellectual environment.

It is also interesting to note that references to God became more frequent in Niccolò's later writings; perhaps he found that increasing age, coupled with domestic and international turmoil, gave rise to a need for a rather more active divine presence than Fortune could provide. As much as he might have been a skeptic, from a religious standpoint Machiavelli appears nevertheless to have been filled with contradictions, a man who shared metaphysical and earthly values, as well as a taste for irreverence, with his fellow citizens.* And Niccolò, who possessed the Florentine spirit in spades, was never one to resist engaging in polemics, cracking an irreverent joke, or taking advantage of a chance to *épater les bourgeois.*

---

* Even the life of the Florentine saint Philip Neri is filled with quips and jokes, however devoid of the typical Florentine nastiness. Saint Philip Neri's ability to change his native spirit into charity is in itself a miracle.

3

~

WARFARE AND STATECRAFT

*When the Cardinal of Rouen told me that the
Italians don't understand warfare, I replied that
the French do not understand statecraft; for had
they mastered it, they would not have allowed
the church to grow so powerful.*
— NICCOLÒ MACHIAVELLI,
RECALLING A VISIT TO FRANCE
DURING THE REIGN OF LOUIS XII

*The thing a ruler must be careful about is to avoid
seriously offending someone in his employment.*
— NICCOLÒ MACHIAVELLI, *THE PRINCE*

I t is no coincidence that Niccolò Machiavelli was nominated to the
Florentine chancery by the Ottanta on May 28, 1498, less than a week

after Savonarola's death, or that the Great Council duly confirmed his appointment to the position three weeks later. Niccolò was still young by Florentine standards, and he had already applied for a lesser position in the same office the previous February, only to be rejected because of his known anti-Savonarolan stance. Now, the ousting of the frateschi had opened the door for a rather more important, and lucrative, position.

Despite his political credentials, however, the reasons for Machiavelli to be chosen over the other candidates remain to some extent obscure. We have no hard evidence that he had special connections with the chancery before his election, though his father, Bernardo, was apparently a close friend of the chancellor, Bartolomeo Scala, and Niccolò himself is reputed to have perfected his Latin under Scala's successor, Marcello Virgilio di Adriano Berti (commonly known as Marcello Virgilio Adriani). It is quite possible that the latter threw his weight behind Machiavelli's candidacy, which was reinforced by the presence in his family of the anti-Medici martyr Girolamo Machiavelli; besides, and probably as telling, Ser Bernardo's lack of involvement in Florentine politics meant that his son had inherited little envy or resentment—and therefore few, if any, enemies to stop the nomination from going through.

It is perhaps not surprising that in his writings Machiavelli emphasized the role played by Fortune in our lives, considering how much Lady Luck had favored him: Though he was from a family of little consequence in Florence, he suddenly had become the head of the Florentine Second Chancery with an annual salary of 128 gold florins, plus the perks that any permanent office carries by law or practice. The job provided Niccolò with the *honore* that had always escaped his father as well as a chance to play a crucial role in steering the Florentine ship of state. The presence of a permanent, albeit unofficial, Medici leadership had meant a concentration of most political decision-making within the Medici family. The advent of the Popular government after 1494 and the establishment of an assembly-based regime caused a slowing down of the political process, a situation worsened by the rapid turnover of executive personnel. Given these circumstances, it was inevitable that the Florentine chancery, with its staff of permanent bureaucrats, should assume a greater managerial role in public matters.

More than once, Machiavelli, while in theory subject to the authority of others, would behave as if he were his own boss, aided in this by both his character and external circumstances. In theory, the First Chancery of the Florentine Republic was supposed to deal with foreign affairs, whereas the Second Chancery dealt with internal matters and the governing of the military. However, in practice such distinctions became blurred, and often things were simply handled by the person with the greatest chance of getting something accomplished, whether owing to connections, influence, or ability. Besides, the fifteen-year-long war in Pisa inevitably meant the growth of the Second Chancery in importance as well as an increase in the power of the *Dieci di Balìa* (the Ten on Peace and Liberty, but usually called "i Dieci"—the Ten), the magistracy in charge of orchestrating Florence's role in the conflict. When Machiavelli became secretary of the Dieci on July 14, 1498, the parsimonious Florentines were getting a two-for-one deal, as he took on the new job and kept the old one without any increase of personnel or expense. Apparently now Niccolò had ten more people giving him orders, but since the members of the Dieci rotated every six months, in practice bureaucrats handled most of its business. In addition, the Great Council could decide not to elect the Dieci, as happened more than once, leaving the administration of all field operations to Machiavelli and his staff.

Managing a war involved more than just deskwork, and in the years to come Machiavelli would spend a lot of time on horseback representing his city. In March 1499 he embarked on the first of such missions, being sent by the Dieci to deal with Jacopo IV d' Appiano, Lord of Piombino. Florence had been facing a series of military emergencies, including a Venetian invasion of the Casentino in northeastern Tuscany, and had been unable to settle the Pisa question. The stingy Florentines, in contrast to a trend common in Italian states, had never been willing to provide themselves with a stable military organization, and in times of need were forced to enlist whoever remained on the market—often not the best troops or commanders, and, in any case, men often devoid of any sense of loyalty toward Florence. Appiano had resented the fact that one of his rivals, Rinuccio da Marciano, had been given a larger command and more money by his Florentine employers, and now he demanded equal treatment. Machiavelli managed to sooth Appiano's ruffled feathers, with the aid of honeyed words and the promise to increase his command by forty men-at-arms. Although he had only been following the Dieci's instructions, Niccolò's first diplomatic mission had been a success, earning him a reputation for both ability and reliability.

The need to appease Appiano went beyond the sphere of immediate military necessity. Florence was surrounded by a plethora of small independent or autonomous polities, some of them situated in key strategic positions and whose rulers practiced warfare as a way of life and survival. Piombino, Appiano's domain, placed on the Tuscan coast, fell into such a category, with the added problem that Jacopo's sister, Semiramide, had married Lorenzo di Pierfrancesco de' Medici. This particular branch of the Medici had formally severed its ties with Piero's side of the family, but the ever mistrustful Florentines felt blood to be thicker than water. Lorenzo and his brother Giovanni may now be known as the *popolani*— "those of the people"—but nevertheless were downright *ottimati* and by some seen as a possible alternative to Piero as rulers of the city in the case of a possible Medici restoration. Besides, Giovanni had become the third husband of a formidable character, the object of Machiavelli's next diplomatic mission.

Caterina Sforza, Countess of Forlì, may have lacked a few qualities, but not grace, beauty, cunning, or toughness. The illegitimate daughter of Galeazzo Maria Sforza, Duke of Milan, at an early age she had married the cowardly and nasty Girolamo Riario, nephew of Pope Sixtus IV and ruler of the town of Forlì in the Romagna region. When Riario fell under the knife of a few disgruntled local noblemen, Caterina had managed to take refuge in the nearby fortress of Ravaldino; to the conspirators' threat that they would kill her children unless she surrendered, she responded by lifting up her skirts on the fortress wall and declaring that she had "the molds" to make more.* Following her second husband's murder, she allegedly extracted terrible vengeance on the culprits' families. A woman with a robust sexual appetite, as witnessed by the abundance of aphrodisiac potions in her recipe book, she married a third time, and to everyone's surprise, to the handsome Giovanni di Pierfrancesco de' Medici. The latter died soon after, but not before the couple produced a son, also called Giovanni, destined to be a worthy chip off his mother's block.

Although legally the ruler of Forlì was Ottaviano Riario, Caterina's son by Girolamo Riario, nobody had any doubts about the real power-holder. Ottaviano had been employed as one of Florence's *condottieri* (mercenary captains) a couple of years before for a salary of 15,000 florins, but then had refused to renew his contract with the excuse that the Florentines had not paid him. Now, as we shall see, with war at her doorstep, Caterina showed interest in revamping the agreement. The Florentines were in a quandary, not wishing to pay Ottaviano more than 10,000 florins, yet unwilling to anger Caterina. Forlì happened to sit on Florence's northeastern border; should any of the Riario fail to produce male offspring, Forlì's lordship could easily end up in the hands of a Medici. In addition, Florence needed soldiers for its war against Pisa and hoped to recruit at least 500 good infantrymen from the countess's domains, the Romagnoli having a well-deserved reputation for being a warlike people. Florence also hoped to acquire gunpowder from Forlì. So, on July 13, 1499, Machiavelli mounted his horse and set off for the Romagna.

Still today with the aid of good weather it is a two-and-a-half-hour drive from Florence to Forlì on an uphill road that is all twists and turns. It took Niccolò three days to reach his destination, having first assessed the condition of the Florentine frontier town of Castrocaro. Following

---

* The authenticity of this incident has been doubted, since Machiavelli was the first to mention it and nothing of the kind may be found in contemporary accounts of the events following Riario's murder. It is, of course, quite possible that Machiavelli got the story straight from Caterina, given that the latter spent the last years of her life in Florence.

his instructions, he reported about the defensive situation of the outpost, adding information about some incidents of local strife. Marcello Virgilio Adriani had given him very specific orders, a demonstration that the chancellor still believed his pupil needed guidance, despite all his intelligence and acumen; indeed, under Adriani's precise directives the only latitude left to the young Niccolò remained his discretion in "using adequate words and employing the phraseology you consider best." The Florentine authorities knew the countess to be a very pointed customer.

Machiavelli met Caterina on the 17th, but from the very beginning the negotiations proved difficult. The countess, not without reason, pointed out that the Florentines were notoriously bad employers and that she had received better offers from the Milanese. This may have been an exaggeration, but in truth the duke of Milan, Ludovico Sforza, desperately needed every soldier he could lay hands on. Charles VIII of France had died in 1498, and his successor, Louis XII, had renewed the French pretenses on Naples, adding a dynastic claim on Milan. It was no secret that Lombardy would be the objective of Louis's impending campaign, the king having publicly struck an alliance with Venice for this purpose.

The sovereign had also managed to get Pope Alexander VI on his side, the lecherous pontiff agreeing to dissolve Louis's marriage—on grounds of nonconsummation—and in return receive for his son Cesare Borgia the duchy of Valentinois and the hand of a high-born French lady. For good measure, Louis had also made peace with Spain, renewed the truce with the empire, and struck a deal with Philibert of Savoy, since he needed to pass through Philibert's domains to reach Milan's borders. To counter such a threat, Ludovica Sforza had been enlisting soldiers at a frenzied pace, and Caterina, who happened to be his niece, had some very good recruiting pools. This, of course, worked very well for Caterina, since now she had two suitors in hot competition for her services.

Machiavelli tried to convince the countess to accept Florence's terms, but she—stressing her family's "honor"—pointed out that the Florentines were offering less generous terms to her son than the other captains in the Republic's pay. After a week of hard bargaining, seeing the daily departure of soldiers for Milan, Niccolò raised his bid to 12,000 ducats. Caterina appeared to agree, prompting Machiavelli to write confidently to the Ten that a deal had been struck. But suddenly the countess performed a volte-face, asking for assurance of Florentine military aid should the Venetians decide to attack her territories, adding that "the more one discusses matters, the better."

Niccolò had not the authority to negotiate such conditions; indeed, he did not hide his displeasure "with words and gestures'" about Caterina's attempt to force upon him a fait accompli. There could be no doubt that his mission had been a failure, although back home his efforts were much appreciated and his letters praised. Once he returned to Florence, he could not resist inserting into his report to the Dieci the barbed comment that all the problems with Caterina could have been avoided if the Republic had fulfilled its obligations toward her son in the first place. Machiavelli certainly had a point, but at the same time he appears not to have grasped the complexity of the Florentine political and financial situation—the first of many examples of his tendency to put theory before practice.

In any case, Niccolò's report could well be considered an internal document of the Florentine chancery, given that since the previous May the Ten had existed only through the office's permanent staff. The war against Pisa had been going badly, with the Florentines becoming increasingly angry about the heavy tax burden imposed on them to pay for a conflict that appeared to be going nowhere. Public opinion clamored for the conquest of Pisa, with Florentines on the one hand wanting a vigorous campaign, but on the other having little stomach to pay for it. The Dieci had always been a stronghold of the *ottimati*, and very soon rumors started circulating that the war was simply part of an aristocratic plot to bankrupt the city and wreck the popular regime. As a result, when in May 1499 it became necessary to elect a new Dieci, the Great Council simply refused to comply; the handling of the conflict fell on the bimonthly elected Signoria. Given that, inevitably, the chanceries would be doing most of the daily work, for a young and ambitious man like Machiavelli this was a golden and uncurbed opportunity to create his own power base within the administration.

Since the previous year the Florentine commander in chief had been the condottiere Paolo Vitelli, scion of a warlike family from Città di Castello on the other side of Florence's southeastern border. Vitelli had started off with a show of energy, taking a number of enemy fortresses around Pisa (and after the conquest of Buti cutting off the hands of captured artillerymen) and repulsing the Venetians in the Casentino. This success, however, had forced him to abandon the Pisa venture—just as the Venetians had planned—allowing the beleaguered city to strengthen its material and human defenses. Florence would never have managed to retake Pisa under these conditions if Venice had not decided to strike an agreement with the French, allies of the Florentines, against Milan.

Freed from the pressures of the Casentino front, Vitelli resumed the siege of Pisa, conquering enemy strongholds and subjecting the city to an intense artillery bombardment, at the same time requesting more and more money for his troops. On August 10, Vitelli's troops assaulted the breach previously created by the Florentines' guns, only to be forced back—although not by the Pisan defenders. The assailants had loudly expressed their intentions to put the captured city to the sack, something Florence had expressly forbidden, not wishing to get a ruined city and an even more hate-riddled populace. With difficulty, Paolo and his brother Vitellozzo managed to countermand their order, being forced to club their men into obedience and arousing the indignation of the many battle-thirsty Florentine youths who had volunteered to serve before Pisa. The Pisans quickly repaired the breaches and manned the walls, while Vitelli, despite orders to renew his attack, made no further move, and the besiegers' camp broke up on September 1.

Vitelli's inactivity derived partly from a military reality contrasting with Florentine political goals, but also from the fact that Florence shared the burden of Vitelli's *condotta*, or mercenary contract, with France. No sooner did Louis XII start preparing his campaign against

Milan than he started pressuring Florence to ally herself openly with him. In the face of the Republic's reluctance to comply, he quietly stopped any sort of payment for Vitelli's troops, at the same time putting pressure on Paolo to protract the siege of Pisa.

There were also strong suspicions in Florence about Vitelli's ultimate loyalty, and indeed, at the time of the Casentino campaign, he had received an offer of 40,000 ducats by Piero de' Medici—then attached to the invading Venetians—for transferring his allegiance. Although the Florentines possessed no hard evidence of any treasonable dealings by Vitelli, the latter's inactivity turned suspicion into certainty. The government's subsequent actions, however, were less motivated by justice than by cynical realpolitik, as Vitelli provided an ideal target for popular wrath over the Pisan debacle. And if the plot against Paolo was hatched by the executive, the responsibility for its implementation, if not indeed its inspiration, can be laid at the doorstep of the de facto head of the Dieci, Niccolò di Ser Bernardo Machiavelli.

On September 10, Machiavelli wrote a peculiar letter to the Florentine commissioners with Vitelli's army, ordering them, among other things, to fortify the village of Cascina but to send the inhabitants to Florence, and to keep the troops in the field short of pay. If the commissioners suspected something foul to be afoot, they certainly received confirmation of such when they learned that two other commissioners, Braccio Martelli and Antonio Canigiani, had been sent "to put that army in order and regulate expenses." Still, the new Florentine officials must have had doubts about their instructions, since Niccolò, as the executive's mouthpiece, needed to remind them on the 16th that "it is necessary to do as such," adding that "we cannot risk our security and reputation." On the 19th, Machiavelli again reiterated the government's orders to the commissioners, but this time he put the matter into context politically:

> The only thing that remains for you to do is to act according to the common desire to restore the city's reputation and destroy its enemies, insomuch as the other powers—especially the Most

Christian King [of France], on whom Italy's destiny depends—holds us in esteem for keeping both our soldiers and our enemies under control. Thus we can handle our own business and in no way are we less reputable than any other Italian state.

Like his fellow citizens, one of the things Machiavelli feared most was being seen as a dupe, and the young Florentine Republic could ill afford to become an international laughing stock, especially on matters of foreign policy. Despite repeated requests, they had refused to openly aid Louis XII for fear of angering the duke of Milan and his allies—as they shared a common border with a few of the latter. By July, a French army had crossed into Milanese territory, capturing every fortress in its path, and Duke Ludovico Sforza, deserted by his friends and allies, could offer but a token resistance. Even before Milan fell on September 6 it had become clear that a French victory was only a matter of time; to make matters worse, now Cesare Borgia had a French army at his disposal for implementing his plans of conquest. In the wake of all this and their failure at Pisa, the Florentines had few options left by which to restore their crumbling prestige.

A sense of urgency, if not to say desperation, started to appear in the missives of the Ten's secretariat to the Florentine commissioners: "Quick, quick, do what is necessary," reads a letter of September 25, most probably dictated by Machiavelli himself. Finally, on the 28th, believing him to be sufficiently weakened by the departure of many of his unpaid troops, the commissioners called Paolo Vitelli to Cascina with an excuse, promptly arrested him, and sent him bound to Florence. Getting wind of what had happened, his brother Vitellozzo managed to trick the officials who had been sent to capture him and find refuge behind Pisa's walls. Florence would pay dearly for this blunder.

Once in Florence, Paolo was viciously tortured to make him confess his treasonable actions, but despite the brutal treatment Vitelli refused to say a word. At this point the Florentine authorities had a real problem on their hands: They had no evidence, no confession, and a renowned soldier of fortune, not likely to forget such an insult if freed. Machiavelli himself would later turn this very practical quandary faced by the Republic into theory, stating that "men ought to be pampered or eliminated." Most of his fellow citizens would have agreed, one Florentine bluntly affirming: "I consider that we should not proceed in fairness, for that is not a way to handle affairs of state."

In essence, Vitelli's innocence or guilt was irrelevant: Once he had been arrested, political expediency warranted his execution. Besides, a lot of Florentines were more than happy to believe Paolo's culpability, to the point of considering his refusal to confess as evidence of wrongdoing. It should also be added that the Vitelli brothers had strong personal links with the city of Pistoia, then in a state of civil war. Florence's inability to find a solution to the Pistoiese crisis strengthened the need for a show of force and the removal of a potential threat to its security. Paolo Vitelli had become a convenient scapegoat for Florence's political incompetence, and on the evening of October 1 a general exultation followed the news of his decapitation.

In this show of political muscle the Florentines were probably following the example of the Venetians, who in 1432 had executed their leading military commander, the Count of Carmagnola. It is possible that Machiavelli himself suggested such a course of action, being familiar with Carmagnola's story as reported in Flavius Blondus's history—one of the books owned by Ser Bernardo. Unfortunately, whereas Venice had gained respect and credibility through Carmagnola's death, Florence's reputation collapsed after Vitelli's. For one thing, the Venetians had a record of being tough but fair when dealing with their hired soldiery, and service under their banner was keenly sought. The Florentines, in contrast, were known to be bad employers and paymasters, and Vitelli's execution added treachery to the equation. Florence's behavior in the Vitelli matter, far from resulting in a renewed respect for the Republic, produced instead widespread criticism.

A few days after Paolo's death, Machiavelli got hold of an intercepted letter from a Lucca official and felt compelled to write a stinging reply to salvage his city's reputation. Still, the sarcastic rejoinder displays an animosity beyond the limits of intelligent propaganda, making one wonder if Niccolò had a rather more personal stake in the matter. After roundly accusing the official of calumny, malice, stupidity, and ignorance—and adding an oblique threat to Lucca's government should it persist in spreading such news—Machiavelli engaged in a series of logical summ-ersaults to justify Vitelli's execution, stating that either for his treason or his incompetence he deserved "endless punishment."

Despite the bombastic tone, Niccolò must have understood that Flor-ence was in no position to impose its will on anyone, and that, maybe, Vitelli's judicial murder had been a mistake after all; indeed, some years later Machiavelli would call it Florence's "revenge" for Paolo's failure. Whatever the case, if Niccolò, as it would appear, had been the engine of the entire affair, then he had committed the first of a series of political errors.

Florence's hopes that Vitelli's execution would restore its credibility with the French were to be rudely shattered. At the end of September, Louis XII agreed with the pope to place a portion of his army at the dis-posal of the pontiff's son for the conquest of Romagna, part of a plan by Cesare Borgia, Duke of Valentinois, for creating his own state in central Italy. With the excuse that the lords of Rimini, Pesaro, Imola, Faenza, Forlì, Urbino, and Camerino—all papal vassals—had not paid their feu-dal dues, Alexander VI issued bulls forfeiting their fiefs. Louis managed to limit these actions to those who had recently backed the duke of Milan, and Cesare proved accommodating to the request, both he and the king not wishing to alarm the Venetians.

In the middle of November, Cesare began his campaign by attacking Caterina Sforza's domains, rapidly taking town after town. The citadel of Forlì proved a tougher objective, the feisty Caterina holding out until the middle of January 1500 before surrendering on terms to the French. For the Florentines the loss of Forlì was a bitter blow, and not just be-cause it had become a Florentine protectorate, with Caterina vainly ask-ing to enter the anti-Milanese league. With no army, let alone a commander, Florence could do little to help, and now it had a powerful and aggressive neighbor that was ready to exploit the city's military weak-ness at the first occasion. Luckily for the Republic, the attempt of the duke of Milan to stage a comeback meant that Cesare could not count anymore on French support and was forced to stop pursuing a policy of conquest—at least for the time being.

Ludovico Sforza's effort to regain his duchy proved short-lived. Betrayed by his Swiss troops, the unfortunate duke fell into the hands of Louis XII and ended his days a prisoner in France eight years later. The Florentines, in the meantime, had signed a treaty of mutual support with the king under the terms of which Louis XII promised to provide 600 heavy cavalry and 6,000 infantry for the conquest of Pisa. Florence agreed to furnish 24,000 ducats a month for three months, this substantial sum being considered a necessary investment to force the Pisans to surrender. The French mercenaries, Swiss and Gascons, started their march from Piacenza in May under Jean de Beaumont, but moved slowly, leaving a wake of destruction in their path. By the end of June they reached Pisa and began setting up siege lines and gun emplacements.

Fear of the "French fury" had compelled the Pisans to seek terms, Beaumont being happy to accept a conditional surrender of the city. The Florentines refused, suspecting Louis XII of having some secret design to take the city for himself—a decision that Machiavelli, with the benefit of hindsight, would later hotly criticize. On June 29, an artillery barrage knocked down a 100-foot-wide section of Pisa's walls. However, when the French attempted to storm the breach the next day, they discovered that the Pisans had built a gun-bristling earthen rampart behind the wall. In the face of these new defenses, Beaumont's troops declined to continue the assault; besides, they had discovered Florence's military weakness and decided to exploit it to their advantage. With their commander unable to keep discipline, the unruly French mercenaries drove off the Florentine victuallers; wandering soldiers of fortune were continually attaching themselves to the army and, backed by Beaumont's officers, demanding to be paid for their services.

Florentine commissioners Luca degli Albizzi and Giovanbattista Ridolfi had been attached to the French army, and they were soon joined by Machiavelli. Niccolò witnessed firsthand the unruliness of the French mercenaries, yet he remained deeply impressed by the military worthiness of the Swiss. Later he would recall how the Swiss had exalted the virtues of their military organization, comparing it to that of the ancient Romans and bragging that the king of France owed every victory to them. One day, they said, they would decide to fight for themselves. Sharing as he did with most of his contemporaries a deep love for antiquity, Machiavelli was continually trying to find similarities between his own age and a—albeit, largely mythical—Roman past; indeed, in public opinion current events were often read or interpreted in the light of incidents that had happened in the classical age.

Niccolò believed that the military prowess of the Swiss derived from their being "the only people today living like the ancients, as for religious life and military organization." However, the Swiss fell short of the Roman example, since they were organized in a "league" without a dominant city and, most of all, because their confederate organization permitted them to be hired as mercenaries by different powers, like the "Aetolians" of old. It would be during the Pisa war that Machiavelli would start building his ideas on military and political organization, even, one could say, developing a few bees in his bonnet about both.

At the beginning of July, the 4,000 Swiss mercenaries were due to receive their monthly pay of three ducats each, but at this point, the 2,000 Gascons, who were supposed to receive their wages a couple of weeks later, clamored for immediate satisfaction, demanding a raise from two and a half to three ducats. The Florentine commissioners were in no position to satisfy these requests, prompting the Gascons to desert en masse. Seeing the situation, Ridolfi left for Florence with the excuse of being ill, leaving Albizzi and Machiavelli to face a situation that was becoming uglier by the hour.

On July 9, a group of soldiers who had unofficially enrolled in the army went to Albizzi demanding three months' pay in a very menacing manner. Having asked for two days to find the sum, the startled commissioner was promptly seized, and Machiavelli was informed that Albizzi would be detained until the money arrived. Niccolò immediately sent a desperate plea to the Signoria on the commissioner's behalf, but Luca, terrified for his life, could not wait for an official response and agreed to sign a personal bond for 1,300 ducats in order to purchase his release. The Florentine camp broke up, and the elated Pisans soon occupied a number of points outside the walls, capturing artillery worth 3,000 ducats.

For Florence it had been a humiliating defeat, and as a result the Great Council decided to once more elect a Dieci to handle the war effort. However, the assembly's mistrust for the institution meant that the Ten could now hire only a limited number of troops for short amounts of time, and only with the approval of the other offices of the Republic. Moreover, the Dieci were not permitted to strike alliances unless the Signoria, the colleges, and other institutions agreed. True to style, the Florentines wanted to have their cake and eat it, too.

The military operations at Pisa had ended ignominiously, but another front remained open for Florence. When Louis XII heard what his troops had done he became positively livid because of the loss of face, and on July 27 he wrote an apology to the Republic for what had happened. Florence, however, did not wait for the missive; the Signoria had decided on July 18 to send two envoys extraordinaire to the French court. They would be Francesco della Casa, who had succeeded Albizzi as commissioner, and Niccolò Machiavelli—the latter, ostensibly, because he had been present at the contested events, but also because, in the absence of his institutional political overseers, his position as secretary of the Ten made him the de facto head of Florence's war effort. In any case, the two men were instructed to make their way posthaste to Louis XII to present their version of the facts before someone else provided the king with a different story.

Della Casa and Machiavelli took eight days to reach Lyon, where they met Lorenzo Lenzi, who, with Francesco Gualterotti, served as Florentine ambassador in France. Gualterotti had already left for Italy, and Lenzi steadfastly refused to accompany the newcomers to Louis, commenting acidly to the Florentine Signoria that now there were people "able to handle every important business," yet expressing satisfaction that someone else would be handling the sticky situation—"something which I desire as much as those in Limbo the coming of Christ." The only help he consented to give consisted in a briefing about the French court in which he recommended, among other things, that they seek the support of Cardinal Rouen (George d'Amboise, Archbishop of Rouen). He also warned them to be careful about attacking Beaumont's behavior.

Having received the advice, the two envoys set out to provide themselves with adequate attire and a retinue before meeting the royal person. Unfortunately, even on this occasion the Republic had demonstrated its usual monetary short-sightedness, providing its ambassadors with only a paltry daily stipend. Machiavelli's was less than his companion's; in fact, they deducted Niccolò's stipend from his normal salary. The Florentine authorities had also provided the two envoys with an advance of 80 florins, but by now that money had evaporated.

In the meantime, the king had moved from Lyon for fear of an outbreak of the plague, forcing the two Florentines to chase after him. Only on August 6 did they manage to catch up with the royal cortege at Nevers; but if they hoped to receive satisfaction for what had happened at Pisa, then they must have been very disappointed. Neither the king, nor his ministers, nor Rouen showed much interest in past events. They noted that the Florentines were also to blame, and said simply that now it was necessary to continue in the enterprise against Pisa for the sake of everyone's credibility. The Florentine envoys understood perfectly that the king wished the Republic to pay for the French troops at Pisa, and the meeting broke up with nothing accomplished.

The same happened four days later at a meeting with Rouen, and in any case, the king was becoming increasingly irritated with Florence's obduracy about his troops' wage. Given that neither Machiavelli nor della Casa could speak French, and that neither the king nor Rouen knew Italian, the whole matter had a slightly comedic aspect to it. But Louis knew he could afford to be a bully, realizing perfectly well the extent of the Republic's dependence on his goodwill for the reconquest of Pisa. Niccolò would describe the situation in cutting terms:

[The French] are blinded by their own power and by their immediate interest, and believe worthy of their esteem only those military powerful or ready to provide cash. This is very damaging for
Your Lordships [the Signoria], since they believe [Florence] to
lack these two qualities. They consider you worthless, believing
you impotent and the disunity and dishonesty of their army to be
the consequence of your bad administration.

Both he and della Casa found themselves in the unenviable position
of having to deal face-to-face with an increasingly angry sovereign, but
with no ambassadorial mandate allowing them to negotiate a settlement.
Machiavelli would pester the government to send someone with greater
diplomatic authority. This proved more difficult than expected, since
everyone in Florence elected to a post that would allow them to take on
such a task declined to do it: "I am deterred by the nuisance and the
cost," Luca degli Albizzi wrote in a private letter to Niccolò.

At least Machiavelli's request for more money had been approved.
But the cash necessary for administrative expenses was slow in arriving.
Niccolò thought that bribery should be used to make friends at the
French court, but of course there was no money for the bribes. Both en-
voys were so frustrated that at one point they even threatened to leave
for Italy without the government's authorization. To make matters worse,
della Casa fell ill and had to go to Paris to get his ailment cured, leaving
Machiavelli to fend for himself.

In the following two months Niccolò had more than one chance to
meet with Louis and Rouen, and he ended up becoming quite close with
the latter, with whom he could converse in Latin. The topic most discussed was the arrival of the new ambassador from Florence with the
Republic's answer about the pay for the French troops, but Machiavelli
sensed that the French were losing their temper when one day the cardinal retorted, to Machiavelli's promise of the diplomat's imminent arrival: "We shall all be dead before he gets here, but we shall see that
others die before us."

The threat could not have been clearer: News had arrived about Cesare Borgia's military preparations against the Romagna lords, but without French protection Florence would be at the mercy of the ambitious Valentinois. Luckily, fear of Borgia prompted the Florentines to find the long-awaited ambassador, and no sooner had Machiavelli delivered the news to the court than a royal envoy was dispatched to Borgia warning him not to attempt anything against Florence. Even better, the Republic decided to cave in to Louis's requests, promising to pay 10,000 ducats of overdue wages at once and the rest over time. The king appeared displeased that the full sum would not be delivered immediately, but he understood the futility of strangling the goose of the golden eggs.

During his conversations with Rouen, Machiavelli had sensed that the French had no real interest in seeing Borgia succeed, although the ambitious cardinal needed the support of Cesare's partisans for his scheme to become pope. Niccolò tried to warn Rouen about how Borgia and the Venetians were attempting to thwart France's designs over Italy, but the cardinal simply replied that "the king is very prudent indeed: He has long ears but is short in trust; he listens to everyone, but has faith only in what he can verify." Machiavelli's words were falling on barren ground, and he was very relieved when, with the arrival of the Florentine ambassador, he finally received the authorization to return home. He arrived in Florence on January 14, 1501, having acquired a wealth of experience and quite a few ideas that would follow him for years to come.

4

TWO FUNERALS
AND A WEDDING

And so Belfagor, having returned to Hell,
testified about the evils one encountered by
taking a wife.
—NICCOLÒ MACHIAVELLI,
LA FAVOLA DI BELFAGOR ARCIDIAVOLO

Quite a few things had happened back in Florence during Machi-avelli's absence, and indeed the stars of the year 1500 had not fa-vored him. Just before going on his mission with the French army at Pisa he had lost his father, and while in France, his sister Primavera had died. This last death became a source of worry for Machiavelli because, as his brother Totto would write with a concern that any good Florentine would have shared, Primavera had passed away without leaving a will, and so all her belongings had gone to "those people"—her Vernacci relatives. Niccolò had a personal stake in his sister's finances, since in 1497 Ser Bernardo had made him one of the representatives to deal with her dowry, now that she had become a widow, in order to "exact all payments from the Monte [delle Doti]" (Public Dowry Fund).

To make things even more worrying, Primavera's son Giovanni had been seriously ill. Although he appeared to be recovering, Totto was keeping his fingers crossed that the lad would reach his fourteenth birthday—"and from then onward he shall legally be able to testate" (as one would expect from a good sport, Giovanni reached maturity). Both Niccolò and Totto knew all too well the bitter quarrels that could erupt over inheritances and for the sake of family unity wished to avoid this danger as much as possible. Indeed, the careful Ser Bernardo had made sure to settle all of his property before his death—with his eldest son receiving the bulk of the estate, for what it may have been worth—precisely for that reason.

It was not the first time that Primavera had caused headaches for her kinsmen. In October 1479 Bernardo Machiavelli had discovered that his fifteen-year-old daughter, presumably a headstrong lass, was determined to marry Francesco di Giovanni Vernacci, eight years her senior. "Determined" is actually an understatement: Niccolò's father had found himself cornered by the two young people and could accept the fait accompli only by calling a notary and drawing up a marriage agreement, after which Francesco "gave the ring" to his new bride. The elder Machiavelli would later tell Francesco's father that the whole thing had happened against his will, although we may suspect him being slightly disingenuous about this in order to appease Giovanni Vernacci, miffed that the whole thing had happened without his consent. In any case, it was out of the question that Primavera and Francesco start cohabitation, given the girl's youth. Besides, Primavera's dowry at the Monte delle Doti had not yet matured.

Some years before, Bernardo had put down enough money for his daughter's dowry to yield a sum of about 500 florins, payable not earlier than June 1483; until then, Primavera would have been a financial liability for her father-in-law. Giovanni sniffed at the small amount of money provided by the bride's family, compared with the sum brought by his elder son's wife; twenty years earlier, the *gran dame* Alessandra Macinghi Strozzi had tartly described a dowry of 1,000 florins as befitting "an artisan." Besides, it was customary for the Monte delle Doti to provide only 20 percent of a dowry up front and the rest in Monte bonds, and years could pass before they were delivered, Florence's substantial public debt not allowing otherwise.

Ser Bernardo had agreed in the nuptial contract to fork out some 200 extra florins in cash plus provide a trousseau for his daughter, although this hardly appeased Giovanni Vernacci, who for all intents and purposes considered his son Francesco's match with Primavera a *mésalliance*. Over the next three years Giovanni tried to squeeze more money out of Ser Bernardo, only to be systematically stonewalled by the latter with the retort that such concessions would bankrupt him. The elder Machiavelli could also have reminded Vernacci of a maxim by the humanist Leon Battista Alberti: "Modest, sure, and immediately payable dowries are to be preferred to large ones, yet uncertain and payable over time." Both fathers must have been aware of the plight of many a Florentine husband, reduced to dire straits because they were unable to collect their promised large dowries. Perhaps for this reason, in the end Giovanni Vernacci gave in, and, in the words of Ser Bernardo, the two parties "remained satisfied."

Stingy as he may have been, Primavera's father realized that he needed to spend for his daughter's turnout, providing her with a rich garment and other items for a trousseau worth about 21 florins, plus a painting of the Blessed Virgin destined for the nuptial bedchamber. Not to be undone by his father-in-law, Francesco Vernacci—despite Giovanni's misgivings—bought for his future wife a sumptuous dress worth 15 florins. Vernacci could afford to pay in cash, whereas Ser Bernardo had to arrange installments. This sort of lavish expenditure was all too common in Florence: Visible wealth, in this case in the form of clothing, was displayed not just to underscore social standing but also as a form of public spectacle.* In the words of historian Julius Kirshner: "Socio-cultural logic dictated that Florentine fathers and husbands, independently of their personal wishes, invest considerable sums in adorning their daughters and wives." Needless to say, such spending sprees could be taxing even for wealthy individuals, and Ser Bernardo must have shed bitter tears every time he sent his son Niccolò to pay a merchant one of the installments for his daughter's trousseau.

The experience made a deep impression on the young Machiavelli, who years later would mock this need for showing off in his short story "La favola di Belfagor Arcidiavolo" (The Tale of Belfagor, the Archdevil). The tale opens in Hell, where Pluto notes how many male souls blame their wives for their misery. An infernal parliament decides to send the archdevil Belfagor to Earth to investigate the matter. Belfagor, in the guise of Roderigo of Castile, arrives in Florence with a goodly sum and a train of infernal spirits disguised as servants. He then proceeds to marry a woman by the misleading and at the same time ominous name of Onesta Donati. (One can translate the name as "Modest Gifts"; incidentally, the Donati were an old but impoverished Florentine family). Soon her extravagant demands—"dressing her in the most recent fashion and providing her with the newest things that so often change in our city"—her wastefulness, and grasping relatives reduce poor Belfagor to penury and debt.

Fleeing the clutches of creditors and magistrates, he is rescued by the peasant Gianmatteo and in return grants him the power to drive devils out of possessed women. Belfagor enters the bodies of various females and comes out at Gianmatteo's request, and the peasant's fame as an exorcist makes him rich in a short time. However, when Belfagor refuses to exit from the king of France's daughter, Gianmatteo is threatened with death by the irate sovereign, but the wily peasant accomplishes the task all the same by telling the archdevil that his wife is coming to reclaim

---

* In the mid-1960s an old-timer from our country estate in Chianti would recall when my great-grandfather would arrive with a coach-and-four, adding that then "gentlemen were really a source of pleasure" (*Allora sì che i signori davano soddisfazione*).

him. Terrified by the prospect, Belfagor rushes back to Hell, where he proceeds to relate the woes of marital life.

The main problem with Belfagor, and the source of all his troubles, according to Machiavelli, is that he is in love with his wife and "could not stand to see her sad or unhappy." The misogynistic attitude developed in the story was not unique to Machiavelli; nor confined to Florentine males. Alessandra Macinghi would warn her son about the perils of falling in love with one's wife, particularly if she lacked a brain, adding, "A man who's a man, makes a woman a woman." Niccolò would have agreed, and when comparing Fortune to a woman would state that "to subdue her, one needs to conquer and browbeat her." However, Alessandra Macinghi also maintained that "good [female] companionship soothes a man's heart and body," and Machiavelli would add that men who "don't have women in their house live like animals."

If marriage could be a source of woe, it nonetheless had a practical side; political rights passed only through one's legitimate offspring. By 1501, Machiavelli had reached the respectable age, by Florentine standards, of thirty-two, and he held a job that gave him both dignity and a decent stipend. Sometime that August, Niccolò tied the marital knot with the lady of an old and distinguished family: Marietta, daughter of Luigi Corsini. The Corsini lived close to him, just two streets to the west, and though not exactly the greatest family in Florence, they were socially a notch above Niccolò's branch of the Machiavelli (and would dramatically improve their standing over the next two centuries). The marriage appears to have been convenient for both parties. On one hand, Niccolò's link to the Corsini took him one rung up the social ladder; on the other, Marietta's family could benefit from Machiavelli's political connections. The Corsini, on the whole, were known for their pro-Medici sympathies, and in 1497 Marietta's uncle, Roberto, had been barred in perpetuity from holding public office for his indirect involvement in the del Nero conspiracy.

Whether the match was personally advantageous to Marietta herself remains debatable. Certainly there were drawbacks to being married to Niccolò. For one thing, at least until he worked in the chancery, he would often be absent for months on end, leaving his wife to run matters at home—quite a burden for anyone devoid of a substantial household staff, as they were. Marietta clearly felt abandoned by Niccolò, who tended to put matters of state before his family, not even bothering to be at home during the last days of some of his wife's pregnancies. In addition to all her domestic and motherly chores poor Marietta also agonized about her husband's well-being—in every sense—something that Machiavelli apparently found somewhat irritating. Her letter of November 24, 1503, is telling in this respect:

> My beloved Niccolò. You mock me but unfairly, for I would flourish much more if you were here. You know all too well how happy I would be if you were not down there [in Rome], especially since I am told about the epidemic ravaging the place. You may imagine how glad I may be, not being able to sleep day or night.—the happiness I get from the baby. I beg you write to me more often than you do, for I have received but three letters. Do not wonder why I have not written to you: I'm not angry, but have had no chance because sick until now. The child is well and looks like you: white as snow in complexion, but with hair as black velvet and is hirsute as you. And because of this resemblance, I find him beautiful. He is lively as a one-year-old; he opened his eyes no sooner he was born and screamed the house down. But our daughter is ill, and please try to return. . . . I will be sending you a doublet, two shirts, two kerchiefs and a towel that I am sewing at present.

Marietta may have spoken the truth about not being angry, but in the previous months she had more than once vented her spleen at her spouse's behavior. Biagio Buonaccorsi, Machiavelli's friend and a colleague in the chancery, was often the recipient of Marietta's ire: "She says she will not write and grumbles endlessly," he wrote; "her gripe is that you promised not to stay away for more than eight days."

If the prolonged absences were not enough of a strain on his wife's nerves, Machiavelli's spendthrift tendencies surely were, especially when it came to fine clothes. Marietta simply went berserk on at least one occasion upon discovering that her husband had ordered a cloak for himself made of very expensive material, worth in excess of five ducats. Admittedly, Machiavelli's position demanded a certain amount of external display, and Niccolò at the time was representing the Republic at Cesare Borgia's court; he may have felt that better attire would make a greater impression. Even so, the expense involved appears excessive; besides, everyone knew Niccolò's taste for fashionable clothes, and one cannot but compare this with the rather modest garments he wore in his youth. Buonaccorsi once quipped that Niccolò would be capable of having a doublet made out of precious cloth intended as a diplomatic gift; Marietta evidently did not share Biagio's sense of humor.

Besides, it appears that at the beginning of the marriage her husband displayed a rather lackadaisical attitude about getting her dowry money from the Monte. Buonaccorsi would write to his friend on December 21, 1502: "She curses God, believing that she has thrown away her body and her property; for your soul's sake. Please arrange for her to receive her dowry like all other women; otherwise we shall not see the end of this." At the time Machiavelli had rather more pressing needs to attend to— following Borgia's path of conquest across the Romagna, a road that would ultimately end in the dramatic events in Senigallia on New Year's Eve 1502, when Borgia had a number of his officers executed for suspected treason. But Niccolò was not singling out his wife or her finances for neglect; he displayed the same careless attitude when dealing with official matters, and often even in keeping in touch with colleagues and friends. Indeed, self-involvement appears to have been an ingrained feature of his character.

Marietta would probably not have limited her curses to the Almighty had she suspected her husband to be more than a little unfaithful—or a downright philanderer. During his lifetime he would retain a keen eye for women and engage in a number of affairs, some of them long-standing and others occasional. In his correspondence we find mentions in particular of a courtesan called Lucrezia, known as "la Riccia," and later the well-known singer Barbera Raffacani Salutati. The former would provide him with sexual solace before his fall from power and some much-needed comfort afterward; for the latter he would write the comedic play *La Clizia*, and his feelings for her apparently went beyond mere physical pleasure. She appears in fact to have been entrusted with the secret code that Machiavelli used to correspond with his friends. A few years after his death, she would write to one of her former lover's friends asking for help in a running quarrel with some members of the Corsini family. It may be just a coincidence that Marietta belonged to the same kin as Barbera's "molesters," but it is not impossible that the Corsini could have taken umbrage at the notoriety of Niccolò's relationship with the actress.

Machiavelli's roving sexual appetite would lead him to maintain "occasional" (*alla sfuggiasca*) liaisons with numerous women, and, in typical Italian fashion, he did not hesitate to boast about them—or even to engage in self-mockery on the subject: Florentines love to make fun of themselves as well as others, though they do not want to be the target of jokes. In a now well-known bawdy letter to Luigi Guicciardini, Niccolò told of an encounter with a prostitute whose unbearably ugly features, discovered after the copulation—not to mention stinking breath— caused him to throw up in disgust. The description of the whole episode is so extreme that one is left wondering whether it was not a piece of literary fiction (as certain elements in the text referring to Lucius Apuleius's *Golden Ass* would make us believe), particularly considering that Niccolò was in the midst of telling Luigi a cautionary tale about the risks of letting one's sexual appetite run amok.

It should be remembered that Machiavelli enjoyed quite a bit of notoriety among his friends for his amusing stories, which often had sexual overtones. Once in a letter to Francesco Vettori he would describe the misadventures of Giuliano Brancacci, who having hooked up with a lad and found out that the rent-boy derived from a family of quality, tried to make the object of his pleasure believe that he was actually Filippo Casavecchia, one of Niccolò's friends. Machiavelli went on to add that Casavecchia, by his adroit unmasking of the real culprit, had caused quite a bit of laughter in Florence "during this Carnival season," and that the phrase "are you Brancacci or Casavecchia?" had become a recurrent joke among the Florentines.

Because of certain words used in the letter, some have suspected the writer and the protagonist to have been the same person. Niccolò wrote that Brancacci was "*vago di andare alla Macchia*" (desirous to go in the bush), and "*il Machia*" happened to be Machiavelli's nickname. Other references in Niccolò's correspondence could imply that he may have practiced "the Florentine vice," as sodomy had come to be known. Francesco Vettori would hint about having been molested by one of his teachers, suggesting that Machiavelli may have suffered a similar indignity, and that from that moment on matters had gone to Hell in a handbasket:

> A father has a son, whom he affirms to raise in virtue; however, he starts by giving him to a teacher who spends all day with him, with the freedom to do with the lad whatever he wishes, and lets him read things that would raise a dead man. The mother keeps him clean and well dressed so that he may be more pleasing, and when he gets older provides her son with a room at the ground floor with a separate entrance and every other convenience, so that he may do as he wishes, invite and bring there whoever he likes. We all behave in such a manner, and those who appear proper err the more in this. Therefore it is not surprising if our young men turn out so degenerate, for such behavior stems from the worst possible upbringing. You and I, even if old men, retain to a degree the habits learned in our youth, and there is nothing we can do about it.

Although tutors did have a reputation for corrupting youths, it may well be that Florentine adolescents tended to find other ways to vent their sexual frustration in a city where unmarried girls were kept under lock and key. Unplanned pregnancies could result in a family's dishonor even when the young lady involved belonged to a household's staff and not a more illustrious bloodline: The case of Ser Bernardo Machiavelli's maid is emblematic in this respect, and in *The Mandrake*, Niccolò informs us about the remedies some Florentines were prepared to undertake to solve such problems. Prostitutes, on the other hand, could be unafford-able to youngsters, who may also have practiced "bugger-my-neighbor" as a form of camaraderie. From the contents of Vettori's letter one could easily believe sodomy to have been the favorite sport of male Florentines; indeed, in another missive Vettori would describe an incident in Rome involving, once again, Giuliano Brancacci and Filippo Casavecchia, but with the one trying to seduce the daughter of one of Vettori's neighbors, and the other her young brother.

It remains unclear to what extent Machiavelli himself had a liking for his own gender, even if—at least according to an anonymous denuncia-tion appearing when Machiavelli was secretary of the Ten—he enjoyed anal sex with "La Riccia." Despite the fact that sodomy carried a criminal sentence, some of Machiavelli's friends (Donato dal Corno, for one) practiced it openly, and to this day sexual deviation is a constant source of jokes among Florentines.* Niccolò himself would poke fun at the habit in his letters, and in *The Mandrake* he would have one of the female char-acters compare the Turkish practice of impaling people with her de-ceased husband's bedtime practices. Thus, Machiavelli's pun about being too demoralized to see "La Riccia," and wondering if instead this mood would have affected him had he planned to see "il Riccio" (a young rent-boy), should not be taken literally, but instead as an example of Niccolò's typically Florentine sense of humor.

To be clear, Vettori had started the letter quoted above by referring to a passage from Virgil about the insane love of the shepherd Corydon for the young boy Alexix, implying that Niccolò had been smitten with an infatuation. Despite the common image of Machiavelli being aloof, cold, and cynical, the same Vettori had unequivocally declared some time be-fore: "I have seen you smitten by love . . . and known how much passion drives you." Yet, Francesco was also replying to a letter by Machiavelli of

---

* In Florence the equivalent of the American threat "I'll kill you" is, albeit not in polite society, "I'll bugger you" (*t'inculo*). Biagio Buonaccorsi used it in a letter to Niccolò (*cazo vinculo*) at a time when Marietta was fuming about Machiavelli's neglect for her.

a few months before, in which Niccolò described having fallen in love with a young woman—according to Roberto Ridolfi the widowed sister of one of his neighbors in the country. But for Vettori, evidently, the difference was minimal: To Machiavelli's declaration about "Fortune" having organized the encounter with such a "creature," he replied that idleness was the source of such emotions, and the simple remedy to this, and the only thing men sought—despite the utterances of the learned and philosophers—was "to fuck." The contrast between *Fortuna* (Fortune) and *fottere* (fucking), is also emblematic of the difference between Machiavelli's and Vettori's attitudes toward women, as well as toward life in general.

Fortune would indeed accompany Machiavelli throughout his life, often in the guise of a female companion: There was "La Riccia," who remained loyal to him in adversity (exciting even Vettori's admiration); Barbera Raffacani, lover and inspiration for some of Niccolò's finest works; and especially the long-suffering Marietta. Machiavelli would pay tribute to his wife's devotion when, in one of his last letters, written in Imola, he would tell his son Guido to greet her, adding: "I have never longed more to be in Florence as now." Over the years, his frequent sexual escapades notwithstanding, daily practice and cohabitation, in good times as well as bad, had turned a relationship born of social convention into marital love and trust. Interestingly enough, both in his first will of 1512 and the final one of 1523, Niccolò chose his wife to serve as guardian of their children if any of them happened to be minors at the time of his death, despite the fact that in the first instance his brother Totto was still alive, and in any case, there were enough male relatives around to fulfill the job, if Machiavelli had so wished.*

---

* At the time, fatherless minors came under the jurisdiction of the *Ufficiali dei Pupilli* (Court of Wards) until they reached adulthood. A father could appoint a guardian to represent his children, in the event of his untimely demise, in their dealings with the Pupilli, with the guardian usually, but not invariably, being chosen from among his male relatives. For instance, Lodovico Capponi, one of Machiavelli's neighbors, appointed his wife instead of one of his brothers as the guardian of his offspring (ACRF, III [B], *Lodovico Capponi e figli*, f. 2r). Machiavelli choice of Marietta over one of his male relatives is eloquent testimony of the trust he placed in her.

In this context the wills' conventional phrase "beloved wife" (*uxori sua dilecta*) acquired a rather more profound meaning than usual. If Fortune was a woman, then Machiavelli had been lucky to find a spouse who, despite what he had once stated in *The Prince*, ultimately had been the victor in the struggle for conquest and submission.

5

~

BE MY VALENTINE

People believed Cesare Borgia cruel;
nonetheless, through his cruelty he redeemed
and pacified the Romagna, restoring it to
peace and confidence. In this sense, if one
considers matters properly, he showed himself
much kinder than the Florentines, who in
order to avoid the label of cruelty allowed
Pistoia to be destroyed.
— NICCOLÒ MACHIAVELLI
ON CESARE BORGIA

"The weakness of our contemporaries, stemming from lack of education and ignorance, makes the wisdom of the ancients appear inhuman or impossible to apply today," Machiavelli would write in his *Discourses*. Like any educated Renaissance man, he had the habit of looking at the past in order to find a solution to present problems, a trait even more pronounced in a person, such as Niccolò, lacking a family tradition of political practice. Yet, it was easy for him to graft his understanding of the ancient past to his experiences of the present: The Roman Republic of old, after all, had invented a formula for statecraft through trial and error. The Florentine Republic, ideally poised to continue Rome's heritage, could reach greatness by applying those well-tested lessons. Though Florence's newly acquired liberty tottered from 1501 to 1503, the city eventually emerged from one of the worst political crises in its history, and these years would be crucial for the development of Machiavelli's political thought.

The domestic and foreign threats the Florentines faced were intimately linked, and it is no wonder that Machiavelli—given his institutional position—would be forced to act as his country's fireman. No sooner had he returned from France than he had to deal with the civil war in Pistoia, which had been festering, with frequent outbreaks of violence, since 1499. Pistoia had always been a source of trouble for Florence, rent as it was between two rival factions, the Panciatichi and the Cancellieri. These large families and their associates also controlled a number of communities in the surrounding rural areas, allowing for the recruitment of large numbers of armed retainers from among the local country folk when needed, and these men could be brought into the city. The burning hatred between the Panciatichi and the Cancellieri had conditioned Pistoia's political life for centuries, and Florence had found it expedient to maintain that division to keep the subject city under control.

The Medici regime before 1494 had been partial to the Panciatichi, and naturally the advent of the Florentine Republic had turned the political tides in favor of the Cancellieri. Yet, the situation was rather more complex than it at first appeared, since a number of important Florentine families had established alliances and clienteles in Pistoia that in no way mirrored those existing in Florence. The Cancellieri, for instance, could count on the support of people who had been staunch *Palleschi* ("those of the balls," with a reference to the Medici coat of arms) under the Medici, and the opposite is true of the Panciatichi. As a result, Florence's policy toward Pistoia, far from being clear cut, would instead be fraught with ambiguity and indecisiveness.

Foreign elements further complicated the picture. The Vitelli of Città di Castello had strong family ties with the Panciatichi; and after the execution of Paolo Vitelli, his brother Vitellozzo is said to have recruited exiles from the Panciatichi to fight with the Pisans, and even sent his own soldiers against the Cancellieri in 1501. In reality, either of the two factions was potentially capable of turning Pistoia into a haven for the Republic's enemies, a nightmare of the worst kind for the Florentine regime.

Matters had come to a head in August 1500, when the Cancellieri, thanks to an adroit use of artillery and the aid of troops sent from Bologna by the local lord Giovanni Bentivoglio, had managed after a week of savage fighting to evict the Panciatichi from Pistoia. However, the latter were far from defeated, and from their strongholds in the countryside they conducted a lively and successful war against their enemies. In the face of these events Florence dithered, the regime apparently pleased with the Cancellieri success but at the same time thoroughly alarmed because the victors were proving less than pliable to the Republic's requests. For this reason, in February the Florentines decided to send four commissioners to Pistoia, although these officials refused to depart until they were provided with an adequate military force capable of cowing the Pistoiesi. Machiavelli tagged along, ostensibly because two of the commissioners belonged to the Ten; however, the presence of the secretary of the Dieci di Libertà e Pace in Pistoia should also be placed in the context of Florence having to face a very serious threat from abroad.

There's no doubt that Cesare Borgia was a man of considerable ability, daring, and ruthlessness. The third son of Cardinal Rodrigo Borgia and the redoubtable Vannozza de' Cattanei, once his father became Pope Alexander VI—Rodrigo blatantly and unabashedly bribing every buyable member of the conclave that gathered after the death of Innocent VIII—he became the strongman in Alexander's schemes, and these were all orchestrated for the purpose of permanently aggrandizing his immediate family. This pursuit required a substantial lack of principles— a requirement Cesare had no problem meeting. For him, deceit, corruption, fraud, and murder were merely part of a very pragmatic approach to politics—and though his contemporaries reeled in shock at some of his exploits, this was more due to their stunning success than to moral qualms.

Attaching himself to the then victorious Louis XII, Cesare had managed to marry into the French royal family, receiving the title of "Duke of Valentinois" (thus becoming known as *il Valentino* in Italy); more important, he could now tap into the military resources of the Valois. In a series of whirlwind campaigns from 1499 to the end of 1500 he had, with his father's spiritual, monetary, and legal blessing—and French troops— brought the unruly region of Romagna (ostensibly part of the papal domains, but in reality ruled by a series of quasi-independent polities) under his control, conquering Imola, Pesaro, Ravenna, and Forlì, where the feisty Caterina Sforza put up a stiff resistance before surrendering.

Borgia had timed his campaigns well, striking when the Venetians— who opposed his expansionist schemes, having their own designs on the Romagna—had their hands full fighting the Ottoman Empire. Even after Cesare received the title of Duke of Romagna from the pope, it was clear that he had a formidable appetite for more territories (as he had for power, money, and women) and that ultimately he intended to become lord of all of central Italy. Not surprisingly, Florence viewed *il Valentino's* progress with considerable alarm, which is understandable considering that his conquests had turned him into a very uncomfortable neighbor for the young Republic.

By the end of 1500 rumors had begun to spread about Borgia's plans to make inroads into Tuscany, with Pistoia as his possible objective. In Florence everyone feared that the Pistoiesi "would throw themselves in Valentino's arms," although nobody could be sure which of the two factions would be the most willing to rally in Cesare's support. On the one hand, it was known that the Panciatichi had been plotting with Borgia's henchmen, Vitellozzo Vitelli and Liverotto da Fermo, for the defeat of the Cancellieri; on the other, the Cancellieri were accused of having dealings with Valentino to evict the Panciatichi from their strongholds in the countryside. Clearly something had to be done, lest the Pistoia crisis cause the downfall of the Florentine Republic, and so, during the *gonfalonierato* of Piero Soderini (March-April 1501), the decision was made to support the return of the Panciatichi.

The latter had enjoyed the support of the Soderini during the past regime, Piero's father, Tommaso, being a staunch supporter of the Medici. Yet, the gonfalonier had for some time been leaning toward the popular faction. Indeed, the people of Florence, "moved by compassion," had taken the side of the Panciatichi, while many of the richest, although not the "wisest," favored their opponents. In April the Signoria took action, recruiting large numbers of irregular troops from the Florentine countryside and sending them to Pistoia together with the Florentine commissioners in charge of carrying out the government's wishes. In this way an uncertain truce was patched together between the two warring groups. An attempt was also made to reform the city's institutions, although the Cancellieri remained in control of Pistoia and the Panciatichi held on to their fortresses in the countryside. Nevertheless, by forcing the main leaders of the Cancellieri to come to Florence, Soderini had managed, albeit temporarily, to defuse the factional tensions within Pistoia.

The Pistoia settlement arrived none too soon. In May, Cesare Borgia, having taken Faenza and executed its young ruler, descended into Tuscany after a foray in the direction of Bologna. Supposedly he intended to proceed to the conquest of Piombino, on the Tyrrhenian coast. Bypassing the weak forces sent to block his advance, he proceeded south, leaving in his wake a devastated countryside. His arrival in Campi, a few miles from Florence, threw the city into a panic. However, not everyone in the city was displeased with Valentino's escapade. Apparently, a group of disgruntled ottimati, led by some of the most active supporters of the Cancellieri, had been plotting to force the government to call a parliament and create an oligarchic regime with the aid of Borgia.

It is possible that they were counting on their Cancellieri allies to open Pistoia's gates to Cesare, but Soderini's actions in the previous weeks had effectively deprived them and Valentino of a crucial power base. Borgia told the Florentine ambassadors that his foray into the Republic's territory had been decided at the insistence of his lieutenants Vitellozzo Vitelli and Paolo Orsini, as the former was seeking revenge for his brother's death, and the latter was trying to pave the way for the return of his relative Piero de' Medici. Playing a prearranged part in Cesare's play, Vitelli reassured the diplomats that he only wished to have his honor satisfied; those "few citizens" on his blacklist need not suffer loss of life or limb. Orsini instead insisted on the advantages the Florentines would gain by employing him in their service.

The ambassadors were unimpressed, believing instead that the objective of the charade had been to create "disunion and division" within the city. Valentino waited in Campi for news of a regime change in Florence, but a delegation of Cancellieri supporters arrived to inform him that the game was up. Frustrated in his ambitions, Borgia decided to turn his attention to easier targets, but not before forcing the Florentines into an agreement whereby they would have to employ him as their captain general for three years, guaranteeing a fixed number of troops and a yearly wage of 36,000 ducats. It would have been a crippling expense. But the Florentines proceeded to promise to repay Louis XII what they owed him for the use of his troops after the unfortunate campaign against Pisa and asked, in exchange, that the king order Cesare to depart. In the face of such powerful pressure, Valentino had no option but to leave, with a useless contract in his pocket, but no money to go with it. For once, the French alliance had served Florence well.

"Favored by the heavens and by Fortune": Thus Machiavelli would describe Borgia in a letter written in mid-May to the Florentine commissioners in Pistoia. Clearly, Valentino intrigued him as much as he scared his fellow citizens, especially because of Cesare's apparent relationship with Lady Luck. However, Niccolò had other things on his plate besides Borgia's good fate. As we have seen, he had traveled to Pistoia in February, and he would return there at least three more times between July and October. The 125 letters written by the secretary of the Ten attest to the amount of attention Pistoia demanded from him; and although

Niccolò would go to the war-ridden city in a subordinate position to the Florentine commissioners, his role as information-gatherer would nevertheless prove crucial for the government.

Admittedly, his memorandum "De rebus Pistoriensibus" (On the matters of Pistoia) does not reveal much about Niccolò's thoughts, being more a collection of facts than a meditation on how to resolve the crisis; nevertheless, it is clear that it contributed to Florence's policy toward Pistoia. The Ten would start a letter of October 26 to the Florentine commissioners with the words "According to what Niccolò Machiavelli has told us this morning, . . . " instructing them to allow the return of "as many Panciatichi as possible" and at the same time to do whatever they could to pacify the countryside. "Since the yokels obey none," this would mean quartering troops in the various communities. The influence of Machiavelli's way of thinking is rather more pronounced in two *sommarii* (reports) written by the Florentine commissioners. In essence, they proposed forming a "popular" government in Pistoia by excluding the most prominent families from power, and ending all divisions by forcing them to change their surnames and coats of arms. In addition, they said, the city should be exempted from all taxation for a decade so that it could rebuild its economy.

These proposals were never carried out, as the Florentine regime preferred to take the usual approach and keep Pistoia divided. The Republican government had neither the material means nor the political will to clamp down on the Pistoiese factions. As Machiavelli would comment some fifteen years later, using examples taken from classical antiquity as a logical template:

> To heal a divided city . . . one may proceed in three ways: kill the leaders, as they [the Romans] did; exile them; or force them to make peace, with the promise to remain quiet. Of these three methods the last is the more damaging, less certain and useless. Taking Pistoia as the best example of such a situation, . . . without doubt the first solution would have been the safest. But since such

executions have in them greatness and vision, a weak republic is
incapable of implementing them; indeed, only after much struggle
will it decide for the second way.

At the time of the troubles in Pistoia, Machiavelli had considered a
more novel solution. In the letter he drafted for the Second Chancery
on October 26, 1501, he suggested that to break the grip of the Panciatichi and the Cancellieri, Florence should recruit two hundred men
from each faction and send them to fight at Pisa. Machiavelli may have
already been thinking about the creation of a future militia, but when
this project saw the light Pistoia would not be included. Instead, Florence
looked to other parts of its domain for citizen troops—interestingly, the
same areas that had provided the makeshift soldiery that had helped to
pacify Pistoia in the spring of 1501.

If the Florentines ever thought that they had seen the last of Borgia,
then they were in for a rude shock. On September 3, Piombino surrendered to Cesare, who now could threaten Florence from the south as
well as from the north. Worse still, Valentino controlled the crucial naval
route from Civitavecchia to Genoa and if he so decided could get troops
to Pisa by sea. But for the time being Borgia appeared to be focused on
finishing the conquest of Romagna, selecting as his next declared objective Camerino, a territory dangerously close to Florence's southeastern
border. To accomplish this design he asked the duke of Urbino,
Guidobaldo da Montefeltro, to furnish him with troops and artillery, a
request that Guidobaldo was in no position to refuse.

Giudobaldo complied, perhaps hoping in this way to keep his own
state from falling into Cesare's rapacious hands. This was wishful thinking, for, as Agostino Vespucci would write from Rome to his friend Niccolò Machiavelli, Valentino had "sent Vitellozzo to do things that
reasonably he'll soon want to do himself," adding that Camerino feared
for itself and Urbino was "on the run." Seeing the writing on the wall, the
Florentines negotiated a new defensive treaty with France. Louis XII
agreed to the deal despite some misgivings—he still expected the Re-

public to pay him 50,000 ducats for the failed enterprise of Pisa, but worried that if he did not come to the aid of the Florentines, they could decide to throw in their lot with Emperor Maximilian of Habsburg. Given that, at the time, Maximilian had sided with the Spanish in the struggle for the kingdom of Naples, Louis desired to keep the route to southern Italy open.

Meanwhile, Valentino had joined the French in their Neapolitan enterprise, leaving his lieutenants to handle his affairs up north. In May 1502, the Florentine government got wind of a rumor that Vitellozzo Vitelli was in cahoots with some disgruntled citizens of Arezzo, always a Medici hotbed, and on the 5th of that month dispatched Machiavelli there to assess the situation, giving him the authority to take any measure he deemed appropriate to ensure Florence's dominion in the area. It is unknown whether Machiavelli actually went or not, no letter of his on this matter having survived or emerged to date. If he indeed did go to Arezzo, then he must have botched the job or underestimated the gravity of the situation.

On June 4, the city rose in revolt and immediately admitted Borgia's troops, led by Vitellozzo, within its walls. The majority of the towns in the Valdichiana, the region that stretched from Arezzo southeast toward the papal territories, also rose in rebellion or surrendered to Vitelli without a struggle. When news of these events spread, fighting once more started in Pistoia. The Florentine commissioners watched impotently as the brutal looting and killing raged, and the Pisans took advantage of the situation to occupy a number of key fortresses. It seemed that the Florentine Republic was on the verge of collapse, and that Borgia needed to give it just another small push. Significantly, Piero de' Medici showed up in Arezzo, apparently to wait for his inevitable return to his native city.

Valentino, however, took everyone by surprise when, with a swift and daring maneuver, he managed to capture the unguarded Urbino, sending Guidobaldo da Montefeltro fleeing with little more than a shirt on his back. Before starting this enterprise he had sent a message to Florence with a request that ambassadors be sent to him for the purpose of discussing matters of great importance. The fearful Republic immediately selected Francesco Soderini, bishop of Volterra, for the task, to be accompanied by the secretary of the Ten, Niccolò Machiavelli. We have no record of the two men previously being acquainted with each other, but the few days they spent together seem to have been sufficient for them to form a bond, possibly cemented by a common political outlook, and in the years to come Niccolò's friendship with the future Cardinal Francesco would pay substantial dividends. The Florentine ambassadors departed on June 22, and on reaching Pontassieve, some five miles outside Florence, they received the news of the fall of Urbino. In their letter to the Signoria, drafted by Machiavelli and signed by Soderini, they could not but underscore Borgia's "ruse and swiftness united with a most excellent success." They arrived in Urbino two days later, in the evening, but were immediately admitted into Cesare's presence.

Borgia, who had a knack for theatrics, received the two emissaries behind locked doors in a chamber dimly illuminated by torches. Displaying both arrogance and guile, he berated Soderini and Machiavelli about Florence's behavior toward him—including failing to pay the 36,000 ducats promised the previous year in Campi—exclaiming, "Your city is ill-disposed toward me; indeed, it treats me like a murderer." He then continued: "I don't like and can't trust this government. You need to change it," adding, "Between us there can be no middle way, you can only be my friends or my enemies." Just to be clear, Borgia reminded the two Florentines that during the past year he could have easily restored the Medici had he so wished, or imposed his own rule on Florence. Although he had refrained from doing so, he wanted to be absolutely sure of the Republic's goodwill toward him, since his territories bordered on Florence's for long stretches.

In reply to this outburst, the bewildered ambassadors defended their government and reminded Borgia about what his men were doing in the Valdichiana. Unabashed, Cesare retorted that he knew nothing about what had happened in Arezzo, but that Vitelli was indeed one of his men and he hoped he would keep up the good work. Moreover, the Florentines should not seek any favors from Valentino, because they did not deserve them. As for his own actions, he scoffed that God and men would forgive him, although he did not care if God did so, while men always forgave winners. At this point the two delegates played their trump card, namely, the defensive alliance between Florence and France. Borgia apparently remained unshaken, answering: "I know far better than you what the king thinks: You will be let down." It was an unproductive meeting, though it lasted two hours, and after it ended the two ambassadors departed "with little satisfaction."

Despite his aplomb, it is clear that Valentino was bothered by the possibility of French intervention in Florence's favor. The next day, in a game of "good cop/bad cop," the Florentine emissaries were visited by two of Borgia's henchmen, Giulio and Paolo Orsini, who tried to convince the ambassadors that the king of France had given Borgia a free hand, provided he acted swiftly, since Louis intended to delay as much as possible sending any military aid to the Republic—Cesare's self-assurance was proof enough of this. Valentino's troops could ride forty miles a day and catch Florence with its guard down. In any case, they added, should Louis decide to intervene, Borgia's troops were so numerous and well supplied with artillery that the French would prefer to fight with and not against them.

That evening, Machiavelli and Soderini had another parley with the duke, who, after repeating the same requests as the day before, issued an ultimatum: The Republic had to give him an answer in four days or else face the consequences of his wrath. After consulting with each other, the ambassadors decided that Soderini should remain to deal with their unpleasant host while Machiavelli rode back to Florence posthaste for further instructions. In reality, they were trying to gain as much time as possible.

In the meantime, the two men had written to Florence describing the events and painting a vivid portrait of Borgia. "This lord is very splendid and magnificent," they said, and so warlike that every great enterprise appears small to him. He never rests if seeking glory or the acquisition of new territories; nor does he know fatigue and fear. He arrives in a place before people know about his departure; he is beloved by his soldiers and has recruited the best in Italy. These factors make him victorious and redoubtable, to which one should add that he has Fortune's constant favor.

Even before Machiavelli and Soderini's mission, as an answer to the Borgia threat the Republic had strengthened Florence's defenses, sending troops under the energetic Antonio Giacomini toward Arezzo in order to block Vitelli's advance up the Arno Valley. The leaders of Florence had also dispatched a diplomat to Louis XII with a request for help. Concerned that Valentino had become too big for his breeches, and fearing him as a future source of trouble, the king agreed to send reinforcements and to order Cesare to abandon Arezzo. Yet the French troops camped near Milan hesitated to move despite Louis's orders, and some Florentines abandoned their city for fear of Vitelli. Others prepared themselves for what they expected to be a siege. To make matters worse, the government seemed incapable of finding an ambassador to send to the French in Milan. Finally, Piero Soderini, then a member of the Ten, accepted the unenviable task and departed alone toward the north of Italy.

The Florentine regime played for time, and as the days passed, Borgia's swaggering started to seem hollow. Francesco Soderini may have been in an uncomfortable situation in Urbino, but Cesare had started to become more pliable, trying to convince the bishop that an alliance with him would actually benefit the Florentines. Probably informed by his friends in France of the Republic's successful efforts with Louis XII, he had tried to downplay its importance; indeed, he attempted to convince Soderini that either the French troops would be too few, leaving Florence at his mercy, or too numerous, proving an unbearable burden for the Florentines. In the letters he wrote to his superiors back home, Soderini said that the duke desired nothing more than what had been agreed to in Campi. The government, however, would have none of it, and the bishop recounted how Borgia's face had changed completely when he received the news that Florence had rejected his proposals. The regime now felt more confident, Soderini having managed to convince the French commanders to march to the Republic's aid.

In Florence, a major constitutional change was under way, having been triggered by the events Valentino had set in motion. The rapid turnover of personnel in the various offices was proving a handicap for political stability; under the Medici this had been less of a problem because although the state was officially run by free institutions, real power had been in the hands of one family and its acolytes. The Great Council may have been more representative of the citizenry at large, but it could not be relied on to make rapid decisions, and for the executive's two-month term did not guarantee any sort of political continuity. Various proposals for constitutional reforms had been put forth in previous years, including the idea of instituting a new council to handle all financial legislation, instead of the Gran Consiglio, but none had ever seen the light. For an example of a stable executive the Florentines once again turned to the Venetian Republic. In Venice, the chief executive, or *doge*, served for life, yet his power was curbed by a series of institutional checks and balances.

Still, the idea of a permanent *gonfaloniere di giustizia* appealed to many: For those aspiring to a *governo stretto* it was a first step in that direction, and for the supporters of a *governo largo* it appeared to be a good way to uphold the existing constitution. Whatever the case, everyone expected the new man in charge to recover Pisa, solve the city's financial crisis, and provide a strong response to external menaces—such as Cesare Borgia. In a *pratica* of July 2, 1502, Pietro Ardinghelli proposed electing a gonfalonier who would serve in that position for life. The Great Council approved the plan without much opposition on August 26, and a list of 236 suitable candidates was duly drawn up. By his actions Borgia had managed to provoke a change of government in Florence, although—just to prove once more that one must be careful what one wishes for—it was not the sort of change he'd had in mind during his colloquiums with the Florentine delegates in Urbino.

6

HOLLOW WORDS

*The natural hatred that His Holiness has
always had for him [Cesare Borgia] is
common knowledge, [Pope Julius II] not
being able to soon forget his ten years in exile.
But the duke allows himself to be guided by a
spirited self-assurance and believes other
people's words to be less hollow than his own.*
—NICCOLÒ MACHIAVELLI,
IN THE AFTERMATH OF
POPE JULIUS II'S ELECTION

The long-awaited French troops arrived in Arezzo at the end of July 1502, and Vitellozzo Vitelli, despite an initial display of braggadocio, abandoned his recent conquests and withdrew, on Borgia's orders, toward the papal territories. Cesare himself had to travel to see Louis XII in Milan to justify his behavior, in the process putting all the blame on Vitelli. The king commanded the latter to present himself in person, but

Vitelli excused himself with a feigned illness. Acrimony, indeed, had become somewhat of an ailment for him: Never one to forget a slight, he deeply resented Valentino for tossing him to the wolves. Besides, like many other petty rulers of central Italy, he had started to feel uneasy with Borgia's ambition, fearing that sooner or he would become its victim.

The relief of Arezzo brought more work for Machiavelli. The Florentines worried that Louis would not return Arezzo and the other territories to Florence until the Republic paid him the remaining dues for the Pisa expedition. Just to confirm these suspicions, the French commander in Arezzo, Imbault, had shown no intention of returning to the city anytime soon and in fact seemed to be doing everything possible to show favor toward its inhabitants. As in the case of the Pisa expedition in 1500, there could be no guarantee that the French commander at Arezzo would follow the king's instructions; but this time the Florentines protested, forcing Louis to replace Imbault with the more trustworthy Monsieur de Langres. Machiavelli traveled with him to Arezzo in mid-August, staying in the city for a few days, and returned there a month later for about a week. During this period the most pressing matters for the Florentines were securing the leaders of the rebellion—as Niccolò would write to the commissioner Piero Soderini on September 8—and convincing the French to leave enough troops in the area to guard the Republic's reacquired possessions. Having agreed to leave behind a force of 150 "lances" (between 750 and 1,000 cavalry), Langres left at the end of September.

The Arezzo revolt would become a seminal moment in the development of Machiavelli's political thinking. A year after the events took place, he would write "Del Modo di Trattare i Sudditi della Valdichiana Ribellati" (On the Method of Dealing with the Rebels of the Valdichiana), an incisive and, to some extent, brutal piece of realpolitik in the form of a memorandum, directed probably to the Florentine government. Taking inspiration once again from his beloved ancient texts, he compared the way Florence had dealt with the Aretine rebels with examples from ancient Roman history. Arguing that men are the same in every era and suffer from the same passions, he said that given a certain situation, their actions will follow a predetermined pattern, and thus the same remedies may follow suit.

When the Romans had to deal with rebellious people, they forgave them if it was expedient to do so, but usually they destroyed their cities and deported the population to Rome, or imported so many foreigners that the original inhabitants became the minority. Inviting the Florentines to imitate "those who have been the masters of the world, particularly in a case where they can teach you to rule," Machiavelli suggested an attitude of leniency for places such as Cortona and Borgo Sansepolcro, but said it would be wiser to destroy the chronically untrustworthy Arezzo and disperse its inhabitants, "for the Romans maintained that rebels should be rewarded or utterly destroyed, and that any other way is fraught with the greatest danger." A year before penning those words, he had written to the Florentine commissioners in Arezzo urging them to capture as many rebels as possible, saying, "Better twenty more than one less, without any concerns for the number or the risk of depopulating the city."

In the second part of the memorandum, with a sudden logical shift, Niccolò moved into the world of contemporary politics. The pressing need for energetic action, he explained, had less to do with potential threats from beyond the Alps than with more certain perils nearer to home: Cesare Borgia certainly intended to make himself lord of Tuscany, and given the fact that the pope, Borgia's father, did not have many years to live, he would likely do so at the first opportunity, entrusting the enterprise to Fortune. For not only was Valentino a devious, fork-tongued schemer of the first degree, but, as Cardinal Francesco Soderini had once said, Valentino and the pontiff would "know the right moment and exploit it to the utmost."

The conclusion of the memorandum is missing, but from the rest of the text one may infer that it reiterated the suggestion about using punitive measures against Arezzo so that it would not again become Borgia's springboard for the conquest of the whole of Tuscany. The memorandum is highly revelatory of Machiavelli's mindset; clearly, his political thinking was already developing along the lines for which he later became famous. He would constantly maintain that since ancient Rome, especially under the Roman Republic, had developed a governing system that had allowed it to conquer the world, anything the Romans had done could—indeed should—be imitated. Of course, Niccolò did not have the monopoly on obsessions with antiquity; however, when analyzing contemporary events, he always reverted to historical precedents to support his case. And the one thing he shared with future political scientists was abstract theorization.

Machiavelli's tone in this document sounds more confident than one would usually expect from a civil servant, and even quite arrogant at times. For example: "[Valentino] has always had little consideration for the Venetians, and even less for you [the Florentines]." But Niccolò knew he could afford such bluntness, as much as it may have irritated his fellow citizens, because of the political changes that had taken place in Florence the previous autumn. On September 22, 1502, the Great Council had elected Piero Soderini as gonfaloniere di giustizia for life, a choice that many applauded. Soderini had a good reputation, partly because he had acquitted himself well on the previous occasion in which he had sat as gonfalonier. He was considered a political moderate, and, although a patrician, had always favored debates in the *collegi* over those in the rather more exclusive *pratiche*. His diplomatic skills were known to all, and because of these, the French had decided to come to Florence's aid that summer. Moreover, there was no chance of him establishing a dynasty, since he had no children.

For Machiavelli, Soderini's election would prove a momentous occasion: Not only had he worked with his brother Francesco, but he had also served under Piero when the latter had been one of the Ten. Niccolò would be one of the first to inform Soderini about his election, in a letter he sent to him while Soderini was still acting as commissioner in Arezzo. In the letter, Machiavelli expressed the desire that the new gonfalonier would soon deliver the goods that Florence expected from him. As time went by, the link between the two men would become stronger, so much so that Niccolò's enemies would brand him as Soderini's "minion" (*mannerino*). Lady Luck apparently still favored Machiavelli; in the future the twists and turns of Fortune would find Niccolò and Piero inexorably linked.

Even before the new chief executive took office, it had become clear that it would not be easy for him to solve Florence's problems. Cesare Borgia had managed to obtain Louis XII's forgiveness in exchange for supporting the French conquest of southern Italy; he had received a green light for the conquest of Perugia, Bologna, and Città di Castello (Camerino having already surrendered to him), plus the subjugation of the powerful Orsini family. This carte blanche strengthened Valentino's position, although legally he would be acting as supreme leader of the papal forces against rebellious subjects. The latter, however, had not remained idle, fearing, in the words of one of them, "to be devoured in turn by the dragon," and on September 25 they gathered in the castle of Magione, near the lake Trasimene, to discuss an offensive and defensive alliance against the duke of Romagna.

It did not take long for Borgia to get wind of these proceedings, and he moved to parry the blow by seeking alliances with Venice and Florence.* After some fruitless debates about whether to send an ambassador to Valentino, the Florentine regime entrusted the Ten with finding a special envoy for the task. The job fell once more to Niccolò Machiavelli, who on October 5 was instructed to travel to Imola immediately in order to renew the Republic's friendship with the duke, although the

---

* Most authors state that the conspiracy took place on October 9, the date when the conspirators formalized their anti-Borgia alliance. However, the Florentine Signoria's instructions to Machiavelli of October 5 clearly mention "the gathering and conference of the Orsini and their associates at Magione." Cesare evidently had a very good intelligence service, or the plotters were utterly careless in their actions. Considering the development of future events, one is tempted to believe the latter. As the Romans would have said: "Those whom the gods wish to destroy, they first turn crazy," something the classical-minded Niccolò would probably have endorsed.

Florentines had already declined to help the Magione group. Machiavelli had to convince Velentino to grant safe passage to Florentine merchants through his possessions, but remain noncommittal when it came to Borgia's requests.

Niccolò departed the following day and arrived in Imola on the 7th, leaving behind servants and baggage in order to travel more swiftly. Still "dressed in riding clothes," he immediately sought an audience with Borgia, who received him rather more amicably than the previous June. After the customary exchanges of courtesies, Valentino proceeded to berate his own rebellious associates, accusing them, in particular Vitelli and the Orsini family, of having forced his hand against Florence the year before, and therefore blaming them for the Republic's recent problems in the Valdichiana. Displaying a huge dose of pride, he belittled his enemies, calling them "a convention of failures" and stating that the king of France and the pope "had lit such a fire underneath him, that other water than them [the rebels] would be needed to put it out." Once the Orsini and Vitellozzo had been removed from the scene, he said, he would be happy to become Florence's ally, although, as Machiavelli noted, he remained evasive about the details of this eventual agreement.

Borgia's assurance appeared misplaced when, in the following days, news started trickling in about revolts flaring up everywhere in the duke's domains. Urbino and Camerino reverted to their former rulers, and on October 17 Valentino's army, under Don Ugo de Cardona and Don Miguel de Corella,* suffered a crushing defeat under Fossombrone at the hands of the lord of Perugia, Gianpaolo Baglioni. At Magione the rebels had agreed to raise 9,000 infantry and 100 light horses, plus a "blank" (i.e., future) force of 700 men-at-arms (Cesare would mockingly say that "blank" equalled "nonexistent"), while Borgia could put together, according to Machiavelli, about 100 men-at-arms and 8,500 in-

---

* Known by the Florentines as "Don Michelotto," Don Miguel de Corella was a Catalan and one of Borgia's chief henchmen, responsible for having murdered many of his master's adversaries by strangulation.

fantry, although he had sent recruiting agents everywhere, including among the Swiss and the French army in Milan. Thanks to these efforts, by the end of the month, and despite the debacle at Fossombrone, Valentino had some 5,400 infantry, 240 heavy cavalry, and 450 light horses, with more troops arriving by the day—a more than respectable army and a testimony to Borgia's efficiency in an emergency.

From the beginning, Machiavelli had correctly perceived that the support he enjoyed from France and the pope meant that Valentino was hardly finished, and on October 9 he had written home to inform the Florentines that if they wished to conclude a deal with Borgia, it would be unwise for them to dither too long: "It is clear that [the duke] is willing to make any sort of agreement." The Florentines, in turn, wrote back to tell Machiavelli that before deciding anything, they would need the approval of Louis XII. Machiavelli could do nothing but shake his head at the missed opportunity and watch Valentino's situation improve. He did, however, warn his bosses that "the later the season, the more difficult it shall be to work this field."

Being at Borgia's court started to have an effect on Machiavelli's thinking, particularly as regards military matters. He had been deeply impressed with a parade of Valentino's 6,000 conscripts, writing home that the duke could raise such a number in his domains—one man per household "ready to serve on a two-day notice." Borgia probably organized the spectacle to impress the Florentine envoy, and there is no doubt that Niccolò was deeply impressed. Yet, his already ingrained mistrust of mercenary troops made him all too ready to accept Cesare's words and overlook a crucial detail: Valentino did indeed raise up men among his subjects for military duty, but these could hardly be labeled as militiamen, being instead, for the most part, tough professionals and veterans of many a campaign. The duke in fact enjoyed the advantage of possessing one of the best recruiting grounds in all of Italy, the Romagna having for centuries been a breeding ground for mercenaries.

Other seeds of what would later become Machiavelli's standing army may have been planted on October 16, when Cesare asked Niccolò to request the Ten to send troops to the border at Città di Castello in order to levy men in the same way he did in his own territories. Machiavelli answered that he doubted the Republic's ability to raise such troops, owing to the lack of men and political will. However, in his letter to the Ten, Niccolò said that Florence should act as Borgia had suggested, adding, "I pray that your lordships not take this as a desire to teach you your business or as a show of arrogance, but consider it instead a natural manifestation of affection such as every man should have toward his country." The Ten answered three days later, informing Machiavelli that they had sent troops to Borgo Sansepolcro with two artillery pieces and that, despite wishing to do even more in reply to Borgia's request, "it is not possible for us to act otherwise." As usual, the Florentine Republic reacted to military emergencies with the tools it could lay its hands on, often old, scarce, and blunted.

Niccolò's comments in his letters to the Ten were appreciated by some, but irritated others. On October 11, Niccolò Valori wrote to Machiavelli praising him for his "direct, appropriate and sincere report, on which one may certainly build," adding, "Your judgment about the situation there is much sought here, as well as your opinion on what is happening in France and about the duke's intentions." Valori, one of the members of the Signoria for September and October, had worked with Machiavelli in Pistoia and had come to appreciate his quick mind and sharp wit, which once again were being turned to the Republic's benefit.

Biagio Buonaccorsi, Niccolò's most faithful associate in the chancery, in contrast, would on more than one occasion express concerns about Machiavelli's bluntness. On October 28, for instance, after reminding his friend to write more often, he warned him that his conclusions about Borgia's situation were "too daring" and had drawn criticism because they were in contradiction with the news that had been circulating in Florence. He concluded that Niccolò should "stick a sock in it,"* that is,

---

* The original expression sounds more like "stuff yourself" (*cazovi nel forame*).

limit himself to a bare narration of events and leave the judgments to others. Buonaccorsi's main concern was not that Machiavelli's analysis might be wrong, but instead that it might ultimately be right, making Florence's many armchair politicians in the Great Council appear ridiculous—and these were the same people who ultimately held the keys of his employment. Buonaccorsi's appeal fell on deaf ears, however, as, time and time again, Machiavelli displayed a knack for provoking the wrong people.

Niccolò had grown to admire Borgia's self-assurance. He found it difficult to obtain information at Fossombrone, however, "for at this court," he wrote, "no one talks about matters that should be kept silent." Cesare minimized the efforts of his enemies, in particular those of the coward Vitelli, whom he described as "only good at destroying defenseless places and stealing from those who dare not react." Yet rumors abounded about the rebels' progress, causing Machiavelli to prudently state, "I can only write about what I hear, and understand but what I may." Borgia's poise seemed to be one huge bluff, but he did agree to allow safe passage for the Florentine merchants traveling through his territories.

For Machiavelli this had been a singular success, since it meant he had managed to fulfill one of the crucial parts of his mandate, yet the Republic appeared scarcely interested in the matter (despite the fact that in Niccolò's commission Florence's Levantine trade was described as the city's "stomach"). Machiavelli's advice notwithstanding, the Florentines believed that Borgia's days were numbered; therefore it would be useless to attempt to reach any sort of conclusive agreement with him: "You are a dick," Buonaccorsi would write in mid-November to Machiavelli, mocking his efforts to get the city to strike an agreement with Valentino.

Yet, Cesare was far from finished; in fact, he was ready to strike back. Despite the rebellions in Urbino and Camerino, the bulk of his domains had remained loyal, thanks to a mixture of repressive measures and good administration. Moreover, the troops sent by Louis XII to aid Borgia were on their way, and the pope had been generous in appropriating the church's riches for his son's causes. The rebels, seeing that they were fighting a losing battle, one by one sought to make peace with Borgia. The Orsini as a group were the first to defect, asking to meet with Valentino in person: "They are making fun of me," the latter told Machiavelli on October 23, after indulging himself in a verbal rampage against the conspirators.

Paolo Orsini arrived in Imola two days later, in disguise, but apparently managed to obtain a reconciliation with the duke. "But I know not his [Borgia's] true intentions," Machiavelli would write, "nor can I see how he can forgive the insult or they [the Orsini family] forsake fear." On October 28, Valentino, Vitelli, and Orsini signed a mutual defense agreement (Machiavelli managed to surreptitiously obtain a copy of the pact on November 10). The former rebels agreed to return Urbino and Camerino, while Borgia promised to enlist them once more in his service—in essence it was an agreement to "forgive and forget," despite the fact that a few days later Borgia would describe Vitelli as a "poisonous snake, the ruin of Tuscany and Italy."

The turn of events had left Niccolò puzzled—and desperate to understand the duke's intentions. "I have to deal with a prince that runs his own shop, and I need time to verify facts lest I write fantasies or dreams," an irritated Niccolò would write, answering the complaint of the Ten about the paucity of letters arriving from Imola. To make matters worse, he had been ill for some time, but his requests to be recalled had been rejected, to the detriment of his household's harmony. Marietta had been furious about his prolonged absence—not to mention the money he had spent on a velvet robe (*uchettone*) he had ordered so that he could cut a better figure at Borgia's court. Biagio Buonaccorsi, who was on the receiving end of Marietta's complaints, found himself also having to fulfill numerous requests from Niccolò, including sending him a copy of Plutarch's *Lives*. Lacking direct information, we may presume that Machiavelli wished once again to search ancient sources to find answers for the enigmatic Borgia's behavior.

By the end of November everything seemed to have fallen into place for Cesare. The French troops had arrived, the conspirators had acknowledged his leadership, and the lords of Urbino and Camerino were on the run. A couple of weeks later, Borgia departed for Cesena with Machiavelli in train, ostensibly because of the lack of victuals in the Imola area, Cesare's court and army "having even eaten the stones." Niccolò, his illness diminished, thanks in part to 25 ducats sent to him by gonfalonier Soderini, confessed that it had been impossible for him to figure out Valentino's true intentions. He warned, however, that "he moves swiftly when his own interest is at stake."

The confirmation of Machiavelli's words arrived a few days later when one Ramiro de Lorqua, a fierce-looking individual who had been Borgia's strongman in Romagna—and a singularly brutal law enforcer—was suddenly seized, thrown into a dungeon, and, three days later, beheaded. At the time, Machiavelli could but speculate about the reasons behind Lorqua's death, guessing that Cesare had turned him into a convenient scapegoat to be sacrificed to public opinion once he had accomplished the task of pacifying his master's domains. Given his ability to gather information, Niccolò could not have missed the fact that Ramiro had been executed on evidence of corruption, embezzlement, and, even more serious, conspiring with Valentino's enemies. And yet, years later, when writing *The Prince*, Machiavelli would state that Borgia's decision to execute Lorqua was but another example of the duke's political ability, since "he wished to show that any cruel deeds that might have happened were not his fault but caused by the brutal nature of his representative." By then, a disgraced Machiavelli desperate for employment had begun to see the merits of Borgia-style inventiveness.

As if the disloyalty of some of his most trusted followers had not been enough, Cesare was facing another serious predicament. On December 20, the heavy cavalry sent to Valentino's aid by Louis XII left for Milan, taking with them "more than half of his [the duke's] forces and three-quarters of his reputation." This unexpected departure sent Borgia's court "into a tizzy," but Machiavelli could not discover the reasons for this departure, despite extensive conversations with the French commanders. Cesare nevertheless continued his march, still having with him about 5,000 Swiss, German, Gascon, and Italian infantry. Although speculations were rife about his next objective, it soon became clear that he had set his sights on Senigallia, which was held by Giovanna da Montefeltro for her young son, Francesco Maria della Rovere, with the aid of the Genoese condottiere Andrea Doria, later a famous naval commander.

Learning of Borgia's advance, all three fled, but not before ordering the castellan to surrender the citadel to Valentino. Cesare arrived at the gates of Senigallia on December 31, being received there by the former rebels Vitellozzo Vitelli, Liverotto Eufreducci da Fermo, and Paolo Orsini, whom Borgia had sent in advance to occupy the town. There is evidence that these individuals were planning to kill their master and that the departure of the French cavalry had actually been planned by the duke himself to lure the would-be murderers into a false sense of security. Be that as it may, once he entered Senigallia, Valentino adroitly maneuvered his troops to separate Paolo, Vitellozzo, and Liverotto from their men; then, at a prearranged signal, the three condottieri were seized and bound by Borgia's soldiers, who then set upon the troops of the captured conspirators.

Machiavelli arrived in Senigallia from Fano that evening to find the town in a turmoil. In a terse message to the Ten, he noted that he believed the captured men would not be alive in the morning. This prediction proved to be correct: That night, Borgia had Vitelli and Eufreducci strangled by Don Michelotto; Orsini survived another three weeks because Cesare and the pope wished to get their clutches on Paolo's family—"so that they can decide to have a nice party," Niccolò would caustically comment. The pope had been informed of his son's intentions on the eve of the Senigallia operation, and no sooner did he receive the news of its success than the leading members of the Orsini faction in Rome were arrested and thrown in jail. The old, blind, and debauched Cardinal Gianbattista Orsini, believed to be the mastermind of the Magione conspiracy, would die there soon afterward—poisoned, according to rumors circulating at the time—the pope having already confiscated all his property.

Machiavelli saw Borgia soon after his arrival in Senigallia, finding the duke in an excellent mood. Cesare told Niccolò that Florence should be grateful to him for having removed "those evil weeds that were polluting Italy" and asked that the Republic send him Guidobaldo da Montefeltro, should the latter seek refuge in Florentine territory. Valentino's assistants later added that it would be appropriate for Florence to send a proper ambassador to Borgia "chosen from among the most prominent citizens." Machiavelli conveyed this request along with another bit of news. Goro Gheri, wanted by the Republic for his role in the Pistoia upheaval, had been apprehended by some of the duke's Spanish soldiers, who were demanding two hundred ducats for delivering him to the Florentine authorities. "Your lordships should consider this case," Niccolò wrote at the end of his letter. The Ten answered a week later, saying that although they wished to get their hands on Gheri, they thought the price for his ransom to be excessive. They instructed Machiavelli to do the necessary haggling to reduce the sum to "80 or at most 100" ducats. Gheri eventually made good his escape. Little did Niccolò know that his path would again cross Gheri's in the future under very different circumstances.

In the meantime, Borgia had decided to settle a few more scores. After evicting Giampaolo Baglioni from Perugia, he turned his attention to Siena, seeking revenge on the city's de facto lord, Pandolfo Petrucci, for his role in the Magione conspiracy. Once more Borgia entertained Machiavelli with the usual request for an alliance with Florence, pointing out that the Republic would have willingly spent 100,000 ducats to get rid of Vitelli and the other conspirators, and so it owed him at least what had been agreed upon at Campi. Florence should uphold that deal "so as not to appear ungrateful, contrary to your custom," he said, adding that Petrucci had been the real mover behind the Arezzo rebellion. In any case, Florence should not worry about Louis XII, since the king had promised to protect Siena, not Petrucci. Borgia had once more started to assume a threatening tone, and therefore it was with relief that Niccolò informed him that the Republic had appointed Jacopo Salviati as ambassador to his court. His task ended, Machiavelli departed for home on January 20.

Back in Florence, Machiavelli would write a detailed account of what had happened in Senigallia. He had already drafted a more succinct report to the Ten on the same subject a few days before leaving Borgia. Given that he had not been present at the arrest of Vitelli, Eufreducci, and Orsini, it is quite possible that he obtained the information directly from Cesare, however, and therefore certain details of the narrative, such as those relating to the craven behavior of Vitellozzo and Liverotto when they were about to be executed, should be taken with a grain of salt.

This document is more of a cautionary tale about Borgia's ruthlessness than an early example of "Machiavellism." Indeed, the report should be read in conjunction with a statement Niccolò wrote a few months later, in his memo "Parole dette sopra la Provvisione del Denaio" (Speech about Providing Money): "We know what sort of people [the pope and Valentino] are, their behavior, and how little we may trust them." Borgia's words and actions clearly impressed Machiavelli, but not necessarily in a positive way. Like any other Florentine, he could not forget the duke of Romagna's blackmail at Campi, nor what he had told the Florentine envoys in Urbino in the aftermath of the Arezzo rebellion, which he had certainly masterminded. As for the execution of his former associates, the manner in which it had been done may have been surprising, but it was hardly shocking: After all, Florentine history was full of similar episodes.*

Machiavelli was back in the chancery on the morrow of his return, most of his work consisting in the day-by-day administration of the Florentine military effort. He also wrote to his brother Totto, who had opted

---

* It should be remembered that Valentino had the legal authority to back his actions, being both duke of Romagna and commander in chief of the papal forces. By executing Vitelli, Eufreducci, and Orsini, he had brought only a few of the Holy See's rebellious subjects to justice. These men, incidentally, were themselves no lambs. Eufreducci, for one, had taken control of Fermo by murdering his uncle's entire family.

for an ecclesiastical career, about Totto's hopes of obtaining a parish through litigation, since the present incumbent of the benefice had gotten it through simony. Pragmatically, Niccolò suggested that Totto attempt to reach an agreement without having to spend money, despite all the evidence his brother could muster, adding pointedly: "You know how many disputed benefices have been gained, and lost, through sodomy—rather a more unfair way." Machiavelli knew the works of the Florentine poet Dante Alighieri and may have recalled his statement: "Laws may exist, but who will enforce them?" Niccolò's contemporaries, even those wearing clerical garb, responded to the customs and practices of their own times, and for this reason Machiavelli suggested that his brother find a few influential people to back his cause, rather than trying to defend any legal rights he might have had.

Niccolò was aware that law was useless unless backed by force, and this was equally true, or even more true, in matters of statecraft. This would be the main theme of the aforementioned *Parole dette sopra la Provvisione del Denaio*, which Machiavelli wrote in March 1503. In this piece, he urged Florentines to dip into their pockets for the sake of their own security—but the document was so forceful in its wording that it was probably never intended for the general public, unless Machiavelli wished to arouse the wrath of the whole city. More likely, it was a memo written for the gonfalonier, Piero Soderini, who at the time was desperately trying to find a remedy for Florence's chronic lack of funds, but had seen all his efforts stonewalled by his small-minded fellow citizens. From January to April, the Great Council refused to pass any tax bills, forcing the government to rely on loans to finance the war with Pisa, employ troops, and pay Louis XII the yearly 40,000 ducats required by the agreement of the previous year.

Soderini had also started to become unpopular. He had to deal not just with the petty members of the Great Council, but also with the advocates of *governo stretto*, not to mention those who secretly wished for the return of the Medici. In addition, grain prices rose steadily from November 1502 to the following May, creating bitter resentment against the government by the lower classes. In this context we can well understand Machiavelli's outburst in the *Parole* against his fellow citizens. He underscored their shortsighted stinginess by the use of examples taken from contemporary as well as past events: If Florence wished to be strong, argued Niccolò, then it had to provide itself with enough forces to be credible, or else risk losing its liberty.*

All this required a long-term financial policy far removed from the day-to-day politicking that the Florentines seemed to cherish so much, comforting themselves with the belief that French aid would always be at hand, and ignoring the fact that in international affairs, might was right. In the end, the government did manage to reduce the interest rates paid by the *Monte Comune* (the institution in charge of Florence's public debt), and, in mid-April, to obtain a further, but smaller, *accatto* (forced loan) to finance the Pisa war. This compromise solution may have appeased the Great Council, but it did nothing to endear Soderini to his fellow patricians, many of whom were among the Monte's biggest creditors.

Just to confirm Machiavelli's words about Florence's misplaced sense of security, on April 28 the Spanish forces in southern Italy inflicted a crushing blow against the French at the battle of Cerignola—one of the turning points in the history of warfare—and a fortnight later entered Naples. Initially these developments did not appear to worry Florence, which in the late spring started a campaign against Pisa with the usual capture of a few enemy fortresses. Others were quicker to see that the balance of power in Italy had changed. The pope and his son Cesare welcomed the French defeat, having become resentful that Louis XII's tutelage was not allowing them to pursue their planned policy of conquest. Alexander VI immediately tried to negotiate an alliance with Spain and attempted to get the money-starved Florentines to follow suit by offering

---

* It is interesting to note how echoes of Machiavelli's words can still be found in the complaints of Florentines today. People say that the city is being run by *bottegai* (shopkeepers) who are concerned only about their daily financial gains, while allowing multinationals to destroy Florence's identity by turning it into a Renaissance Disneyland.

them the possibility to tax the fiscally exempt ecclesiastical revenues in their domains. As further incentive, at the end of May the pontiff made Francesco Soderini a cardinal, a move he believed would strengthen his position with the Florentine government (not to mention the 20,000 ducats people said Francesco had paid for the dignity). The Republic, however, remained steadfast in its alliance with Louis XII, although it had to release the French soldiers in its service and promise to send hired troops to fight in southern Italy—despite the fact that many in Florence were openly accusing the French of having sabotaged the recovery of Pisa in order to continue extorting money from the city.

Machiavelli had spent most of his time at home, except for a brief mission to speak with Pandolfo Petrucci in Siena. Petrucci had been forced by Valentino to flee to Lucca the previous January, but had soon returned home, much to Borgia's chagrin, and Niccolò was supposed to sound him out on a possible alliance between Florence and the pope. The mission proved unfruitful, and the projected treaty never saw the light. In the meantime, Borgia had been up to his usual tricks, in April starting to move some of his military units uncomfortably close to the Florentine border. In July, rebels from Arezzo and other areas of the Valdichiana started to appear on Florence's southeastern frontier, and people believed that Cesare intended to fight for the Pisans.

However, Borgia kept everyone guessing: "The Duke of Romagna," Machiavelli would write on July 14 to the Florentine governor of Arezzo, Giovanni Ridolfi, "is giving money in Rome to his men-at-arms, and nobody knows whether he sides with the French or the Spanish." Luckily for Florence, a large French army had started to descend through Italy on its way to Naples, and on July 31 a gleeful Niccolò informed one of the commissioners in Valdichiana that "these forces are very numerous and should arrive here soon, thus the duke will not dare to attack us." Fortune, once again, had saved the Republic from losing its liberty.

Lady Luck would continue to smile on Florence, but toward others her countenance was about to change. On August 18, Pope Alexander VI died after a brief illness—Machiavelli commented in his *Decennali*

(The Decennials) that with "holy kicks in the rear" he had been joined among the "blessed spirits" by "his faithful handmaidens: lust, simony and cruelty"*—depriving his son of both his political and financial support. Cesare had taken ill at the same time, so seriously that in Florence people believed that his days were numbered. Valentino's ailment did not allow him to move with his usual swiftness, but on the morrow of his father's death he secured for himself several strategic places in Rome, including the papal treasury and the vital fortress of Castel Sant'Angelo, located on the Tiber near the Vatican. The duke's enemies immediately rose up once more, however, and within weeks a number of his recent conquests had reverted to their former lords.

In an effort to avoid losing his other possessions, Borgia threw himself into the arms of Louis XII, obtaining in exchange the king's agreement that he could retain the Romagna. More important, Cesare wanted to make sure that the next pontiff would not be hostile to him—but his new alliance with the French court meant that he could not count on the roughly eleven votes that the Spanish could muster among the cardinals. Also, despite having brought his own troops to Rome, he had no hope of overruling the conclave by force, because the Colonna, Orsini, and Savelli families—all victims of Borgia at one time or another—had all shown up in force in the city. Thus, when the papal electors convened on September 16, it soon became clear that Cardinal d'Amboise—the candidate that the king of France and Borgia supported, despite the fact that the cardinal and Borgia shared a mutual dislike for each other—had no chance of being elected, and as a compromise solution, on September 22, the choice fell on the old and frail Francesco Todeschini Piccolomini, who took the name of Pope Pius III.

The new pontiff issued a few decrees in Cesare's favor but refused to provide him with military assistance, while the duke's enemies clamored

---

* Machiavelli's satire against Alexander sounds rather more ferocious when one recalls the passage in the Gospel according to Luke, where Mary agrees to become the mother of Jesus with the words: "I am the Lord's handmaiden" (ecce ancilla Domini).

for his blood; the Venetians, meanwhile, freed from their war with the Ottoman Empire, had already started to make inroads in the Romagna. To save him from possible murder, the pope allowed Borgia, now deserted by both his friends and his soldiers, to take refuge with a few retainers in the Castel Sant'Angelo. Cesare's already bleak situation did not improve when the new pontiff took his last breath on October 18, less than a month after his election.

As soon as the news of Pius's death reached Florence, the Republic decided to dispatch an envoy to watch the proceedings of the forthcoming conclave, and the choice fell once more on Niccolò Machiavelli, mainly because the government wanted Cardinal d'Amboise to convince Louis XII to release Florence from the obligation to contribute some 400 heavy cavalrymen to the king's Neapolitan campaign. Niccolò was also instructed to attempt to appease Cardinal Raffaello Riario, who had accused the Florentines of favoring the return of Antonio Maria Ordelaffi to the lordship of Forlì, instead of Caterina Sforza's children—incidentally, the cardinal's nephews.* Somewhat incongruously, the Florentines maintained that Ordelaffi's reinstatement had occurred at the request of his present subjects, but that at the same time the Republic feared that otherwise Forlì would have fallen into the hands of the Venetians.

Florence's attempt to walk the Italian political tightrope fooled few and displeased many, as Machiavelli reported from Rome on October 28. The French, in particular, were very unhappy about Valentino's troubles in Romagna and had decided to formally protest what had happened in Forlì. Cardinal Riario bluntly told Niccolò that people always looked at results, not the ways by which these were achieved; since the result of Florence's meddling had been that his nephews were deprived of their rights, the Riario would seek the aid of anyone willing to help them, including the Venetians. As for the matter of the troops for Louis XII, Machiavelli could not get a firm answer from Amboise, the latter being

---

* The Riario had been given Forlì in 1480 by their relative Pope Sixtus IV, replacing the Ordelaffi as lords of the city.

too occupied with the negotiations for the conclave to pay much attention to him. Borgia, still in Castel Sant'Angelo, entertained high hopes that the new pontiff would be one of his friends.

Valentino's hopes were not illusory. He had managed to reconcile himself with the Spanish and had even convinced them to back the candidacy of Giuliano della Rovere, known as Cardinal San Piero in Vincoli from the church in Rome where he was titular priest. It was a bold move on Borgia's part (rather too bold, as it turned out), since della Rovere had been one of his father's bitterest opponents, paying for his defiance with numerous years of exile abroad. Moreover, he had the support of many of Valentino's enemies. Nevertheless, since he was considered the front-runner for the papacy, Cesare considered it expedient to strike a deal with him. Giuliano was all too willing to obtain Borgia's support by promising that, once elected, he would make the duke captain general of the church and support his territorial policies. However, behind Borgia's back, the cardinal did not hesitate to tell the Venetian ambassador that men often behaved according to necessity, but once free from constraints, "act differently." If Valentino thought, as Machiavelli would note, that della Rovere was prepared to forgive and forget all the humiliations he had suffered at the hands of the Borgia, then he was gravely mistaken.

On the morning of November 1, it was announced that Giuliano della Rovere had become pope, taking the name of Julius II. Informing the Florentine authorities about that fact, Machiavelli wrote that Julius II would have trouble honoring the many promises he had made before his election, "many being in contradiction with each other." Julius, however, was quite prepared to dispense with such niceties, and although on the morrow of his election he had confirmed his promises to Borgia, a few days later he had no compunction about telling the Venetian ambassador that there was no need to remind him not to support Borgia's ambitions in the Romagna. That province belonged to the church, and those who held territories there did so as vicars or vassals of the Holy See.

The message was intended for Valentino as much as for the Venetians, who by attacking Faenza had made clear that they desired to take the region for themselves. Cesare had started to feel the ground slip from underneath his feet, and when Machiavelli met with him on November 6, the duke berated him and his government with "words filled with passion and poison": He considered Florence, not Venice, to be his real enemy, and he would soon be laughing at the sight of the weak Florentine state in ruins at the hands of the Venetians; as for the French, they would lose Naples, or in any case be unable to help the Republic. Cardinal d'Amboise, also present during this conversation, took umbrage at these words and retorted: "God never lets sins go unpunished, let alone those of this one here." With the benefit of hindsight—or, as the Florentines would say, acting like "the Brozzi astrologer"*—Borgia's words appear prophetic, particularly as regards the French. Yet, given the vagaries of Italian politics and the uncertainty of warfare, Cesare could not have predicted the French defeat in Naples a few weeks later.

Borgia's ire was not the only problem Machiavelli had to contend with. By now Marietta had resigned herself to her husband's poor letter-writing, but not everyone displayed such tolerance: "We are surprised not to receive more up-to-date news," the Ten would write on November 2—a refrain that Niccolò would hear again and again while in the chancery. While it is true that because of the government's stinginess, Machiavelli was not able to employ fast couriers as much as he would have liked,† he does appear to have been lazy in compiling his official

---

* This expression refers to one Sesto Caio Baccelli, born a few years after Machiavelli's death and famous for predicting the obvious. The Florentines describe wisdom in hindsight as "acting like the Brozzi astrologer, who recognized thorns by touch and shit by its smell" (*far come lo Strolago di Brozzi, che riconosceva i pruni al tatto e la merda dal puzzo*).

† Before the invention of the modern postal system, mailing letters could be cripplingly expensive. People often preferred to entrust their correspondence to individuals who happened to be going to the same place as the documents, rather than, as one character aptly put it, giving them to "these murderers of the postal service" (*questi assassini delle poste*). ASF, MP, 3901, nnf (Cristoforo Bronzini, in Rome, to Demiurgo Lambardi, in Florence, May 10, 1624).

missives. The government expected him to at least pay lip service to bu-
reaucratic conventions by sending regular updates—no matter what the
substance—but it appears that Niccolò had no time for this sort of game
and would admit as much a few years later to one of his friends, when
away on official duty in Verona: "I am stranded here, nobody knowing
anything about anything, and yet in order to seem active I'm busy imag-
ining what sort of rants I can write to the Ten." Rather undiplomatically,
he had already told his bosses once: "I resent being accused of laziness,
having faced perils, discomfort, expenses and fatigue far greater than
what your lordships' salary or my possibility allow."

Machiavelli had started to develop the habit of rubbing people the
wrong way, an unwise behavior, to say the least, and potentially disastrous, if combined with ill-concealed arrogance. While in Rome he received a letter from Agnolo Tucci, a stationer and one of the priors at
that time, telling him to remind Cardinal Soderini about the bishopric
Tucci wished for one of his relatives, adding: "Should it be done without
expense you would earn the gonfalonier's gratitude." It is possible that
by mentioning Piero Soderini, Tucci was trying to impress Machiavelli,
but despite having asked for a quick reply, he got no answer. The gonfalonier, as a matter of fact, had other worries than one of the priors' family ambitions, and when writing to Niccolò asked him only to send
up-to-date information about the events in the kingdom of Naples.

The Republic's other concern was the turmoil in the Romagna, and
Machiavelli followed its development from Rome and provided detailed
news whenever he could get hold of it. Despite this, on November 22
Tucci sent him another missive in which he berated the French for not
having listened to the Florentine's advice "and taken our troops." He also
asked Machiavelli to inform the papal government that the Florentines
would not watch passively as the Venetians took over the Romagna,
"since we believe that this cannot happen without the pope's complicity
and consent."

Once again Machiavelli ignored the letter, forcing a concerned Biagio
Buonaccorsi to beg him to respond: "Tucci is beside himself with fury,"

Buonaccorsi would write on December 4, mentioning how the prior had viciously attacked Niccolò in front of the whole government. Although Tucci had not elicited much sympathy from his colleagues, Buonaccorsi told Machiavelli to be careful, because some people had disliked the positive comments in his reports about Cardinal Soderini. Niccolò became impatient with Tucci: If the man's imperious tone was not enough, he resented the fact that he was acting as if he were the supreme arbiter of Florentine politics, rather than a member of a two-month government. Machiavelli did not like being publicly bad-mouthed by someone he probably considered his social inferior (to make matters worse, Tucci had addressed Machiavelli with the intimate *tu* instead of the formal *voi*).* Dipping his sharpened pen in venomous ink, Niccolò answered the self-important prior, using the *voi* at every step:

> I received your letter of the 22nd; and although I could not make out the signature, I believe I recognized the hand and the style. Nonetheless, even if mistaken I think it appropriate to answer you. You talk about the perils of Romagna, now that Faenza has been lost; you mention that you must attend to your own necessities, since those who should be making decisions are not doing so; you believe the pope is involved; you worry about French affairs; you remind me to be thoughtful and conscientious, etcetera. All these affairs have been treated in official correspondence to me, and my extensive replies are available; however, not wishing to let you

---

* Machiavelli used the *tu* when writing to his children, but otherwise, even when writing to his closest friends, he invariably employed the *voi*. The *tu*, however, could be a way to emphasize rank—for instance, when addressing a social inferior, or in the case of a Florentine governmental body writing to an official. Tucci, although one of the priors, was not writing in the government's name, as much as he may have liked to believe so, and thus became an easy target for someone like Machiavelli who, despite a pronounced disregard for accepted conventions, had a keen sense of his social and administrative position.

down again, I shall go over these matters again at your request. I
shall write in the vernacular, just in case I used Latin in my letters
to the chancery, even if I don't believe so.

Machiavelli's sarcasm could not have been more blatant. Since he
never wrote his official correspondence in anything other than Italian,
he was in effect calling Tucci an uncouth and preposterous fool. The rest
of the letter simply underscores this, as Niccolò caustically went over
every point Tucci had raised in his missive, ending with a parting shot:
"I do not believe that anyone who is supposed to tell the truth would
write differently." The "prudent and discreet" Machiavelli—to use the
words of Niccolò Valori at the time of the Pistoia troubles—had been
replaced by an often conceited individual, confident of his position because of his mentors in powerful places. His enemies could only bite the
bullet and wait.

Time, however, had run out for Cesare Borgia. Seeing him abandoned
by everyone and refused a safe conduct even by the weak Florentine Republic, it had not taken long for Julius to renege on his promises to
Valentino with the excuse that the latter had become a rebel by refusing
to return some of his possessions to the Holy See. Brought to Rome
under virtual arrest, he was later moved to Ostia, but managed to escape
to Spanish-held Naples. Ferdinand of Aragon and his wife, Isabella of
Castile, who could not forgive Borgia's pro-French policy—let alone his
criminal character—had him sent as a prisoner to Spain, Luis XII having
already stripped him of his French titles and possessions.

Escaping yet again, Cesare sought refuge with his brother-in-law, Jean
d'Albret, King of Navarre, for whom he would die fighting in the course
of a petty skirmish. At the time of his downfall everyone expressed relief,
glad to be rid of such a monster—"a basilisk," Machiavelli would call him
in his *Decennali*, who "whistles sweetly to ensnare his enemies." Only
later, when Niccolò's fortunes had taken a turn for the worse, would he
start to appreciate Cesare's realistic, if brutal, approach to politics, stating
unequivocally: "If I were a new prince, I would imitate Valentino's deeds
on every possible occasion."

7

A MOST BEAUTIFUL THING

*And everyone agreed that such a beautiful
thing had never before been organized in the
city of Florence.*

—LUCA LANDUCCI,
ON THE FIRST PARADE OF THE
FLORENTINE MILITIA, MAY 2, 1505

The Italian political and military situation changed abruptly on December 28, 1503, when the Spanish, under Gonzalo de Cordoba, the victor at the battle of Cerignola, crossed the river Garigliano south of Gaeta and won a resounding victory over the French forces entrenched there. That Piero de' Medici had drowned in the Garigliano while trying to ferry artillery back to Gaeta was hardly a consolation for the Republic, and as Louis XII's remaining troops retreated north toward Milan, Machiavelli may have recalled Borgia's words of a few weeks before: Not only had the French lost the kingdom of Naples, but they were in no position to help their Florentine allies.

In a quandary, with the Pisa war stagnating, the Venetians becoming more aggressive in the Romagna, and rumors abounding about the Spanish making inroads into Tuscany, the Florentine government raised troops in haste, but before taking more active countermeasures it first needed to know the king of France's intentions. Machiavelli had just returned from Rome, but on January 19 the Signoria decided to send him to the French court to assist the Florentine ambassador, Niccolò Valori. Machiavelli's previous experience there, as well as his relationships with some prominent characters close to the king, probably influenced the decision, although officially his mission was to renegotiate Florence's contribution to France's military effort.

According to their instructions, the two diplomats were to be very frank with Louis about Florence's situation and find out whatever they could about his future plans, pointing out that by helping the Republic, the king could also preserve his own possessions in Lombardy; otherwise, the Florentines would be forced to consider switching their alliance to Spain (an empty threat, as everyone knew it would mean the return of the Medici to Florence). When passing through Milan on his way to Lyon, Machiavelli was to meet with the French governor there and ask him to protect Tuscany until the king had managed to reorganize his forces. Maybe because of his reputation for slackness in his correspondence, Niccolò was told to "write immediately, adding both your thoughts and opinions," although nobody doubted the urgency of the situation.

The meeting in Milan proved inconclusive. The French authorities there were convinced that once the Spanish saw Louis's navy and his army in Lombardy, they would not dare to move. Furthermore, they believed that the Sienese would resist, the pope would be "a good Frenchman," the Swiss would stay home, and the Venetians would "return to their fishing." Unimpressed, Machiavelli bluntly retorted that fleets on the sea and armies in northern Italy would not protect Tuscany; as for the pope and the Sienese, they would want to see what sort of aid the king intended to send before committing themselves. From a friend in

Milan, actually a soldier in Louis's service, Machiavelli learned some rather more disquieting news: The king had no money, few men-at-arms, and even less infantry, and people doubted he would be able to find enough resources to protect Lombardy—let alone his allies—while his enemies were strong and at the ready.

Having paid lip service to his instructions, once in France, Machiavelli, true to style, would be happy to let Valori do most of the writing, and given the latter's rank, nobody could contest such a formally impeccable decision. Moreover, the two Niccolòs liked and trusted each other, having worked together in Pistoia some years before. Valori clearly admired Machiavelli's abilities and had been his constant advocate among those who counted in Florence. Still, even he, while praising Niccolò's work more than once, had reminded him about the importance of observing formalities.

"Your reports are much praised," Valori wrote on October 28, 1502, at the time of Machiavelli's mission at Borgia's court. "But to make things absolutely clear, we wish you would write more often." Machiavelli's disregard for keeping in contact eventually soured his relationship with Valori, despite the latter having become the godfather of one of Niccolò's children. "Its seems that we have turned our fellowship into hostility," Valori would later lament with Machiavelli, complaining about not receiving any replies to his missives. Machiavelli would have reasons to regret personal slights like this one later on, once the need for support from friends arose.

Arriving in Lyon on January 27, Niccolò immediately went to see Valori, and the next day the two met with Cardinal d'Amboise, since the king was ill. Machiavelli exposed the Republic's perils and needs, stressing the trust the Florentines had in Louis XII and asking what sort of help they could expect from him. "Speaking in a lively manner," Niccolò added that should friends fail her, Florence would have to reach an agreement with her enemies. Amboise did not take kindly to such words; red in the face, he raved about the Florentines even having such thoughts in times so difficult for France. "Displaying all his ability," Machiavelli pointed out that to save Tuscany from the Spanish, the French should man its walls: the pope, Siena, and Perugia. Amboise retorted that he could count on the pontiff and Siena, but as for Perugia, it belonged to the pope.

The next day, the cardinal mentioned the negotiations for a truce between France and Spain, but whatever the results of these parleys, he said, Florence should not worry about its safety. The two diplomats got similar answers from the king and other court officials, and having received, on February 11, the news that the truce had been signed, Machiavelli announced his return to Florence. The only thing he and Valori had managed to obtain was a rather vague promise that the Republic would be included in the treaty. It had become clear that Florence could not count on France's aid in an emergency. Meanwhile, the city's military unpreparedness had turned into a milking cow for anyone wishing to exploit its weakness.

The Florentine taste for factionalism did not help the situation. By now, far from being a unifying figure, Piero Soderini had become a source of division within the city. He had been supported in his election by the *arrabbiati*, but could also count on the support of the moderate Republicans, and among his friends figured a number of old *frateschi*, such as Bernardo Nasi and Antonio Canigiani. Nonetheless, a substantial group of Florentines resented his rule, some for personal reasons and others because supporters of the *governo stretto*—Soderini's use of large *pratiche* carrying little favor with these people. Many old Savonarolans were also disappointed with Soderini's unwillingness—as they saw it— to restore the city's moral purity, and some extreme Republicans desired a more energetic stance against those who openly or in secret favored a Medici restoration.

Among the gonfalonier's most prominent opponents stood Alamanno and Jacopo Salviati, two powerful, rich, and well-connected cousins with many adherents within Florence's political bodies. Their dislike for Soderini had grown over time, seeing that he did not heed their advice but instead preferred the opinions of those "men of lesser intelligence and quality" who were more pliable to his will. Besides, the fact that the gonfalonier would now stay in office for life caused resentment among many men who might otherwise have been candidates for the position. Soderini had also been behind the removal of Ser Jacopo da Martino, a friend of the Salviati cousins, from the *Tribunale di Mercatanzia* (the Merchant's Court), with the accusation that the Salviati had been using Ser Jacopo to try to take control of Florence's business network.

Finally, the gonfalonier may have suspected the Salviati of being crypto-Mediceans, given that Jacopo had married Lucrezia, sister of the defunct Piero and of Cardinal Giovanni, while Alamanno's sister, Cornelia, had married Giovanbattista Ridolfi, whose nephew Piero was the husband of Contessina de' Medici, Lucrezia's sister. There is no evidence that the Salviati ever supported the return of the Medici during this period, but Soderini could not risk aiding—in his vision—potential snakes in the grass. Significantly, under his rule the Salviati cousins, while holding a number of important governmental positions, were never elected to the Signoria.

Soderini's conflict with the Medici had a strong personal slant, given that in Rome, his brother Francesco and Cardinal Giovanni de' Medici were each trying to attract into their fold as many Florentines as possible of those residing in the eternal city. After the death of his brother Piero, Giovanni had become the leader of the exiled Medici, proving himself an able politician, and was close to Pope Julius II. Giovanni and Francesco Soderini disliked each other, and the Medici cardinal used his influence with his fellow citizens in Rome to create opposition to the gonfalonier's regime in Florence. Given the ties between the Salviati and the Medici, the activities of the latter abroad could easily be perceived as an attempt to create a fifth column in Florence.

However, by and large Piero Soderini's enemies preferred to work within the Republic's political system rather than against it—for the sake of prudence, if nothing else. The people who did not share this attitude preferred to stay out of the limelight, quite a few gathering around the gonfalonier's old enemy Bernardo Rucellai, who held an intellectual court of sorts in his garden—the Orti Oricellari—where Neoplatonic philosophy and political reforms were discussed. Rucellai and his circle looked back at the golden days—as they saw them—of the fifteenth-century Florentine constitution under the Medici. With many other Florentines they shared an admiration for Venice's political organization, but favored a far more aristocratic constitution than the supporters of the Great Council.

The struggle between the Salviati cousins and Soderini erupted at the beginning of 1504 over the choice of Florence's military commander. The Salviati supported the candidacy of Giampaolo Baglioni, but he happened to be a friend of the Orsini (who had managed to recoup their power after Alexander VI's death), who in turn had strong links with the Medici. Soderini and his followers preferred Fabrizio Colonna, whose family had been hostile to the Orsini for centuries. Colonna, however, happened to be in the service of Spain, and Florentines marveled that a pro-French government would make such a choice. The official, if weak, reply to this objection was that hiring Colonna would in no way damage Florence's special relationship with Louis XII, and in any case would prevent the Spanish from attacking the city. In the end, Colonna's demands proved excessive, and his ties with Spain too strong. As a compromise solution it was decided to engage Baglioni along with other condottieri of Soderini's choice, notwithstanding the fact that all these men happened to be political, and often personal, enemies.

Soderini did manage to get the Florentines to approve a tax proposal so that the government could pay for the renewal of the campaign against Pisa, and in the teeth of the opposition of the Salviati, he got one of his friends, the no-nonsense and experienced Antonio Giacomini, appointed as commissioner in the field. Giacomini displayed his usual energy, capturing a number of fortresses and pestering the government to order a direct attack against Pisa. The city had been holding out, thanks to supplies sent by Lucca, Siena, and Genoa (despite Genoa being a French protectorate) via the mouth of the Arno River. The Florentines had retaliated as best as they could by ordering raids into Lucca's territory to ensure that its citizens, as Machiavelli would write to Giacomini, "will not provide even a glass of water to the Pisans; and since you know that the Lucchesi have been keeping them alive, you have made it clear that this should stop and if necessary you'll go get them within Lucca itself."

But the operation against Pisa came to a stop when prisoners revealed that there were more than 2,500 fighting men manning the walls; they added, however, that the inhabitants feared the Florentines would divert the course of the Arno River, and so deprive them of their outlet to the sea. These admissions may have been part of a disinformation plan concocted by the Pisans to forestall the Florentines, but whatever the case, Soderini swallowed it whole and proceeded to pursue the idea. Experts were consulted for their opinion, and they confidently reported that with 2,000 workers and enough lumber, fifteen to twenty days would be sufficient to build a dam upstream and deviate the Arno into two previously dug canals. The *pratiche* convened to discuss the scheme declared it to be "nothing if not a daydream," but Soderini managed to garner popular support for what appeared to be a cheap way to end a costly war. As it would turn out, by wanting to have their cake and eat it, too, the Florentines ended up both hungry and empty-handed.

On August 20, Machiavelli wrote to Giacomini ordering him to start the works to change the course of the Arno, but the commissioner was far from convinced that it was a wise decision: "Your Lordships shall see," he replied five days later, "a daily increase in problems, for its is misleading to believe it may be done with ease." There is evidence that Machiavelli himself had misgivings about Soderini's master plan, for a report by Biagio Buonaccorsi among Niccolò's papers contained the damning opinion of the condottiere Ercole Bentivoglio, who scotched the whole scheme based on sound engineering principles. "Nonetheless," Buonaccorsi would add, "these clear and flawless reasons were ignored. The results have proven who was wrong."

Disgusted with the whole venture, Giacomini resigned on grounds of ill health, while Machiavelli, whatever his doubts, spent the rest of the summer issuing orders for its completion.* But, after weeks of toil, deviating the Arno ultimately proved impossible (provoking Francesco Guicciardini's snide remark "as foreseen by all the wise citizens"). Some 7,000 ducats had been wasted on the project, owing to Soderini's insistence that the plan would eventually succeed. The gonfalonier made another mistake when he offered full pardons to those Pisans wishing to surrender. This allowed the Pisans to get rid of all the so-called "useless mouths" (women, children, and the aged) while the local peasantry accepted the pardon only to go on aiding Pisa in secret. Soderini's prestige had been severely damaged by these debacles. His enemies in the city started to raise their voices against the way he handled public affairs, and those in Rome looked for a chance to bring down the Republican regime.

Machiavelli tried as hard as he could to stay clear of factional controversies, despite the fact that by now he had a reputation for being firmly in Soderini's camp. Although he was undoubtedly an independent-minded person, like any Florentine with brains he realized that politics were a difficult and potentially dangerous game; besides, although Soderini could rely on a substantial group of adherents within the city's institutional bodies, so could his adversaries. The gonfalonier could still muster up support for some of his nominations and provisions, but every time this involved a lot of maneuvering, pleading, and cajoling—which were not always successful. The Ten often included people vociferously opposed to Soderini's policies, and Machiavelli had to be careful about antagonizing his direct superiors. In fact, he would need as much support as he could get for his own pet project, one that had been occupying his mind for some time: making Florence militarily independent through the creation of a city militia.

---

* Much has been made of Leonardo da Vinci's involvement in the project, although Machiavelli's correspondence at the time is hardly revelatory in this regard. Leonardo had been employed by the Signoria to paint a huge fresco, *The Battle of Anghiari*, on one of the walls of the Great Council's hall. It is possible, but by no means certain, that the classical references included in Leonardo's notes for the painting (which the artist never finished) could be evidence of Machiavelli's involvement in the project.

This idea had long and tangled roots, arising out of a combination of Niccolò's archaeological mindset, his own experience in Pistoia, what he had seen at Valentino's court, and the bitter realization that his native city had time and time again been exploited by sovereigns, petty lords, and untrustworthy condottieri. The ancient Rome he so loved had grown to greatness thanks to the civic virtue of its inhabitants, embodied, as Machiavelli saw it, in their national army. This is what had allowed the city to survive crisis after crisis and laid the groundwork for the creation of an empire. The reviled Cesare Borgia, moreover, had also been successful because of his reliance on his own subjects in arms rather than on hired professionals—or at least that is how Machiavelli saw it. In reality, as we have seen, Machiavelli failed to understand the professional nature of Borgia's militia.

In his first *Decennale* (Decennal) written in 1504 and printed at the beginning of 1506, Machiavelli summarized, in verse, ten years of Italian history, and in particular the woes that had befallen Florence for her reliance on equally unreliable foreign arms and non-native mercenaries. Just to make himself absolutely clear, Niccolò ended his poem with an appeal to his fellow citizens, buttressing it with one of those references taken from the ancient past so dear to the humanists, and by now part of Florence's cultural milieu: "Your path would be easier and shorter / if you reopened the temple of Mars." He had already made a similar statement, if not so classical in its style, in the "Parole dette sopra la Provvisione del Danaio," in which he argued that to preserve their liberty, the Florentines should rely on themselves and keep their own swords by their sides, rather than waiting for the French to help them.

However, Machiavelli did recognize that any solution to this problem had to be one tailored to Florence's situation. He would state as much in his *ghiribizzi* (fantasies) to Giovan Battista Soderini, one of the gonfalonier's nephews, of mid-September 1506, which contain themes Niccolò would later elaborate in *The Prince*. In essence, by using examples taken from the ancient and recent past, Machiavelli pointed out how rulers and individuals sought different answers to predicaments in apparently similar circumstances. Machiavelli used the examples of Hannibal and Scipio, as the former had established his authority in Italy through despotism and cruelty, while the latter did the same in Iberia through piety and compassion. Niccolò had evidently already been criticized for his faith in classical sources, for he immediately added: "But since there is not the habit of using the Romans as a model, it should be remembered that Lorenzo de' Medici disarmed the people in order to keep his grip on Florence, while Giovanni Bentivoglio, to hold onto Bologna, armed them instead."

By referring to Lorenzo de' Medici, Machiavelli underscored the need for the Florentines to create a national army for the sake of their own liberty at a time when this subject was being hotly debated in Florence. It is unclear when Machiavelli first came up with the scheme for the creation of a militia, but we know that by the spring of 1504 he had been discussing the matter with Cardinal Francesco Soderini. In May of that year the prelate wrote to him that the militia idea had started to encounter opposition in some quarters: "an unfortunate attitude in a matter so good and necessary; one cannot be suspicious of a force raised not for private but for public benefit." Soderini urged Niccolò not to give up, "for what is denied at one time, may be given at another." Circumstances would confirm the cardinal's prediction.

In March 1505, the Florentine forces under Luca Savelli suffered a serious defeat outside of Pisa, with the Pisans retaking much of the countryside they had previously lost. The next blow fell in April, when Giampaolo Baglioni announced that he would be quitting the Republic's service. The defection of Florence's most important condottiere put an abrupt halt to all operations in the field, and on April 8, Machiavelli received instructions to go forthwith to Baglioni's camp to find out the real motives for his decision. Niccolò arrived on the 11th and confronted the erstwhile commander, "prodding him in every way" to force him to reveal his reasons. To the secretary's chagrin, Baglioni proved rather more serpentine than expected, and despite "changing his countenance" a few times, he stuck to his version of the story: The Florentines, he said, had employed some of his enemies, and in any case, he had to protect Perugia; besides, he had shown his contract with the Republic to a number of lawyers, all of whom had agreed that he had no obligation to remain in his post.

Machiavelli blew his stack, vehemently declaring that such disloyalty would inevitably damage Baglioni's reputation more than his loss would damage the Republic: He would become "a lame horse that no one would want to ride." As for his legal opinions, Niccolò essentially told Giampaolo to shove them up his backside, "for these matters should not be judged by doctors of law, but by governments." He warned Baglioni to reconsider his decision, "for this matter weighs more heavily than the whole of Perugia." Putting together the few admissions he had managed to extract from Baglioni with what he had learned from other people in the camp, Niccolò became convinced that the unfaithful condottiere was in cahoots with some of Florence's enemies. The notorious Goro Gheri was also in the area, and this added to Machiavelli's suspicions.

In fact, Baglioni had been co-opted in a plan hatched by Cardinal Ascanio Sforza, the Orsini, Bartolomeo d'Alviano—one of the foremost Italian captains in Spanish pay—and Pandolfo Petrucci to restore the Medici regime in Florence and then use the city as a springboard for the grand operation of evicting the French from Lombardy (Cardinal Ascanio had a personal stake in the enterprise, as his brother, Duke Ludovico, had been dispossessed by Louis XII and held as a prisoner in France). The conspirators knew they could count on supporters within Florence among those families with strong ties to the exiled Medici, or from individuals, especially young patricians, who hated the Republican regime. But, once again, the Republic had luck on its side. Sforza expired suddenly at the end of May, saving Florence and ruining the hopes of the Medici, at least for the present.

In the meantime, the government had been desperately looking for someone to take Baglioni's place, even mentioning Alviano as a possibility. Soderini once again put forward the name of Fabrizio Colonna, but agreed to entrust the matter to a twelve-man committee convened for the purpose of choosing a replacement. The board instead voted for

Francesco Gonzaga, Marquis of Mantua, the candidate of the Salviati—
Alamanno Salviati at the time being a member of the Ten. The terms of
the agreement were duly drawn up, and on May 4 Machiavelli departed
for Mantua to conclude the ratification of the contract. Little came of
this mission, since Gonzaga decided to drag his feet on the number of
troops he was supposed to provide and refused to fight the allies of the
emperor or the king of France.

The government also decided to send an envoy to Gonzalo de Cordoba in Naples, but when Machiavelli's name was proposed, among others by his friend and relative by marriage Piero del Nero,* it was decided
that to avoid offending Cordoba someone of greater social standing
should be sent. Niccolò instead departed for Siena to thank the lord of
the city, Pandolfo Petrucci, for having warned the Florentines of Alviano's imminent arrival in Tuscany. The government's suspicions of
Petrucci following his surprising volte-face is clear from Machiavelli's instructions: "Use your usual good judgment to discover that lord's true
intentions." Niccolò soon found Petrucci to be very eel-like indeed, and
the numerous letters he wrote—for once—in the week he spent in Siena
drip with frustration and annoyance.

It did not take long for Machiavelli to discover, for example, that Pandolfo was "a man whose face reveals little or nothing." He wanted to convince the Florentines to forsake their right to the town of Montepulciano
(occupied by the Sienese in the aftermath of the eviction of the Medici
from Florence), and though he desired an alliance with Florence had no
intention of stopping Alviano from passing through Sienese territory.
Petrucci's deviousness left Niccolò "very confused," and when he confronted him with all his contradictions, Pandolfo simply answered that
"just to be on the safe side, I run matters by the day and judge them by
the hour, because I trust time more than intelligence." Niccolò had met

---

* Piero's kinsman Francesco del Nero had married one of Marietta
Machiavelli's sisters. As we shall see, the del Nero connection would prove of
crucial importance for Niccolò in the years to come.

his match in Petrucci and left for home without gaining anything—except the impression that the man could not be trusted.

While in Siena, Machiavelli received the news that Cordoba had forbidden Alviano to invade Tuscany, but when informed of the fact Petrucci had shrewdly said simply that "reason would dictate that Alviano should obey and stay quiet, but men do not always follow reason." The lord of Siena's prediction proved to be correct when Alviano, ignoring Cordoba's orders, landed with a large force near Piombino. Once again, in the hour of most need, Florence found herself isolated. The French refused to intervene, with the excuse that Florence had not paid the money agreed to in the alliance treaty, while Francesco Gonzaga declined to serve, saying that Louis XII had not yet approved his contract with the Republic. The only forces that Florence had at its disposal were a few thousand cavalry and infantry in the Maremma region under Antonio Giacomini and Ercole Bentivoglio, deployed there to block Alviano's advance along the coast toward Pisa. (The number of Spanish soldiers in Piombino makes one suspect that Alviano and Cordoba were really in agreement, Cordoba not being able to intervene directly because the truce between France and Spain included Florence.)

In mid-August, the fire-eating Giacomini informed the government that he intended to seek battle, and although the Ten urged prudence, on August 17 he engaged Alviano near San Vincenzo. Unexpectedly—and thanks to Bentivoglio's timely intervention—Alviano suffered a crushing defeat, losing many men and all his baggage. An elated Soderini ordered the captured banners to be hung in the Great Council's hall, and overruling all dissenting voices, managed to collect enough money to fund a direct attack against Pisa led by Giacomini and Bentivoglio. The decision satisfied few, as many people doubted Bentivoglio's abilities despite his contribution to the recent success. Moreover, his appointment as commander in chief could very likely antagonize the other condottieres in Florence's service. Machiavelli's confidential letter to Giacomini of August 27 would prove ominous in this respect and revelatory of what the Florentines had to contend with in their dealings with hired soldiery:

Keep secret what I am writing to you. This morning the *pratica* has decided to bestow the baton of command on Messer Ercole, but intends to postpone announcing this for a day or two to find a way to appease Marco Antonio [Colonna], fearing he may raise hell. Two things need to be done: first, Messer Jacopo [Savelli] and Messer Annibale [Bentivoglio] should send someone here to let people know that the glory for the victory is not all Ercole's, since several days ago he sent word asking that his valor be publicly proclaimed; second, you should write to some powerful friend that Marco Antonio does not intend to be divisive, or to be backed, as it is commonly believed, by Jacopo and Luca [Savelli]—since this assumption has delayed Messer Ercole's appointment. To sum things up, Jacopo and Annibale's honesty [for not taking credit for the recent victory] has made this third man [Ercole] too insolent and given him excessive prestige. You can remedy this mess; and tear up this letter.

Inflated condottieri egos were not, of course, a uniquely Florentine problem in a world where honor and reputation went hand in hand. But whereas other Italian states had found ways to deal with their hired mercenaries' tantrums, Florence did not possess a hand firm enough to keep order in its military nursery.

Machiavelli's analysis was realistic, if perhaps a bit too optimistic. By September 9, artillery fire had managed to open a breach in the walls of Pisa, but when ordered forward, the Florentine infantry refused to move with the excuse that the breach was too small—in reality because their pay had not arrived and Giacomini had proven to be a tough disciplinarian. Three days later, after yet more pounding, which had caused the collapse of yet more masonry, Giacomini again ordered the assault, but once again the Florentine troops declined to advance. Cordoba, in the meantime, had managed to bring a number of Spanish infantry into the city, and Bentivoglio was proving unable to exercise any authority over the recalcitrant soldiery. (Significantly, two of the rebellious companies belonged to Jacopo Savelli and Marco Antonio Colonna.)

In a fit of rage, Giacomini threatened to turn the artillery on the mu-
tineers and wrote stinging letters to the government inveighing against
the poltroons. When, in return, he received orders to abandon the siege,
he announced that he would resign his commission and return home.
Machiavelli, who liked and trusted Giacomini, warned him that he would
be facing a hostile populace, as the Florentines, thwarted of a success
that everyone had taken for granted, would wish to make him a scapegoat
for the disaster. "For the Lord's sake stay where you are," he would write
on September 23, "and I pray you not to depart without leave, so as not
to give these many treacherous* and envious individuals a pretext to go
on howling." Its is significant that the main attacks against Giacomini
came from those who disliked Soderini and the Republican regime, such
as the Salviati and the Rucellai. In any case, the gonfalonier was blasted
for being rash and imperious, and for backing an enterprise that wiser
men had thought unreasonable. The failure of the Pisa expedition had
shaken the Republican regime's credibility to its roots. Clearly a solution
had to be found lest another debacle made it collapse completely.

Florence had only itself to blame for failing to build a credible military force. All Italian polities employed professional soldiers, but during
the course of the fifteenth century the major states had developed administrative systems to keep their mercenaries well disciplined and in a
state of readiness. Florence, however, had been slow to imitate the example of Milan or Venice in this regard, its citizens being unwilling to
spend money for defense in peacetime, preferring to keep taxation low
and avoid increasing the public debt. The political bodies in charge of
military affairs had very little authority, and in any case came into existence only in times of war. As a result, when hostilities did break out,
the Florentines were often forced to rely on the dregs of the mercenary
system—not the most skilled, efficient, or reliable people in the first
place, and usually low in morale because of Florence's unwillingness or
inability to provide regular pay.

---

* Machiavelli uses the word *traditori*, literally "traitors" in contemporary
English; however, this appears too modern and misleading a translation.

Machiavelli's lambasting of soldiers of fortune as faithless, cowardly, and avaricious individuals is revelatory of a specifically Florentine problem rather than one typical of Italy in general. In any case, Niccolò needed to downplay the importance of mercenaries in order to argue for his idea of a conscript army that Florence could control with ease. The inability of the Florentines to enact a drastic reform of their military administrative system meant that they would always be at the mercy of their hired soldiery and France's aid. But both the mercenaries and France had proven unreliable, and unless an alternative solution could be found, Pisa would be lost forever, and with it the Republic.

As an old proverb goes: "Three things are impossible in this world: to square a circle, make a dog's bed and teach a Florentine." Soderini may have had this in mind when, desperate for a solution to the crisis in Pisa, he started to become interested in Machiavelli's project of establishing a city militia. However, he knew that if he brought the plan to public attention, it would be mercilessly shot down by his fellow citizens, who always seemed to resist novel ideas. The gonfalonier could not risk another public humiliation, and therefore, probably at Machiavelli's suggestion, sought an alternative course of action.

The Florentine constitution gave the Ten the authority to conscript men as auxiliaries in times of war, and at the time of the Pistoia and Arezzo upheavals they had ordered the recruitment of troops in the Republic's dominion. This legal loophole allowed Soderini to bypass Florence's legislative bodies and proceed unopposed to enact the militia scheme, with the added advantage that in case of failure the responsibility would fall squarely on the shoulders of the Ten and their secretary.

Having received the appropriate commissions for the task, Machiavelli departed for the Mugello at the end of December 1505. On January 2, 1506, he wrote to the Ten from Borgo San Lorenzo about his recruiting success: "These people like the idea very much, and are eager to make it work." He had managed to enlist hundreds of locals, "and these young men come willingly," he wrote. His optimism was somewhat dampened when he arrived in Ponte a Sieve, as he found the surrounding area "in disorder and with little food"; moreover, the inhabitants of Petrognano refused to enlist because those of a rival community had. Niccolò met with the son of a certain Andreasso, one of the local bosses, who told the secretary that no one would come unless their leaders were convinced to enroll—provided the Republic remove their criminal sentences.

Nonetheless, Niccolò must have been proud of his accomplishments, particularly when the new recruits started training "in the Swiss manner." It was like a dream come true. On February 15, a select group of militiamen paraded through Florence among cheering crowds, elegantly dressed in a uniform of white and red (the city's colors), "equipped with breastplates, some carrying pikes and others handguns." Soderini's opponents could only look on in anger and dismay in the face of this fait accompli.

The militia may have been born, but its path still remained filled with obstacles, political as well as administrative. Despite the February parade having favorably impressed many citizens, others harbored serious doubts about the whole venture. Suspicions about the real scope of the new military force only increased when the gonfalonier proposed the infamous Don Miguel de Corella (Borgia's former strangulator in chief) as commander of the force. To determine the extent of the opposition to this, Soderini sent Machiavelli to sound out some prominent citizens, including his adversaries. When, among others, Piero Guicciardini, Giovanbattista Ridolfi, and Francesco Gualterotti unequivocally scotched the idea, Soderini managed to convince the Council of the Eighty to appoint Corella as *bargello* (police constable) for the Florentine countryside. Many of Soderini's opponents were certain that the gonfalonier intended to use the militia to become lord of the city, a conviction that caused Bernardo Rucellai to leave Florence for Avignon. At the time, nobody really knew Bernardo's real motives, but some suspected that he feared the discovery of his dealings with the exiled Medici. Rucellai had been more of a nuisance than a serious opponent, and Soderini could be happy to see such a gadfly gone.

According to one source, Rucellai felt he had been let down by some of those whom he considered his allies in the battle against Soderini. The previous summer, when Soderini had attempted to take Pisa, the widespread support for the enterprise had caused some of the gonfalonier's enemies to seek a rapprochement. In the early months of 1504, Soderini had conducted secret negotiations to marry his great-niece, Maria, to Pierfrancesco de' Medici, whose branch of the Medici family had managed to remain in Florence by siding with the Republic, and who, incidentally, also happened to be Caterina's Sforza's nephew by marriage. Pierfrancesco was also related to the Salviati, and a marriage to Maria Soderini would weaken his ties with the gonfalonier's enemies. The Salviati got wind of the scheme in time to stop it, but two years later they found it expedient to favor the marital alliance, predicting that with Florence's conquest of Pisa, Soderini's prestige would increase.

One can therefore understand why Rucellai would not relish the prospect of becoming politically isolated in a city that he felt was going down a slope that would end in despotism. The militia coming under the control of one of Borgia's former lieutenants seemed but a further step in that direction. It is unlikely that Soderini ever thought of becoming Florence's sole ruler, however, as much as he resented people who opposed his politics. Furthermore, it is nearly certain that Cardinal Soderini first suggested Corella's name, wishing to find "some inflexible and strict official like Manlius Torquatus." Although Don Miguel could hardly be defined as an example of Roman *virtus*, the cardinal and his brother saw him as the right man to discipline the fledging militia lest it should turn into shambles.

Francesco Soderini would emphasize this point in a letter to Machiavelli on March 4, 1506, stressing that the new army's credibility depended on the soldiers obeying orders, and agreeing with Niccolò about the need to establish an appropriate judicial authority with extensive territorial jurisdiction. Pending legislative approval of a more specific set of rules governing the militia, Don Miguel, as bargello, would see that the conscripted soldiers obeyed the government's commands.

The militia, however, could not stay permanently in a state of legal limbo, and there always existed the risk that Florentine politicians would decide to end it for good. Debate abounded in Florence about the new force. Although nobody disagreed in principle on the positive aspects of having a standing army, many nonetheless expressed concerns about what incentives the militiamen should be offered, so that they would serve willingly, and what kind of discipline they should be subjected to so that they could be kept in order. The city's political bodies had trouble settling these matters.

Machiavelli's first *Decennale* was a piece of skillful propaganda written to convince the Florentines that speedy approval of the appropriate legislation would be in their best interest. The work proved popular enough to cause the appearance of a pirated edition, forcing Machiavelli and his friends to undertake legal action to protect the author's intellectual property. In a letter to Niccolò of February 25, 1506, Ercole Bentivoglio thanked him for sending him a copy of the *Decennale*, showering it with praise and encouraging the author to continue on the same track: "For we are grateful that these truths will be read by those who shall come after us, so that knowing our own and our time's misfortune they shall not blame us entirely for not preserving Italy's honor and repute."

By putting the blame on misfortune, Bentivoglio had found a convenient way of justifying his own shortcomings. But as much as he might have been flattered by these words, Machiavelli had set his sights on other targets: On November 9, 1505, he had sent the manuscript of the poem, accompanied by a flowery letter in classical Latin, to none else but Alamanno Salviati, eulogizing him for his past contributions to the Republic's defense. Machiavelli may have been trying to curry favor with Soderini's enemies at a time when the gonfalonier's fortunes were at a very low ebb, as a result of the recent Pisa debacle. But at the same time, the pragmatic attitude of the Salviati toward Soderini a few months earlier had demonstrated a degree of political flexibility, something that Niccolò wished to encourage for the sake of his militia scheme. Alamanno Salviati, however, had already developed something of a loathing toward the secretary, openly calling him a "scoundrel" and boasting that when he had been part of the Ten, he had made sure that Machiavelli would receive no commission. Given the circumstances, backing one of Soderini's projects, especially one with Machiavelli's imprint, would not have benefited the Salviati.

Even in the absence of official regulation, the Ten were busy putting flesh on the militia's bones. People were induced to enlist with the promise of pardon for any past crimes or misdemeanors, and in June some five hundred militiamen were sent to the Pisa front—not with very good results, apparently, given that Machiavelli had to dispatch Don Miguel with his company to restore discipline and infuse some steel in the conscripts. More or less around this time, Machiavelli composed a memorandum, probably at the government's request but evidently intended for a wider readership, in which he spelled out everything he considered necessary to put the militia in order. Not one to mince his words, he opened with an artillery barrage of obvious, if unwelcome, truths:

> I shall ignore the disputes on the opportunity or not to give the country a military organization, for everyone knows that empires, kingdoms, principalities, men—from the highest in rank to the commander of a boat—cannot do without authority and strength: You have little of the former, and none of the latter. The only way to obtain both is to pass a law to regulate the army and keep it in order. Do not be misled by the more than one hundred years you have lived without the above, for if you analyze the past and the present you shall understand how it is impossible today to preserve your liberty in the same way as we used to do.

Machiavelli went on to analyze the structure of the Florentine state and discuss where recruitment should take place. Florence, for one, was not a good breeding ground for infantrymen, for its citizens would prefer the more prestigious cavalry, and in any case were more used to commanding others than to obeying them. The *distretto* (i.e., the Republic's territories outside the dioceses of Florence and Fiesole) included rebellious places such as Arezzo: "For Tuscan character is such that if one should realize that he could be his own master, he would want no one above him, especially if he had weapons and his liege none." Only the *contado* (i.e., the Republic's territories roughly corresponding to the dioceses of Florence and Fiesole) remained, being abundant in population, dependent on Florence, and devoid of large fortified settlements that could become hotbeds of unrest. Recruitment should be widespread, to boost the Republic's military reputation, and conscripts from various *bandiere* (local companies) should be grouped together under a constable for training purposes. These officers should not come from the same areas of the men they commanded, and in any case their appointment limited to just one.

As for the conscripts themselves, they had to be kept under control through discipline and regular training, and punished more severely than civilians for any infringement of the law. Finally, an appropriate magistracy should be created to run the militia in peacetime, but control would devolve to the Ten in the event of a war. Once the militia was established in the *contado*, it would be easy to do the same in the cities. Niccolò ended with a parting shot: "And then you shall see the difference between chosen men and the corrupt soldiers you have now; for the unruly child, reared in brothels, is corrupted and becomes a mercenary, but if well raised and schooled shall bring honor to himself and his country." Seeped in classical history and the culture of ancient Rome, Machiavelli judged everything according to the standards found in antiquity. For him, the honesty of the militiamen must mirror the civic *virtus* of Rome's citizen army under the republic—a crucial factor that allowed Rome to survive and ultimately triumph in the face of adversity. Nonetheless, the reference to brothels in connection with mercenaries sounds peculiar when coming from a man like Niccolò, who frequently consorted with prostitutes.

A few months later, Machiavelli would reiterate the same points in another memorandum and rebut a series of objections raised in the interim. Choosing a few conscripts, or only those willing to serve, would be couterproductive: One could never be sure about individual attitudes, even in the case of a select force of about 2,000 men. As for the expense of the whole operation, it would be limited to the officers' pay—no great sum. Pikes were cheap to make, and other weapons could be kept in stockpiles ready for use. It would be useless and expensive to pay the rank and file other than in the field, for the small sum allotted to each individual would not be enough to satisfy him or make him more disciplined.

Moreover, the expense would be an excessive burden for the various communities. Instead, Machiavelli proposed that exemption from taxation should be given as a reward to those who deserved it for performing some valorous deed, which would cause the others to aspire to the same: "And in any case it always works to encourage people's hopes, and have something in store when you need them." Finally, the drain of men would not reduce the economy of any single area, given that no more than one man per household was to be conscripted; on the contrary, the increase in discipline would help security and foster a sense of belonging to the Florentine state. Machiavelli knew that money-saving arguments strongly appealed to the tax-burdened Florentines, who would welcome the chance to fight a war on the cheap.

Over the summer, the opposition to Machiavelli's project waned, partly because the Florentines had started to take a liking to the army, and also because the turnover of personnel in the various offices favored Soderini's friends. Niccolò, in the meantime, had been constantly canvassing for its approval. Thus, on October 5, while following the pope and his retinue toward Bologna, he would write to the Ten: "If your lordships had seen the infantry of the Duke of Urbino and Nanni [Morattini], you would not be ashamed of nor despise your own militia." Niccolò's continuous insistence on the benefits of a militia started to have its effect, and on October 11, Biagio Buonaccorsi informed him that his comments had "given a bit of grease to the launching of this galley," adding that the changes in the composition of the Ten had created a much more favorable climate for the approval of the militia law.

Finally, on December 6, 1506, the Great Council and the Council of the Eighty approved, by a landslide, the institution of the *Nove uffuciali dell'ordinananza e milizia fiorentina* (the Nine Officials of the Florentine Militia), usually known as the Nine, the magistracy in charge of administrating Florence's national army in peacetime. The law itself embodied the majority of Machiavelli's suggestions, although the limit of 10,000 militiamen is evidence of a compromise solution between those, like Niccolò, who wanted general enlistment and others who instead favored a more selective recruitment.

The militia law also provided a series of checks and balances. In the event of war, the Ten would take over the militia. Commissioners chosen by the government would supervise the behavior of the commanders in charge of the various units, the election by the Nine company officers in turn being subject to the approval of the Signoria and the Council of the Eighty. To guarantee the Republic's authority, the militia would be policed by a force made up of professional soldiers and commanded by a foreigner. Don Miguel de Corella had fulfilled that role until then, but the many abuses of his authority would soon cause him to be summarily dismissed from his post, and his violent life ended shortly afterward in a brawl with some of his fellow countrymen.

For Machiavelli, the passage of the militia law represented an unequivocal personal victory, enhanced by the fact that he would become the new body's secretary. Cardinal Soderini would express his satisfaction in a letter of December 15, 1506, in which he described the provision "as coming from God" and praised Niccolò's "great role in it." Certainly, the Florentines would still have to depend on professional soldiers, especially for the mounted units of their army: The militia was an infantry force, and therefore could be drilled with relative ease, while it took a lifetime to train a man-at-arms. However, Machiavelli clearly intended to address this matter at the right moment. In the meantime, he could be more than satisfied by having gotten the Florentines to accept something new. Opposition to the new army would subside over time, after it became clear that Soderini could not manipulate it at will; indeed, many of the gonfalonier's enemies would at one time or another be part of the Nine. However, the animosity of Soderini's adversaries toward Machiavelli undoubtedly increased after this success, as future events would prove.

Assessing the militia's true contribution to Florence is not easy, especially after its disastrous failure in the field a few years later. Criticism have been leveled at the army's out-of-date equipment and training methods, which were influenced by the Swiss victories in the Burgundian wars of 1474–1477: Firearms were limited to 10 percent of the militiamen, and there was a heavy reliance on the massed-pike formation. The edge of this fighting technique had been blunted at Cerignola by the

Spanish massed volleys and light infantry armed with sword and buckler. However, at the time, this lesson still had to seep in. Even the celebrated Fabrizio Colonna—whom Soderini had twice put forth as his candidate as commander of the Florentine forces, and who later would be one of the interlocutors in Machiavelli's *Art of War*—bluntly stated that the Spanish success had been due to fieldworks rather than to "the soldiers' behavior or some commander's prowess."

It should be added that the pike was the best weapon for raw recruits, especially since these were supposed to drill once a month. Unfortunately, the Florentine militia never trained as a body; even the *mostre grosse* (greater musters) held twice a year involved only a few companies at a time. Moreover, the obsession of Florentine politicians with the risk of a coup d'état resulted in an unwieldy command-and-control structure, and the rapid rotation of company leaders never allowed them enough time to get their men to know them—Machiavelli believing that in this way, the conscripts "shall always be uncertain about their commander, and recognize public rather than private authority." The binding oath sworn on the Gospels by the militiamen during general musters could do little to compensate for these shortcomings, or for the absence of any form of payment for the conscripts. But since the Swiss had built a victorious army with even greater limitations, because of the virtual independence of each canton in their confederation, it made sense to believe that the same could be achieved in Tuscany. After all, according to Machiavelli, the Swiss military organization could be compared to that of ancient Rome, and he was convinced of the possibility to instill Roman-style civic virtues in the militiamen.

Ironically, Niccolò would also note how the Swiss had been defeated in southern Italy when the Spanish light infantry had penetrated under the pikes, slaughtering their enemies at close quarters, akin to what the Romans had done with the Macedonian phalanx. But then, Machiavelli would always remain undecided where to find an exact modern replica of ancient Rome.

8

THE ARMED PROPHET

*And so it happens that all armed prophets
win, and the unarmed are ruined. For . . . the
character of populations varies; and while it
is easy to convince them of something, it is
difficult to keep them persuaded. And so one
should see that once they no longer believe,
they should be convinced to do so by force.*
—NICCOLÒ MACHIAVELLI, *THE PRINCE*

The militia was not Machiavelli's sole concern during the summer of 1506. It was said that Pope Julius II had thrown Peter's keys into the Tiber so as to get a better grip on Paul's sword, and there is no doubt that the pontiff had a very strong warlike streak running through him. From the beginning of his pontificate he had declared his wish to reclaim the church's lands lost for various reasons during the previous decades, but in order to do so he had to play his hand carefully, particularly with the Venetians, who now held a number of towns in the Romagna. Julius, however, had graduated from the same finishing school as his uncle, Pope Sixtus IV, one of the most egregious nepotists and most corrupt individuals ever to sit on the papal throne (being up against some very stiff competition). Despite his vile temper, Julius had learned through trial, error, and even exile to bide his time and choose the right moment to strike. He combined all these characteristics with a daring imperiousness and swiftness in implementing his plans that left his contemporaries bewildered, Machiavelli included.

By 1506 Julius had decided to retake Perugia and Bologna for the church, evicting in the process their respective lords, Giampaolo Baglioni and Giovanni Bentivoglio. To achieve this he ably managed to get Louis XII's support by hinting that he would otherwise seek an alliance with the emperor and conspire to evict the French from Genoa. The Florentines were also on his list of potential helpers, and by exploiting the running fight between Cardinals Soderini and Medici for papal favor, he induced the former to promise him Florence's military assistance. Of course, Cardinal Francesco had no such authority, and thus his promise to the pontiff put his brother Piero in a sticky position. He had no desire to offend *il papa terribile* (the terrible pope) with a refusal, but getting the approval of the appropriate political bodies was an entirely different matter.

The gonfalonier's arguments about the Republic's need to stay on good terms with Julius and the French did not convince his adversaries, who opposed sending troops for the pope's cause in the hope of embarrassing Soderini. However, being unable to present a united front, they had to yield to the majority's will and finally agreed that a diplomat be chosen to carry a cautious reply to the pope. The message was that just now Florence could not afford to deprive itself of soldiers without the risk of leaving the Pisa front unmanned, but that Florence would send the requested aid once the pontiff was "on the move." Once again, the choice fell on Machiavelli to carry out this mission.

He departed on August 25 and three days later wrote from Civita Castellana that he had seen the papal army in Nepi. Julius appeared to be satisfied with the Republic's answer. While visiting the local fortress, "the rarest thing in this world," the pope also told Niccolò that Florence should not worry about Louis XII forsaking his promised support, because of his alliance with Giovanni Bentivoglio, or that Julius lacked determination to achieve his goal. As for the Venetians, he had ignored their offers of aid in exchange for Forlì and Ravenna, although he had also disregarded the requests of some exiles from Forlì, who, Niccolò would comment, "believe they are being sent from Herod to Pilate." The pontiff's single-mindedness and energy impressed Machiavelli as he watched him ride at the head of the army.

Machiavelli witnessed another example of Julius's character once they reached Perugia. Giampaolo Baglioni had surrendered on terms, agreeing to allow a papal garrison to enter the city and man its gates. But the impatient Julius entered Perugia before his soldiers, virtually placing himself and his cardinals at Baglioni's mercy. Somewhat alarmed, Niccolò wrote to the Ten: "If he [Baglioni] will not harm the man who has come to despoil him of his state, then it will be out of good nature and humanity. I will know how this matter ends in a week." Baglioni observed the terms of the surrender, however, leaving Machiavelli wondering why someone with such a conspicuous criminal record—which included parricide and incest—failed to exploit an opportunity to capture the pope and his retinue.

At the time, he believed that Baglioni, having listened to the advice of his friends, and faced with the choice to save "by force or through humbleness," had opted for the second alternative. Only later, in the *Discourses*, and after Julius had caused Niccolò's downfall from power, would Machiavelli berate Baglioni's cowardly behavior by refusing to perform "an action worthy of eternal fame that everyone would have admired, for he would have been the first to prove to the clergy how despised are people who live and govern as they do." But by then Machiavelli's misfortunes had soured his ingrained Florentine anticlericalism.

From Perugia the papal army proceeded north, while the pope impatiently awaited the arrival of the aid promised by Louis XII and Florence.

Once he received news that the French troops were on their way, the pontiff showed visible elation, and, true to form, proceeded to mistreat the ambassadors sent by Giovanni Bentivoglio. When the diplomats presented the pope with a list of privileges his predecessors had granted to Bologna, he answered that he wanted to see for himself how the citizens lived and make changes if things there were not to his liking, adding menacingly "that he had forces of such quality to make not just Bologna, but the whole of Italy tremble." The pope was, to an extent, bluffing, since the French and Florentine soldiers had not yet arrived. On the pontiff's insistence, Machiavelli wrote to Florence to provide the promised troops immediately, while Julius grumbled about the time it would take for these soldiers to reach him.

In reality, by the standards of the time up to then, the papal campaign had proceeded at a rapid pace, so much so that Machiavelli had some problems receiving mail from Florence: "To Niccolò Machiavelli in Forlì, or where the Devil he may be," Biagio Buonaccorsi would address his letter of October 11. The pope had by then arrived in Forlì, but from this point onward, he would have to pass through the territory of Venetian-held Faenza in order to reach Bologna. Just to play it safe, he decided to make a detour through the lands of the Republic, not bothering to inform the Florentine government in advance of his decision, and forcing Machiavelli on the saddle to prepare the way for the papal train. Traveling along twisting mountain roads, Julius bypassed Faenza and arrived in Imola, Machiavelli having arrived there ahead of him on October 20. There he encountered the Bolognese ambassadors, who bemoaned Florence's military assistance to the pope, forcing Machiavelli to say, laughing, that Bentivoglio had taught the Florentines "to go with the flow," and the Bolognese could blame only themselves for what had happened.

Since Bologna had in the past fueled the flames of the Pistoia troubles and had on more than one occasion assisted Cesare Borgia against the Florentines, Niccolò could not conceal his smug satisfaction, thinking that payday had arrived for Bentivoglio. However, Niccolò would not witness Julius's triumphant entry into Bologna, which occurred on November 10, having been recalled to Florence on October 26. The length of time he had spent with the papal court had evidently been a source of jokes within the chancery, at least judging from a letter, written in mock curial style, of October 1, 1506, by one Giustiniano and an unidentified individual who signed only as "your buddy":

> Most singular and magnificent master: Since here we understand your good and happy condition with Your Magnificence's utmost satisfaction as for honor, dignity, and pleasant conversations with those appropriate to and befitting your nature, of which there is not penury but instead fertile abundance, and by them liked, loved, and pampered, and also thanks to sumptuous living on the most choice, healthy, and delicate foods your stomach may digest (since you have consumed or are consuming more than usual, be careful: The atmosphere there is not thin like here, but the thinnest, smooth to the touch, pleasant and soft, as we have learned from your magnificent and most honored associate-in-chief), we cannot on the one hand but congratulate you and be most happy for your sake (despite feeling a little envy, unlike you, who have none), but on the other we fear that all this partaking of pleasant air, subtle pleasures, and delicate food will make you so fat and lazy that you'll forget about us, as you have already done, not come home, and, worse still, take priestly orders and become a thoroughly up-to-date curial clergyman. May God help you and make you happy.
>
> We are anxious to hear the news from your side of the world, the best dishes, whether newborn calves or domestically raised mountain kids; and each of us wishes to know what's going on in Pesaro.
>
> From here no other news, except that the Arno is flowing downstream as usual.
>
> Farewell. We send our best to your magnificence *per infinita secula seculorum.* AMEN

Machiavelli's friends were poking fun at his taste for luxury and dislike for the clergy, these sorts of humorous exchanges being a common feature of a chancery staffed with cultivated, worldly individuals possessing the typically wicked Florentine sense of humor. We know, for instance, that during his diplomatic missions Machiavelli had a habit of sending back jokes and witticisms that made everyone "dislocate their jaw with laughter." None of these comedic pieces has yet emerged, but an example of what they must have been like is contained in Machiavelli's statutes of an imaginary confraternity, which satirized the many religious institutions that existed in Florence at that time. Entitled "Capitoli per una compagnia di piacere" (Statutes for a Company of Pleasure) and composed sometime after 1504, it can be taken as an example of the exchanges that went on in the chancery and of Niccolò's biting wit.

The rules of this made-up association, open in its membership to both sexes (real confraternities were single-gendered), prescribed, among other things, incessant tattling and "always speaking ill of each other." Female associates were supposed to go at least every week to "the Servi" (the Servite friars of the Santissima Annunziata—Machiavelli, as is clear from The Mandrake, considered them a bunch of lecherous rascals), or else "suffer the penalty of double attendance there." Should one of the women be considered too beautiful by at least two witnesses, she had to lift her skirt "four inches above the knee," while a good-looking man had to "prove that he did not have a kerchief or other stuffed inside his breeches." Any woman with a mother-in-law had to poison her within six months, and use the same medicine for those husbands "who don't perform their duty." Penalties for breaking the rules included, for women, "to be sent to live among the friars, and men in a monastery," or "beholding the Giant in the Square [Michelangelo's David, placed there in 1504] wearing spectacles"; or, for men or women, "staying for half an hour with his/her arse in the air, and everyone must give it a fart." Though humorous, the Capitoli is also telling because it reveals flaws that were all too common among the Florentines, including the tendency to indulge in envy and gossip as well as a lack of genuine religious devotion. But far from elevating himself to the lofty rank of a moral judge, Machiavelli preferred to chuckle at vices he also shared.

Unfortunately for his own sake, Niccolò did not limit his laughter to widespread habits—something everyone could accept—but instead would use his razor-sharp pen against specific people. In around 1504 he had started to write *Le Maschere* (The Masks), a comedy in the style of Aristophanes, in which, "under the guise of invented names," he savagely lampooned a number of his contemporaries. Although this composition has been lost, because Machiavelli's grandson Giuliano de' Ricci refused to copy the few—and nearly illegible—fragments he had discovered, it is more than likely that Niccolò shared some of the juiciest passages with his friends, Marcello Virgilio Adriani having encouraged him in the first place to write the play. If any inkling of this satire ever filtered out of the chancery's walls—which is also more than likely, in a tongue-wagging city like Florence—it would have caused Machiavelli's targets to have an extra reason for hating him. In any case, by the end of 1506 quite a few people felt that Machiavelli had become too big for his upstart boots and needed a lesson in humility. They soon would have a chance to give him one.

The emperor* Maximilian I of Habsburg had been involved in Italian politics since the end of the previous century, and although often distracted by problems within his own domains, he had never ceased in his attempts to enforce the rights he thought were due to him. He had bestowed the duchy of Milan to Ludovico Sforza, and thus had not taken at all well his imprisonment by the French, or the latter's occupation of what he considered an Imperial fiefdom. The Holy Roman Empire and France had been at loggerheads ever since the death in 1479 of Charles the Bold of Burgundy, which had led to war between the two sovereignties

---

* Technically speaking, Maximilian became emperor-elect only in 1508, his official title as heir presumptive to the Imperial throne being "King of the Romans." However, at the time people commonly referred to him as the emperor.

over inheritance issues. Moreover, Maximilian saw northern Italy as part of the empire, something that had only stiffened his determination to evict the French. He also wanted to teach the Venetians a lesson to repay them for their arbitrary—as he believed it to be—occupation of the Veneto and parts of Lombardy, not to mention the lands the emperor considered belonging to the church.

In 1502 ambassadors from the Imperial court had arrived in Florence asking for military aid and funds. The government had politely declined the request, but the visit nonetheless left its mark: Displeased with Louis XII's behavior toward the Republic, some Florentines began to consider the possibility of an alliance switch in Maximilian's favor. Soderini systematically backed the union with France, but once again, the Florentines were destined to be let down by their favored partner. When Genoa revolted against Louis's overlordship of their city in November 1506, the king asked Florence for troops, in exchange promising help for capturing Pisa. The Florentines duly obliged, but when, after Genoa's recapture, the time came for the king to honor his debt, he refused to move south, using, as an excuse, Maximilian's planned descent into Italy.

Adding insult to injury, he suggested that the Republic use mediation, through himself and the king of Spain, to reach a settlement with Pisa— the last thing the Florentines wanted to hear. As a consequence, and under the pressure of angry public opinion, the Florentine government started to discuss the possibility of finding new allies, or in any case trying to get on Maximilian's good side without offending the French. For this reason it was decided to send a *mandatario* (an official with limited diplomatic powers), rather than an ambassador, to the Imperial Diet that had assembled in Constance in April 1507. Soderini had wished to entrust Machiavelli with the mission, but his decision aroused a storm of protests among the *ottimati*, who maintained that Machiavelli's social standing made him unfit for the job.

Notwithstanding the fact that these people included a number of the gonfalonier's enemies, who thus intended to embarrass Soderini, they had a point: In a world based on very definite hierarchies, the social standing of an individual could make a difference, regardless of his other skills, in the outcome of such a mission. Thus, sending a mere secretary to the Imperial court would be a diplomatic faux pas of the first degree, possibly producing the opposite of what the Florentines were hoping for. Soderini's opponents had their way, and on June 25 the government dispatched Francesco Vettori to Germany.

In a way this represented a compromise solution, for although Vettori was not one of Soderini's friends, there is no evidence of him being a committed opponent of the gonfalonier (unlike his brother Paolo, who loathed Soderini with a passion). Moreover, Vettori had held a number of posts within the Florentine administrative and political structure, and in any case, the lack of full diplomatic mandate made his limited experience in international affairs less telling.

No one felt the gonfalonier's defeat in the matter more than Machiavelli himself. Although he did not cherish the idea of traveling beyond the Alps, he nonetheless had suffered a public humiliation and clearly thought he had been let down by those he had believed were his friends, especially Soderini. He must have felt very sorry for himself indeed— unreasonably so, perhaps, given that at the end of July he received two letters—both to an extent trying to console him, but also containing some sound advice.

Filippo Casavecchia, whom he trusted, gave him a long list of examples taken from classical antiquity and more recent Florentine history of friendships that turned into enmities, something he considered to a degree inevitable "due to the passage of time." Casavecchia added the barb that "in most cases, the ruin of cities is caused and generated by intimate friendships that are practiced daily," which is a good example of the twisted sense of humor so common among Florentines. He also stressed the need for conducting relationships with civility and moderation, not only for the sake of longer-lasting friendships, but also "to avoid those suspicions and jealousies that are all too common in a city such as this one." Casavecchia was clearly trying to tell Machiavelli how his behavior had alienated people who otherwise might have supported him, and warning him that, for his own good, he must not in any way estrange himself from Soderini or hold a grudge against him. "Be patient about the triumph in Germany," Casavecchia wrote, once more citing references from classical history, "for those who boast, having robbed you of it, cannot and will not succeed in Asia."

Alessandro Nasi would reiterate the same idea in a letter to Machiavelli of July 30, 1507. But while Filippo had taken a rather lofty tone, Nasi exhibited a rather more earthy approach:

> My dear and not unlucky Machiavelli, now that you've gotten over it. In your letter of the 23rd you wrote in a very enlightening manner, but I do not intend to reply for lack of time and because the person writing has not much paper. I would be happy if you would shit on the Imperial commission, now that you have recovered, and believe that it is best for you to be in Florence rather than in krautland, something we can chat about when we meet.
>
> Matters will eventually come to a head, and it will happen the same way as with those children whose parents sometimes allow them to play around with something that makes them very happy, and then this becomes the reason to remove it from them. For honest, God-fearing, and civic minded people are likely to make the best decision whatever the situation, be they rich, poor, of good or lesser standing as one may choose.

Nasi ended with an all-too-familiar refrain: "And if in the meantime you should decide to write, it would not be a mortal sin," yet another reminder to his friend about the need to keep up healthy relationships if he wanted to get the "honest, God-fearing, and civic minded" on his side. If some people, like Nasi, were prepared to shrug their shoulders at Machiavelli's apparent indifference, others could take umbrage instead— as Niccolò had just learned at his own expense.

Machiavelli spent the rest of the summer overseeing the establishment of militia units and the movement of troops and victuals across the Florentine domain. He also received a long letter from Don Miguel de

Corella in which the author attempted to justify his own actions, evidently hoping to forestall his dismissal (some Florentines grumbled that it would have been better to have him executed, lest Florence should have to face a vengeful and embittered enemy in the future—the ghost of Paolo Vitelli still hovered over the city).

For Niccolò, the only break in routine was a short mission south of Siena that August to inform the government about the arrival there of Cardinal Bernardino Caravajal, who had been sent by the pope to Germany to assess Maximilian's real intentions, but Niccolò did not manage to get much news other than gossip. The one thing everybody seemed to agree on, and not just in Siena, was that Maximilian would be descending into Italy at some point, the Imperial Diet having voted to raise the necessary troops for the enterprise. Dark clouds appeared to be gathering beyond the Alps, and Florence needed to find a safe haven should the storm break.

Ever since his arrival at the Imperial court, Francesco Vettori had been encountering serious difficulties while trying to fulfill his mission, mainly due to the limitations of his negotiating powers, coupled with an inability to speak any German (curial Latin could compensate somewhat, but Vettori's lack of linguistic skills meant that he could not hobnob with the Imperial officials as much as he would have liked). The emperor wanted money from the Florentines, and though Vettori had rejected some of his most preposterous requests, he did believe that an offer of 30,000 florins could soothe Maximilian's hostility toward the Republic. Vettori's task had been complicated, however, by the representatives of the other Italian states, who were constantly pouring poison into the emperor's ear about Florentine subsidies to Louis XII, thus allowing the French to remain in Italy. Meanwhile, unconfirmed rumors had the Medici making substantial offers to Maximilian to favor their return to power. In frustration, Vettori wrote to the government asking that a proper ambassador be sent "to negotiate and conclude." The emperor had lowered his own requests to 50,000 ducats, but wanted them immediately, declaring that otherwise the Florentine representative should not dare show his face again.

The request put the Republic in a quandary: Should they send an ambassador and pay, thus alienating the French, or refuse to dispatch both the diplomat and the money, thus provoking Maximilian's displeasure? A *pratica* convened to discuss the matter, and those present agreed to send Alamanno Salviati and Piero Gicciardini to the Imperial court, giving them full diplomatic powers. Guicciardini, however, refused to go, stating that it would be a poor bargain to gain Louis XII's inevitable hostility along with Maximilian's uncertain aid. After further debates, the pratica also rejected the idea of extending Vettori's negotiating powers, but agreed that he should be given new and more complete instructions.

Soderini had been waiting for a chance to redress the wrong done to his faithful Machiavelli the previous June. With the excuse that it would be dangerous to send the orders to Vettori via normal courier, he suggested that Niccolò should travel in person to deliver the message. This time the gonfalonier's enemies could find no reason to oppose his request, although suspicions abounded that Soderini and his friends had favored their minion's election because they were sure that he would report matters "according to their projects and plans." In other words, the committed pro-French gonfalonier had every intention of sabotaging any sort of agreement with Maximilian to please Louis XII.

Machiavelli departed immediately, carrying with him the government instructions for Vettori: an offer to Maximilian of 30,000 ducats, to be raised to 50,000 should need be, paid in three installments, and to be delivered only when it was certain that the emperor would be on the move to Italy. In exchange, Maximilian had to promise to respect Florence's liberties. Soderini had been right about the perils of sending the missives by ordinary methods, for once Machiavelli reached Lombardy the distrustful French authorities submitted him to a thorough personal search, forcing him to tear up the government's orders.

Traveling through the Swiss Confederation, he penned his opinions not only about its admirable defense organization, but also its inhabitants' love for liberty and desire to remain independent from any other power. Always on the lookout for classical references, Niccolò would later describe in the *Discourses* the Swiss as being "the nearest to the ancient Romans in their behavior toward religion and military attitude." This experience only reinforced his belief that the same results could be obtained in the Florentine state with good laws and habits. In Constance, Niccolò met with the celebrated composer Heinrich Isaac, who had married a Florentine. Machiavelli, as already noted, held music in high regard, and had possibly listened to Isaac's performances when he had been in Florence during the Medici regime.

Niccolò also began to comprehend how difficult it would be to solve the diplomatic problems he would soon be facing when he spoke with the Savoyard ambassador about Maximilian's intentions. "You wish to know in two hours what in many months I have not been able to fathom?" the envoy had answered, adding that the emperor kept his plans close to his chest, and in order to understand matters in full one would need to have spies everywhere. With these sobering words in mind, Machiavelli proceeded toward Innsbruck, hoping to find Vettori there.

En route he encountered troops marching in disorder, something that confirmed his previous impression about the empire being a hodgepodge of virtually independent polities, each with its own agenda. Maximilian had good soldiers but little money, and nowhere could he get the necessary funds for a prolonged campaign in Italy. Indeed, far from rectifying this situation, the Diet of Constance had produced instead a lot of "hot air" (*un berlingozzo*).*

Niccolò finally caught up with Vettori in Bozen and informed him of the contents of the destroyed letters. Probably mindful of his recent political misadventure, and for once paying heed to the advice of his friends, Machiavelli did everything he could to put Vettori at ease. In his first letter to the government he stressed his desire to return home, but the Ten answered that this was up to Vettori to decide; the latter insisted that Machiavelli remain until the end of the negotiations, saying, "for his presence is necessary, although if needed, and should the road be safe, I'm sure that he will face any risk and toil for the love of Florence." The

---

* *Berlingozzo* is the name of a cake that used to be made in Florence during Carnival. However, the verb *berlingare* meant making useless chatter.

perils were very real, given that the emperor had launched his troops against the Venetians; Machiavelli could very well end up in the war zone. Moreover, Niccolò's presence must have been a solace for the lonely Francesco, who needed a secretary as well as someone with skills in information gathering.

We have no evidence of Vettori and Machiavelli having been in contact before this date (despite having been schooled by the same teachers), but they got along famously. They had similar literary aspirations, had grown up in the same neighborhood, and, one should add, shared a strong taste for women. Also, Vettori endorsed, albeit not without reservations, Machiavelli's militia project, something Niccolò must have found refreshing coming from one of the *ottimati*. No doubt Machiavelli realized the opportunity of cultivating Vettori at the time, given the latter's family connections with people opposed to Soderini (Bernardo Rucellai was Francesco's uncle), but from the start there appears to have been a genuine feeling between the two men. This, together with the personality traits that they shared, helped to bridge the gap between them in age and social background, allowing not just for a close collaboration during the time they spent together at the Imperial court, but also the development of a long-lasting friendship destined to have very long-term results.

A number of dispatches sent from Vettori to Florence from January to June 1508 show evidence of Machiavelli's contributions. Francesco always signed the missives, as warranted by his official position, but often Machiavelli would insert passages in his own handwriting. Occasionally the opinions of the two differed, as the letters prove. Even after Maximilian had received a thorough licking at the hands of the Venetians, Machiavelli could write confidently about the empire's strength, but in the same dispatch Vettori expressed his doubts about Germany's real power. Nevertheless, these differences were always kept within the frame of civilized debate: "Niccolò and I have discussed these matters," Francesco would write to the Ten on one occasion, an explicit recognition of Machiavelli's talents, and later he would state that "had Niccolò departed, I would have seen less than what I managed to see." Vettori, however, possessed a more down-to-earth attitude than Machiavelli, preferring practice to theory. This difference between them would emerge time and time again later on in the many friendly and constructive epistolary sparring matches between Francesco and Niccolò.

The two envoys faced an uphill battle at the Imperial court. Everyone knew that Maximilian disliked Soderini for his stance in international politics, and the previous summer the emperor had written to Alamanno Salviati asking him to use his influence in Florence to detach the city from Louis XII. He apparently considered it useless to ask the gonfalonier the same question because of Soderini's well-known commitment to the French alliance. Moreover, Maximilian's Florentine counselor, Pigello Portinari, happened to be steadfastly opposed to Soderini, and given Machiavelli's association with the gonfalonier, his presence at the Imperial court hardly helped to improve matters. When Vettori introduced Machiavelli to the emperor, the latter called Portinari and under his breath asked him "who this newly arrived secretary was."

Pigello may have been the source of the malicious rumors going around Florence about the true scope of Machiavelli's mission, and his lack of status proved to be a handicap, just as some had feared. "I would have sent Niccolò to follow the Court when it moved to Trent a few days ago," Vettori would write on February 14, 1508. "But these people [Maximilian and his advisers] would take umbrage and we cannot antagonize them. Maybe neither of us shall remain in Germany, but in the meantime we have to obey this country's customs." In the hierarchically structured empire, Vettori could not afford to delegate his official functions, even less so to a man who could be perceived, his talents notwithstanding, as a social upstart.*

---

* The Florentines scoffed at the exaggeratedly obtuse attitude displayed by the Germans toward social rank and its associated symbols. Franco Sacchetti tells about the case of a German knight challenging a Florentine to a duel because the two happened to carry the same crest on their helmets. The Florentine got out of the predicament by selling his own crest for a profit to the German, "who felt as if he had conquered an entire city."

The initial offer of 30,000 ducats was refused by the Imperial advisers, and the Florentine envoys raised the sum to 40,000, hoping in this way to make the emperor somewhat better disposed toward the Republic. Maximilian, however, thought such a proposal too low "for Florence's preservation and security, considering the city's means as well as other factors," and asked for a loan of 25,000 ducats to be paid immediately. Vettori protested to his superiors that even if the Republic found the sum, "the payment would be certain, but the aid not," adding that should the Venetians defeat the emperors, this money would be lost, but should Maximilian emerge victorious, he would raise his demands to in excess of 60,000 ducats. Even more cutting would be Machiavelli's comment that, considering the emperor's financial needs, "if all the tree branches in Italy produced coins as fruit, it would not suffice."

Vettori did not have the power to pledge funds without his government's authorization, and in any case, weeks would pass before the authorities made a decision and communicated it to their representatives. In the meantime, Machiavelli and Vettori followed the Imperial court as it moved through Tyrol. Days and weeks passed, and they encountered more and more troops moving south. Meanwhile, news of Venetian successes trickled in, the Republic went on playing for time, and Machiavelli went down with a kidney stone—a serious enough ailment to worry Vettori. When Niccolò expressed his desire to return to Florence, Francesco had neither the power nor the will to stop him. Conveniently enough, at the beginning of June the Venetians and the Imperialists agreed to sign a three-year truce, Venice taking home swaths of northern Friuli, parts of the Italian Tyrol, and the strategically important port at Triest. With the roads now clear, Machiavelli was soon riding home. He arrived there in record time—despite the kidney stone—making it by June 16, 1508.

His experience at the Imperial court would bring Machiavelli to compose the "Rapporto di cose della Magna" (Report on German Affairs), a peculiar document that he would rewrite and expand twice in the years to come. More than any of his other writings it reflects the contrast existing in Machiavelli between the down-to-earth analyst and the abstract theorist. His description of the emperor's chronic lack of sufficient funds, the difficulties he faced in controlling his subjects, and his tendency to change his mind according to the latest advice was spot-on; less convincing was the description of the Germans, despite their wealth, as frugal, unsophisticated people who refrained from constructing elaborate buildings, dressing well ("spending two florins in ten years for clothes"), and owning chattels, satisfied with eating bread and meat and having a heating stove at home. This rustic life, of course, made for good soldiers and lovers of free institutions. Here the influence of the *Germania* by the Roman writer Cornelius Tacitus is evident; besides, Machiavelli had never traveled to places like Nuremberg or the Hansa cities in the north. His experience was largely limited to parts of Switzerland and the Tyrol—incidentally, the places most suited to confirming his classical-minded prejudices.

Machiavelli would have no time to rest, being very soon sent to supervise Florence's *guasto* (scorched-earth) operations on the Pisa front. The Florentines were determined to get Pisa by starvation, direct attacks having failed, hoping that the pressure from the hundreds of famished refugees from the surrounding countryside within their walls would force the Pisans to capitulate. Just to be sure that no supplies reached the beleaguered city, the Republic employed Genoese corsairs to patrol the nearby sea routes. Matters, however, were complicated by the intervention of Louis XII, who demanded that the Florentines stop operations, threatening to back his demand with troops, with the excuse that Pisa had placed itself since 1494 under the protection of the French crown; in reality he worried that Florence's success would attenuate its dependency on France; moreover, and probably more to the point, he wanted to teach the Florentines a lesson for their flirting with Maximilian.

The Republic protested that the alliance of 1502 allowed it to recover the lost lands of its dominion. This protest fell on deaf ears, however, and Florence instead was forced to pay 100,000 ducats to Louis, and another 50,000 to King Ferdinand of Aragon (not to mention bribing various ministers at the two courts), to guarantee their neutrality in the Pisa war—"filling everyone's throat and open mouth," Machiavelli would acidly comment in his second *Decennale*, berating the European sovereigns for their apparently insatiable hunger for money. Meanwhile, the legal-minded Francesco Guicciardini concluded, with a mixture of bitterness and realism, seeing the Pisans abandoned by those who had promised to protect them: "The power of money can today achieve much more than the respect for honor."

It is unlikely that Louis lost much sleep over his devious actions, or that he and Ferdinand of Aragon intended to keep their word once they received Florence's subsidies: A week is a long time in politics, and changing situations could justify any sort of behavior. However, soon Florence would have the singular good fortune of not having to contend with any external power in her struggle for the recovery of Pisa.

Maximilian had not succumbed to the humiliation he had endured at the hands of the Venetians, and the pope's rage increased daily at seeing Venice holding on to lands he considered to be the church's. In addition, the Spanish king resented the occupation of certain ports in southern Italy by the Venetians, while Louis XII needed the emperor to recognize Milan as a French fiefdom and wished to recover the duchy's eastern territories from Venice. As a result, in November 1508 the representatives of the above powers met in Cambrai to discuss a possible crusade against the Ottoman Empire. The negotiations proceeded rapidly, and a month later the so-called League of Cambrai was formed, with war against the infidels as its main objective. But the Ottoman campaign was not to take place before the Venetians were defeated, all the signatories agreeing on Venice's territorial usurpations.. For the immediate future the Florentines could only welcome the treaty, not only because it gave them a free hand against Pisa, but also because the Venetians would now have their hands too full to interfere in Tuscan affairs. Dark clouds were gathering over Italy, but in the meantime, another storm had broken out in Florence.

The Medici had not lost all hope of returning to their native city, and realizing that force would lead nowhere, decided to try other means. Cardinal Giovanni de' Medici had managed to ingratiate himself with the pope, and upon his request Julius II spoke to the Florentine ambassador in Rome about the wish of Giovanni and his brother Giuliano to be readmitted into the city; should this be refused, then at least their niece Clarice, daughter of the deceased Piero de' Medici, might be allowed to marry in Florence. After consultation, the Signoria told the ambassador he should refrain from conveying such messages in the future, and to inform the pope that the exiled Medici were getting far better treatment than what they deserved. Determined to marry Clarice to a Florentine, in early 1507 the cardinal sent his sister-in-law Alfonsina, born an Orsini, and Piero's widow, to Florence, ostensibly to reclaim her dowry—legally owed to her from the Medici possessions confiscated by the Republic. But the real reason was to scour the city for a suitable son-in-law among those whose influence within the law-making bodies could favor at least the mellowing of the legal proscriptions against her family—no easy matter, despite Clarice's more than substantial dowry of 6,000 florins: In 1506 Soderini had had one Francesco Pitti charged with treason for considering such a match.

Clarice had allegedly already been offered in marriage to one of Soderini's nephews, but the gonfalonier had backed out for fear of the negative effects such a match would have on his image in Florentine public opinion. The person who turned out to be prepared to take the risk was Filippo Strozzi, the scion of an illustrious lineage traditionally opposed to the prospective bride's family, a number of the Strozzi having suffered persecution and exile under the Medici. Once Filippo's decision became public, in November 1508, despite his attempt to keep it secret (a nearly impossible task in Florence), the Strozzi rose as a body to oppose it in the name of their long-established enmity with the Medici. With good reason, they feared the liaison's political consequences.

Despite the pressure from his kin, Filippo did not budge, asserting that tearing up the marital contract would bring him personal dishonor, the hatred of Clarice's family, and the obligation to pay a penalty of 2,000 ducats. He did not mention the obvious fact that he would also be losing his fiancée's dowry, money he badly needed, given that much of his father's substantial fortune had been poured into building one of the most impressive *palazzi* in Florence* (while not all Florentines would have endorsed Machiavelli's statement about Fortune being a woman that needed to be controlled, they nevertheless would have agreed about controlling a woman's fortune).

In an attempt to stop the marriage, Soderini had Filippo called in front of the Otto di Guardia (the Eight of Watch, Florence's police magistracy), while the city split in two factions between those who opposed the Strozzi-Medici match and those who favored it. From Rome, Julius II wrote to the Signoria requesting that it allow the union to take place, receiving in turn the curt reply that the pope should mind his own business. Soderini viewed the whole matter as an attack against his power, and possibly as part of a plot to allow the Medici to return. In no time the *tamburo* of the Eight (the box where anonymous denunciations were placed) filled up with anti-Strozzi accusations; tempers flared, and the marriage became the favored topic of gossip.

In front of the Otto, Filippo skillfully defended himself, pointing out that neither Giovanni nor Giuliano de' Medici had ever been declared *ribelli*, rebels against the state; in any case, female members of a family had always been exempted from the penalties associated with sentences of this kind leveled against their male relatives. Filippo used the example of the Pazzi women, who had been allowed to marry Florentines after their kin had been proscribed following the 1478 conspiracy against the Medici regime. Efficacious as these arguments may have been, Filippo's enemies had executed their own counterbarrage. The potentially most damaging shot was an anonymous denunciation believed at the time to have been penned by none other than Machiavelli himself, so skillful its wording.

According to this document, since Piero de' Medici had thrice attacked the city, all his immediate kin were to be considered rebels according to the Republic's laws; therefore, Filippo should be punished for

---

* The Strozzi had started to build their palazzo at the end of the 1480s and, in the face of the serious economic crisis that hit Florence during these years, continued its edification through the next decade. Savonarola would thunder from the pulpit against people "who build their houses with gold, silver, and the blood of the poor"—a hardly veiled reference to the Strozzi's architectural venture.

consorting not with a rebel's daughter, but indeed with someone who was a rebel herself. The danger of this reasoning could hardly be underestimated: For one thing, where did Piero de' Medici's kinship (*stripe*) end? By stretching the argument far enough, everyone tied by blood to Clarice, the Salviati, the Ridolfi, or the Rucellai could eventually end up in the rebels' cauldron. All this went against established law and practice, and although doubts remain about Machiavelli's authorship, the fact that at the time people were convinced of it must have further alienated those already ill-disposed toward the secretary.

In the end Filippo managed to sway the Strozzi in his favor and build up enough support in the city to get off the hook. The Otto acquitted him of conspiring against the state, limiting any other penalty to a 500-florin fine and his confinement to Naples for three years. Soderini had also failed in his attempt to have him condemned by the Signoria, and the new government that took office in January 1509 proved even less manageable in this respect than the previous one (Neri Capponi, Filippo's brother-in-law, happened to be one of the priors). The Strozzi-Medici marriage proved a singular defeat for Soderini, and the gonfalonier's standing sank even further than it had already, having been lowered a few months earlier by another political failure. The master of the Altopascio, Guglielmo Capponi, had been canvassing in Rome to be nominated archbishop of Florence, meeting the opposition of Soderini and his brother, Cardinal Francesco, partly out of personal loathing for the highly unlikeable Capponi—an animosity exacerbated by a long-standing rivalry between the two families*—and partly because the cardinal coveted the position for himself.

---

* Since the fifteenth century the Capponi, especially Guglielmo's branch, and the Soderini had been engaged in a struggle for political control of the *gonfalone* (district) of the Green Dragon in the quarter of Santo Spirito. There is also evidence that Guglielmo's grandfather may have played dirty with the Soderini over the inheritance of the famed statesman Niccolò da Uzzano (d. 1433). The running fight between the two families could be one of the reasons for Tommaso Soderini's loyalty toward the Medici, as well as for his son Piero's preference for the Florentine political middle class versus the *ottimati*.

The gonfalonier managed to get the Signoria to convince Julius II to block Capponi's appointment, but Soderini, to avoid the accusation of having acted out of private interest, had to swallow the nomination of the well-respected Cosimo de' Pazzi, instead of his brother, to the Florentine see. Although the Pazzi had been fierce opponents of the Medici in the fifteenth century, Cosimo received his post because of Cardinal Giovanni's influence. Coupled with Filippo and Clarice's marriage, this episode demonstrates the Medici's ability to create a pressure group in their favor within Florence. As for Machiavelli, the Strozzi marriage would in the long run prove beneficial for him in a way he could hardly have imagined.

The final campaign against Pisa started in earnest in February 1509, with the Florentines hoping to finish the job before summer, while those who were able to put spokes in their military wheel were otherwise engaged. Machiavelli had once more been sent to the front with instructions to organize the blockade of Pisa: "We have placed on your shoulders this entire matter," the Ten would write to him on February 15. Displaying his usual carelessness, Machiavelli chose to ignore the presence of the good-natured Florentine commissioner Niccolò Capponi, despite the latter keeping him constantly informed of his activities, to the point that both Soderini and Buonaccorsi were forced to remind him about the need to maintain good social relations with his political and military superior. Machiavelli paid lip service to this advice, writing as little as possible to Capponi and continuing with his usual behavior.

His attitude evidently did not go down well with some people in Florence, provoking the Council of the Eighty to nominate two other commissioners to aid Capponi, one of them, significantly, being Machiavelli's old enemy Alamanno Salviati. The three commissioners and Machiavelli, meeting on March 10 at Cascina, decided to pitch three camps around Pisa to stop any troops or victuals from entering the city. In desperation, the trapped Pisans sent a delegation to Jacopo Appiano, Lord of Piombino, asking him to mediate between them and the Florentines and requesting an envoy from Florence to discuss the terms of surrender. Believing that the Pisans were only trying to gain time, the Ten decided to send Machiavelli instructions to "explore this matter with the necessary prudence, and give away as little as possible."

When the Pisans met Machiavelli they immediately protested having to deal with a mere secretary rather than citizens of rank, a statement that made Machiavelli, always sensitive about the dignity of his position, hit the roof, as confirmed by the grinding tone of his letter to the Ten. The Pisans requested the preservation of their lives, property, and honor, adding that otherwise, no deal would be possible, and offering as surety the whole of the countryside outside their walls. To Appiano, in the presence of a delegation of country folk, Machiavelli curtly remarked that he had been tricked by the Pisans, who clearly had no intention of surrendering. Addressing the delegation, he told them how much he pitied their simple-mindedness in playing a lose-lose game: If the Pisans won, they would send the yokels back to their fields without giving anything in return for their help, but should the city be taken by storm, an increasingly likely possibility, the country people "would lose their property, life, and all the rest."

The prospect of their city being put to the sack terrorized the envoys, and one of them started shouting that these were not proper words to use and that Machiavelli was attempting to spread division among them. He could not have been more right, for a yokel called Giovanni da Vico cried, "Peace, we want peace, ambassador," while Appiano scolded the Pisans for their devious behavior toward him. Later, the lord of Piombino told Machiavelli that he had given the delegates a proper dressing-down and that they were willing to agree to Florence's terms, pending their fellow citizens' approval. Believing that Appiano wished only to boost his own position as a mediator, Machiavelli shrugged off the proposal and rode off. Florence had victory firmly in its grasp, and for once he could afford to be haughty.

With grim determination, the Pisans held on for another two months, while the steel ring around their walls tightened by the day. The orders from the Ten were to take no prisoners, and the besieged threatened to answer in kind. But the promises of the Pisan leaders about imminent relief sounded more hollow by the day, causing protests and rioting.

Machiavelli had been doing his part in the siege operations, constantly bringing instructions, reinforcements, and pay to the various besieging units, and on April 16 he proudly told his superiors that the militia units at the front were "among the finest infantry one may find in Italy."

Not everyone appreciated this flurry of activity, in particular those people who resented Machiavelli's arbitrary exercise of power. Alamanno Salviati in particular fumed at what he considered Machiavelli's lack of respect for his superiors, once exploding in verbal abuse over the leave the secretary had given to some soldiers. Informed of this, Machiavelli wrote a resentful letter to Salviati; in reply, the commissioner denied having insulted Niccolò and said he had simply lost his temper because the commissioners had not been informed in advance of the decision. It would appear that Machiavelli had learned a lesson, since a number of the letters written by the commissioners to the Ten at the time of Pisa's surrender are in his handwriting. Given his known opinions on the matter, he could well appreciate Salviati's concerns about the risks of weakening the authority of the Republic's representatives over the military; yet, Niccolò's confidence in his own talents would increasingly lead him to ignore the advice, opinions, and feelings of others.

Finally, on May 20, a delegation from Pisa met with Alamanno Salviati, and the next day the delegates departed with him to Florence. It took five days of discussions to hammer out the capitulation agreement and a couple more days to get it ratified. Although the formal surrender had been set for June 4, two days before that the famished populace started to stream from the gates seeking food in the camps. As the victorious Florentines prepared for their triumphal entry into Pisa, the Ten were careful to provide Machiavelli with the necessary funds to pay the troops selected for the occupation. They were to receive one-third of their due, lest the disgruntled soldiery decide to serve themselves at the expense of the unfortunate Pisans. The last thing Florence needed was to have soldiers running amok in the city. Although the Pisans had subscribed to what amounted to an unconditional surrender, the Florentines had realistically decided that generosity with their defeated foe would be more profitable than revenge: The Pisans were allowed to retain the same liberties they had enjoyed before 1494, including their fiscal privileges.

Later Machiavelli would condemn Florence's decision to negotiate Pisa's surrender, attributing it to the commissioners' incompetence and their inability to " blockade or storm" the city—how different the result would have been if Antonio Giacomini had been in charge! Yet, there is no evidence that Machiavelli viewed positively Florence's conduct at the time of Pisa's capitulation, and his post factum criticism sounds more like a propaganda attempt to back a political agenda than an honest evaluation of actual events.

Machiavelli's signature appears under Adriani's in the capitulation document, and he could justly be proud of his accomplishments as he beheld the militia preparing to take part in the victory parade through the conquered city. (In reality, the Florentine levies had accomplished little in the field, but at least they had saved the Republic the trouble and expense of hiring large quantities of professional infantry.) In any case, the triumph planned for June 6 was postponed until two days later, astrological conjunctions being the probable cause of the delay; indeed, the humanist Lattanzio Tedaldi had written to Machiavelli on June 3 suggesting the right hour for the entry. As the Florentine populace exploded into joyous celebration at the news of Pisa's fall, Machiavelli's friend Agostino Vespucci wrote to him: "If I did not think your pride would be swollen, I'd dare say that with your battalions you did sterling work, helping not to delay but on the contrary to accelerate the restoration of what belongs to Florence."

Not everyone agreed, however. A lot of people resented the fact that Soderini had tried to take all the glory of the victory for himself, and Machiavelli's own success did nothing to soothe the animosity against him. Filippo Casavecchia would sense Machiavelli becoming more isolated, even if he never doubted his ability: "I do not believe that idiots will understand your thinking, while the wise are few and far between; you understand what I mean, even if I'm not good at saying it. Every day I discover you to be a greater prophet than the Jews or any other country ever had."

9

COUNCIL AND
CONCILIATION

*Your Lordships can well believe, as they do in
the Gospel, that should war erupt between the
pope and this king, they will not be able to
avoid taking sides—all the relations you may
have with both contenders notwithstanding.*
—NICCOLÒ MACHIAVELLI TO THE TEN,
AUGUST 9, 1510

The juggernaut of the League of Cambrai had started rolling the previous April with the French invasion of the Venetian mainland; soon thereafter, Julius II issued a bull of excommunication and interdict against Venice in an attempt to isolate the city both spiritually and politically, while his troops advanced unopposed through the Romagna. Smelling blood, the rulers of Ferrara and Mantua joined the invaders, bringing the league's forces in the area to some 50,000 men.

Against this impressive array the Venetians could put together some 35,000 soldiers, half of the infantry being militia, even though the pope's enmity had not allowed them to recruit in the papal territories.

To lead their army they had chosen the old but solid Niccolò Orsini, Count of Pitigliano, but unfortunately with the daring Bartolomeo d'Alviano as second in command. Pitigliano had devised a strategy of attrition, hoping to gain time by wearing down his adversaries without engaging them in battle. Alviano, however, had different plans, and on May 14 the Venetian rearguard under his command engaged the French at Agnadello, suffering a crushing defeat. With half of his forces gone, and many more of his troops deserting by the day, Orsini could do nothing but retreat toward Venice, abandoning most of the mainland to the invaders.

Bergamo, Brescia, Verona, Vicenza, Padua, and Treviso fell in quick succession, and to everyone it seemed that Venice itself would soon follow suit. Niccolò Machiavelli, in Chapter 12 of *The Prince*, would attribute the defeat of Agnadello to Venice's reliance on mercenaries, forgetting, or wishing to forget, that the Venetian hired soldiery had performed with great bravery, some units preferring to succumb to a man rather than surrender. But by then Niccolò had developed something of an obsession for citizen armies and wished to whitewash the recent disastrous performance of Florence's militia—the ultimate cause of his fall from power.

The Imperial forces under some of Maximilian's vassals had occupied large portions of the Veneto, but at this point Louis XII, having accomplished his objectives, preferred to consolidate the recent conquests, leaving but a token force to continue the campaign. Sensing the change, the Venetians started a series of determined diplomatic maneuvers intended to break the League of Cambrai apart, starting with Julius II. The pope had always been suspicious of Louis XII, and had once said that he "did not wish to become the chaplain of the French"; moreover, he worried about Cardinal d'Amboise's designs on the papacy and was engaged in a heated dispute with the king about appointments to French benefices—the French crown having declared itself the only authority in this matter since the mid-fifteenth century.

Meanwhile, the Venetians had regrouped their forces, and on July 16 they reoccupied Padua with a brilliant cloak-and-dagger operation, concentrating the greater part of their army there under Pitigliano and the feisty *provveditore* (commissioner) Andrea Gritti. Three weeks later, by a stroke of luck, they managed to capture Francesco Gonzaga, Marquis of Mantua, provoking the pope to throw his *birretta* on the ground in a fury when he heard the news. The Venetians, however, still had to contend with the Imperial troops marching toward Padua, reinforced by French and papal contingents. Fortunately, Orsini, while no thunderbolt in the field, possessed the necessary skill and obstinacy to conduct a dogged defense. On September 15, 1509, the siege of Padua began, and in the following days the Imperial artillery would pound large sections of the city's walls to rubble. The Venetians, however, repulsed every attempt to storm the breaches.

After two weeks, seeing that he had made no headway, deserted by his allies, and by now unable to pay his troops, Maximilian lifted the siege. It did not take long for the Venetians to send an agent to the Imperial court to make an offer, oiled with substantial bribes for the emperor's chief counselors. The agent took care to remind Maximilian that his real enemies were the French, but, still smarting under his reverse at Padua, Maximilian declined the offer. In the meantime, however, the Venetians had managed to sow seeds of dissent among their remaining enemies.

Machiavelli had been following the events that were taking place in northern Italy from Florence, and on September 28 he wrote about them to Alamanno Salviati in Pisa. Why Niccolò decided to take this step remains a mystery. One could speculate that he wished to ingratiate himself with the anti-Soderini faction, perhaps because he understood the damage that could come of his close association with the gonfalonier. It could also have been a case, as the Florentines would have said, of "speaking to the mother-in-law so that the daughter-in-law understands" (*parlare a suocera perchè nuora intenda*); in other words, Soderini may have been using Machiavelli's skilled pen to persuade Salviati of the need for Florentines to endorse the gonfalonier's foreign policy—and interestingly enough, the missive is signed by Machiavelli but written by a different hand.

The letter's primary theme is that, whatever happens, the Florentines need not fear Maximilian. This is significant, given that at about the same time the letter was written, the Signoria had decided to conclude an accord with the emperor. Louis XII had insisted that the Republic agree to the treaty because he was concerned about Venice's recovery after Agnadello. He knew his disputes with Julius II would eventually cause the pope to abandon the league. The French king needed as many allies as possible to face the pontiff's growing hostility, and the Florentines had decided to comply with his requests. However, although Soderini's opponents were in agreement about concluding a deal with Maximilian, they also wanted to retain France's favor. Given Soderini's commitment to the French pact, Machiavelli (or his source of inspiration) may have perceived this as the right moment for an internal peace campaign in the name of a general accord about Louis XII's friendship.

Niccolò, however, appeared to have learned nothing from his mistakes, for while, on one hand, his letter seemed to be a demonstration of humility, on the other it displayed brazen conceit. He addressed Salviati with flowery words but proceeded to lay down the law in unequivocal terms: "I understand matters to be this way," he wrote, "and being personally acquainted with these rulers, I'm not afraid of going against the accepted wisdom." After recounting what he knew about the siege of Padua, Machiavelli declined to give his opinion on Maximilian's chances of capturing the city: "For I can't find anyone competent in this field, and everyone follows his own convictions."

However, Machiavelli continued, it did not matter if the emperor was victorious or not, since he would soon face two big disadvantages: the lack of funds and inclement weather. Moreover, he could not hope to destroy Venice completely, nor expect to reach a financially advantageous agreement with the Venetians. In conclusion, Machiavelli said, Maximilian had no other option but to retreat. "I don't see why one should seek an agreement with an emperor who can't take Padua, just for the sake of doubling expenses and prolonging the war," Niccolò wrote. His point could hardly have been clearer: Florence had no need to fear Maximilian, and trying to win his favor was only a waste of money.

Salviati penned his reply on October 4 in a letter that was a masterpiece of malice, worthy of an old saying about Florentines—that they have "Heaven in their eyes, and Hell in their mouths." Alamanno systematically used the familiar *tu*, whereas Machiavelli had employed the formal *voi*, just to underscore the difference in their social and political ranking. After effecting gratitude toward Niccolò for remembering him so dearly and for providing most welcome news, "for here we learn nothing at all except from those vagrants who may arrive every two weeks to a month" (shot number one: Salviati received dispatches from the government and certainly had other ways of gathering information), Alamanno went on to say that the professional soldiers in Pisa maintained that Padua could not be taken by force (shot number two: Niccolò would do best to check his sources). However, Salviati added that, being somewhat like a friar (*fratesco*) in his attitude, he doubted the Venetians would be successful, since the adversities they were facing seemed nearly of divine rather than natural origin, "and thus we should pray God to provide the best outcome."

The mockery in Salviati's words was evident, for by using the word *fratesco* he was poking fun at Machiavelli's well-known dislike for the clergy and the Savonarolans, as well as his trust in natural causes, and reinforcing it with a statement of belief in miracles and God's intervention. (It should be added that in his letter Machiavelli had mentioned that the news from Padua had been brought to Florence by a friar, and therefore Salviati could also be scoffing at the clergyman's reliability.) Alamanno invited Machiavelli to do everything he could to keep the king of France, Spain, and the pope united, "lest one of them should, out of desperation, act in such a way as to ruin the whole of Italy; or the French army remain at other people's discretion, for that would be very worrying."

Salviati then delivers his barbed parting shot: "If I have omitted any-thing, I shall leave it to my doctor to figure it out." But Machiavelli, unlike most of his colleagues in the chancery, had never, at least to our knowl-edge, earned a degree of any kind, and thus Salviati's message may be summed up in one brief sentence: Keep to your place, you arrogant, ig-norant, and misbelieving sycophant. Niccolò's botched attempts at peacemaking had failed miserably, as Alamanno placed the responsibility for anything that might happen to Florence, should their policies fail, squarely on his and Soderini's shoulders.

Florence signed the treaty with Maximilian on October 24, agreeing to pay him 40,000 ducats in exchange for his protection. The first of the four installments was to be paid immediately and the second in mid-November. The Ten selected Machiavelli to deliver the second sum, in Mantua, and instructed him to then proceed to Verona, "or the best place to collect news." As usual, there were grumblings in Florence about the government's choice. On November 3, Francesco Guicciardini wrote to his brother Luigi in Mantua: "No decision has yet been reached about who to send to the Imperial court; and while some would prefer a proper ambassador, I believe that in the end they'll choose a member of the chancery, or maybe Machiavelli." Some Florentines, understandably, would have preferred a figure of greater authority; but since the decision had been taken by the Ten, nothing could be done to change it.

Niccolò arrived in Mantua on November 15 and heard the news that a popular revolt had allowed the Venetians to retake Vicenza. Verona could soon follow suit. After delivering the Republic's money to the Im-perial agents and paying his respects to the marchioness of Mantua—the celebrated Isabella d'Este, who acted as regent pending her husband's re-lease by the Venetians—Machiavelli left the documentation regarding the monetary transactions with Luigi Guicciardini and departed for Verona. He had been fortunate to find Guicciardini in Mantua, the two being neighborhood friends despite the eighteen-year gap separating them. Even more important, Luigi's brother Francesco had married a Salviati, and so Machiavelli had every reason to stay on Guicciardini's good side:

Bust of Niccolò Machiavelli. Although apparently those of a young man, the relaxed features could indicate the bust was molded around Machiavelli's death mask, quite a common occurrence in Renaissance Florence. On the other hand, busts were fashionable items, and Machiavelli may have desired one of himself when he was a member of the Republic's chancery.

PALAZZO VECCHIO, FLORENCE

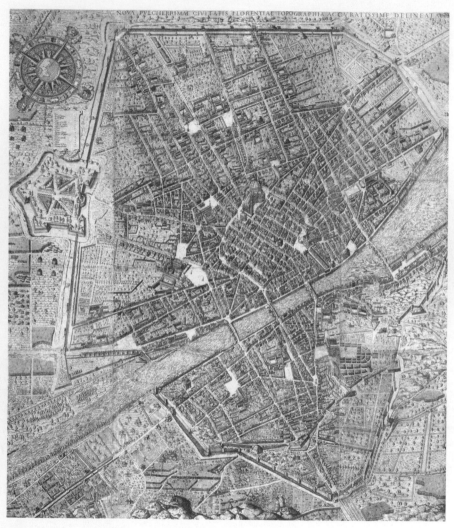

Map of Florence, 1584. Despite having been produced more than fifty years after Machi-avelli's death, Francesco Bonsignori's map depicts a city largely unchanged since Nic-colò's days. Exceptions to this are the large fortress on the far left, the government offices near the river, and the corridor uniting the Palazzo Vecchio with the Pitti Palace, the residence of the Medici Grand Dukes of Tuscany.

SIXTEENTH-CENTURY PRINT (ANTONIO QUATTRONE)

Caterina Sforza at the siege of Forlì. Although a highly inaccurate (for one, the soldier firing a pistol in the background) Romantic portrayal of the countess, it nevertheless conveys some of her feistiness and determination—two character traits that Machiavelli had the chance to witness during his diplomatic visit to Forlì in 1499.

ILLUSTRATION BY TANCREDI SCARPELLI, IN A. RANDI, *CATERINA SFORZA*, (RAVENNA: STERM, 1935)

Paolo Vitelli orders the attack on Pisa. The assault ended in a confused retreat, mainly due to the indecision of the Florentine government regarding whether or not to take the city by storm. Suspicions about Vitelli's loyalty would lead to his arrest and execution a few weeks later, while the Florentines would need another ten years before Pisa finally surrendered.

PALAZZO VECCHIO, FLORENCE (ANTONIO QUATTRONE)

Georges d'Amboise, cardinal and archbishop of Rouen. One of King Louis XII's principal advisors and a superb administrator, until his death in 1510, Amboise was Machiavelli's main interlocutor during the latter's diplomatic missions to the French court. To Amboise's statement that Italians did not "understand warfare," Machiavelli retorted that the French didn't "understand statecraft."

ENGRAVING BY ISAAC BRIOT,
MID–SEVENTEENTH CENTURY.
PRIVATE COLLECTION

Louis XII of Valois. The king of France's somewhat idealized look belies a ruthless, power-thirsty, and cunning character. Machiavelli would a number of times bear the brunt of Louis' high-handed, grasping, and suspicious attitude, which in turn would be the source of serious headaches for the Florentine government.

CHÂTEAU DE BLOIS

Cesare Borgia, Duke of Valentinois. Borgia's benign look could not be more misleading, given his record for cynical politicking and brutality. The ideal example of Machiavelli's "new prince," Cesare in a short time carved for himself a large state in central Italy, until changing fortune caused his dramatic and speedy downfall.

PRIVATE COLLECTION, FAENZA

Vitellozzo Vitelli. Brother of Paolo, executed for treason by the Florentines, and one of Borgia's senior henchmen; fear of Cesare's growing power eventually brought him to conspire against his master. As a result, he became one of Borgia's most celebrated victims, ending up strangled with some of his fellow plotters in Senigallia.

MUSEO DELL'OPERA DEL DUOMO, ORVIETO

Julius II. Raphael's capacity to capture Julius' fierce countenance gives us a hint of what Machiavelli experienced when meeting the "terrible pope." A man of the utmost determination, Julius single-mindedly steamrolled over anybody and anything that stood in the way of his aggrandizement policy.

GALLERIA DEGLI UFFIZI, FLORENCE

Spanish infantry in battle. Although dating from 1535, this picture conveys the same image of steel associated with Spanish soldiers in the sixteenth century. One can easily understand why the poorly trained and badly lead Florentine militiamen took to their heels when pitted against such fighters—Machiavelli's beliefs and hopes to the contrary.

FLEMISH TAPESTRY DEPICTING THE
CONQUEST OF TUNIS (1535).
PALACIO REAL, MADRID

Saying goodbye. A poignant street scene with a man dressed in travelling attire, taking leave from his family. The loving hug given to the little girl is coupled by the wife's anguished look. Machiavelli must have had many such experiences during his time in the Florentine chancery, diplomatic and administrative missions often forcing him to take to the road.

DETAIL FROM THE *PALA NERLI*, CHURCH OF SANTO SPIRITO, FLORENCE

Machiavelli's country home. After being evicted from the chancery, and arrested and tortured for suspected conspiracy against the Medici, Machiavelli though it prudent to retire to his small estate at Sant'Andrea in Percussina. There he would exchange a lively correspondence with Francesco Vettori and write the first draft of *The Prince*.

SANT'ANDREA IN PERCUSSINA (FLORENCE)

The Old Market, Florence. Painted a few decades after Machiavelli's death, it shows a bustling view of Florentine everyday life. Machiavelli spent many an hour loafing about in places such as this one, enjoying the gossip and exchanging jokes with his friends. In particular, the Florentine scene would also provide a backdrop for the *Mandrake*.

PALAZZO VECCHIO, FLORENCE (ANTONIO QUATTRONE)

Giuliano de' Medici. Machiavelli initially believed the good-natured and *bon-vivant* brother of Cardinal Giovanni de' Medici (soon Pope Leo X) to be a possible source of patronage, and at first intended to dedicate *The Prince* to him. Giuliano's departure for Rome, coupled with Medici hostility, dashed Machiavelli's hopes.

AFTER RAPHAEL.
PRIVATE COLLECTION, ROME

Leo X. The pope is shown here with Cardinals Giulio de' Medici (left) and Luigi de' Rossi. An able, worldly, and cynical individual, Leo X enjoyed watching Machiavelli's *Mandrake*. Cardinal Giulio, later Pope Clement VII, would become Niccolò's main patron, commissioning him, among other things, to write the *Florentine Histories*.

GALLERIA DEGLI
UFFIZI, FLORENCE

Leo X and Emperor Maximilian I of Habsburg. The spiritual and temporal heads of Christendom are seen here together in stained glass by Guillaume de Marcillatt. Machiavelli got a negative impression of Maximilian during his diplomatic mission to Germany in 1508. Behind the pope one can see the profile of Machiavelli's once friend, Cardinal Francesco Soderini.

Leo X's entry into Florence. The lavish festivities accompanying the pope's visit into his native city are conveyed in this fresco. Among the characters depicted, one can notice the bearded Lorenzo de' Medici (in front of the cardinals, with black hat and fur coat), the ultimate dedicatee of *The Prince*. To his left, in profile, is the fearsome *condottiere* Giovanni de' Medici.

Barbara "Barbéra" Raffacani Salutati. Machiavelli's mistress, who united beauty with an equivalent talent for acting and singing. Niccolò would write the *Clizia* for her, one of his theatrical masterpieces, first performed in the garden of the wealthy patron Jacopo Falconetti "il Fornaciaio," in whose house Machiavelli had first met Barbara.

AFTER DOMENICO PULIGO. PRIVATE COLLECTION, FLORENCE

Francesco Guicciardini. Machiavelli's close friend in his last years, Guicciardini was in many ways the opposite of Niccolò: down-to-earth, politically able, and with a prominent killer instinct. Yet, the two men got on famously, each respecting the other's intellectual capacity. In addition, Francesco shared with Machiavelli a similar, and very Florentine, sense of humor.

EIGHTEENTH-CENTURY PRINT. COURTESY OF COUNT PIERO GUICCIARDINI

Cardinal Silvio Passerini. Passerini, from Cortona, acted as the de facto governor of Florence for Pope Clement VII. Much disliked by the Florentines, he was forced to flee the city after the sack of Rome in May 1527. Previously, he had given Machiavelli the task to inspect Florence's existing fortifications.

CHURCH OF SAN LORENZO IN LUCINA, ROME

The Siege of Florence. Luckily for Machiavelli, he died before witnessing his beloved city besieged by the forces of Emperor Charles V and Pope Clement VII. The view of Florence is the same that Niccolò would have had when riding in from the south, and the fortified system depicted here is partly the result of Machiavelli's work.

PALAZZO VECCHIO, FLORENCE (ANTONIO QUATTRONE)

A NICCOLÒ MACCHIAVELLI
DELL' VNITÀ NAZIONALE
PRECORRITORE AVDACE E INDOVINO
E D'ARMI PROPRIE E NON AVVENTIZIE
PRIMO ISTITVTORE E MAESTRO
L'ITALIA VNA ED ARMATA
POSE
IL 3 MAGGIO 1869
QVARTO DI LVI CENTENARIO

CASA OVE VISSE
NICCOLÒ MACCHIAVELLI
E IVI MORI IL 22 GIVGNO 1527
DI ANNI 58 MESI 8 E GIORNI 19

Memorial to Machiavelli. The plaque is located where Niccolò's house once stood, on the via Guicciardini in Florence. The gushing phraseology is typical of the Italian *Risorgimento*, praising Niccolò as a pioneer of Italy's unity and national army. One wonders what Machiavelli would have thought of all this hot air. Last but not least, Machiavelli's given age is also wrong.

VIA GUICCIARDINI, FLORENCE

"Send my greetings to Messer Francesco and his gang when you write home," Machiavelli would tell Luigi in a letter of November 29.

When he so desired, Niccolò could be quite amicable; besides, as with Vettori, he and Luigi shared a mutual passion for writing literature, an eye for women, and a taste for bawdy tales. It was to Luigi that Machiavelli would send the letter about his encounter with a horrendous-looking prostitute. He also dedicated a poetic composition to his friend: "The Capitolo dell'Ambizione" (The Poem on Ambition), a description of the woes provoked throughout history by unhealthy desire, recent Italian events taking the lion's share. The poem ended with a warning about ambition, which was already flying over Tuscany spreading fiery sparks over its people: "already swollen with envy in that place / that will burn its land and villas / unless extinguished by a better order or by grace." The reference to "better order" and "grace" were straight out of Dante Alighieri's *Divine Comedy*—beloved by Machiavelli—but Niccolò's rendering also contained a warning to the Florentines: Lack of unity motivated by pride always spells disaster.

Niccolò's opponents had not been idle, for on November 20 Biagio Buonaccorsi had urged him to be diligent in his reporting "to shut the mouths of the bench heaters" (*pancacce*). By the time he received this warning, Machiavelli had already arrived in Verona, where he witnessed the difficulties encountered by the invaders in their attempts to subdue the local population. He cited, among other examples, the case of a peasant hanged for obstinately maintaining his allegiance to Venice, commenting, "and so it appears impossible that these rulers [Louis XII and Maximilian] will be able to hold on to these territories with the locals still living." He also noticed a growing tension between the French and the Imperialists, succinctly stating that "of these two sovereigns, one can wage war but is unwilling; the other is willing but can't." By now he desired only to return home, although the Ten wished him to remain in Verona until receiving further orders, unless his life should appear to be in danger. Finally, recognizing that his task was done, the government ordered him back on December 16, with the added request that he keep his eyes and ears open during the return journey. Little did he know that en route he would receive potentially alarming news.

As he headed toward Florence at a leisurely pace, on the road he received a letter from the faithful Buonaccorsi. "Don't ignore or make fun of this," Biagio wrote in a tizzy, "and for nothing in this world tell anybody else about it." He proceeded to recount the reasons for his agitated state:

> A week ago a masked individual, accompanied by two witnesses, went to the house of the notary of the *Law Keepers* (*Conservatori delle Leggi*) and in their presence served him a writ, warning him that legal action would follow should he refuse to take it, etcetera. The document stated that since your father etcetera, in no way could you keep your position, etcetera. And although legal precedents exist and the law is on your side, nevertheless the climate is such that a lot of people have started to scream and shout about this matter, threatening dire consequences should nothing be done about it, etcetera, and so this affair is on the rocks, needing much help and care. Ever since I've known about it from our friends I have left no stone unturned, working at it night and day, so that I have calmed quite a few tempers. And while we have put to rest those unfavorable to you who have been trying to pull the law their way giving it sinister interpretations, still you have many enemies who will stop at nothing. Everyone talks about the case, even in the brothels, so that we can act publicly even if weighed down by numerous handicaps. Believe me Niccolò: I'm not telling you half of what is being said, and before I managed to produce the law this matter had been considered as already adjudicated. I'm doing whatever possible, and so is Piero del Nero, whom I'm keeping informed of everything, for my actions are being imitated by those who do not wish you and I to be ruined.

Buonaccorsi, on the advice of someone Machiavelli esteemed, also suggested that Niccolò lay low for a while and not show his face in Florence. But Biagio had left much unsaid. What were the reasons for such a furor? Simply put, since Machiavelli's father had been *a specchio*—that is, in arrears with his taxes—in theory his son could not hold any sort of governmental position. However, a law of February 14, 1498, had allowed the recruitment of chancery personnel without the candidates having to be cleared of any *divieto* (legal barrier) they may have possessed. Technically, then, Machiavelli was on solid legal ground. In any case, he felt confident enough of his position to ignore Buonaccorsi's plea, and was back in the city by January 2, 1510. Machiavelli resumed his work in the chancery, and soon he would once more be back in the saddle for another journey beyond the Alps.

It did not taken long for Julius II to change his mind about the perils of French expansionism, as he understood full well that if Venice fell, the papal territories would be the next to go. The pope, however, did not intend to give up the claims that had caused him to join the League of Cambrai, and in the peace agreement of February 15, 1510, between Venice and the Holy See, he had managed to extract every possible concession from the Venetians only because the latter desperately needed to rid themselves at least of one enemy. (The Council of the Ten, the Venetian magistracy in charge of state security, secretly denounced the agreement, reserving the right to do so publicly at the first occasion.)

Moreover, the pope and the Venetians found themselves allied against Julius's former confederates. The pontiff had picked a fight with the duke of Ferrara, Alfonso d'Este, whom he considered one of his vassals, over the salt mines of the Polesine region, and was angered that the duke had refused to abandon his French allies. (The fact that Alfonso had married Lucrezia Borgia, Valentino's sister, did not help.) The pope also resented the occupation of Genoa, as his family came from Savona, then part of the Genoese state. In fact, Julius had trouble having good relations with practically anyone, and by now had become thoroughly obsessed with the French presence in Italy. He is credited with coining the phrase "out the barbarians" (*fuori i barbari*); and although his authorship is probably spurious, the expression nonetheless conveys very well the pope's feelings toward those foreign powers that had turned Italy into a perennial battleground.

Once the news of the treaty between Julius and Venice got out, it infuriated the French and the Imperialists, both determined to destroy Venice's power for good. Louis XII suffered a further blow when Cardinal d'Amboise died on May 25, removing a thorn from the pope's side and depriving his king of a trusted and experienced adviser. Louis did not have a reputation for keeping a close watch on his affairs, and once Amboise was gone, this began to show; those who replaced him lacked the deceased cardinal's ability and drive. A few months later, during a conversation between Machiavelli and the French treasurer, Florimond Robertet, an artist entered carrying the portrait of the defunct Amboise, which prompted Robertet to say that had the cardinal been alive, the French army would be marching into Rome. With Maximilian virtually out of the picture owing to his chronic lack of funds, and Louis uncertain what to do next, the pope and the Venetians could breathe more easily as they prepared for their next campaign.

The papal-Venetian alliance proved a source of considerable embarrassment for the Florentines, as it forced them to rely on a distant ally while facing a potential enemy at their doorstep. Besides, most of the city's condottieri came from the papal dominions; and should war erupt with Julius II this source of military power would be greatly reduced. The Republic came under pressure to choose sides, but the government decided to employ its usual waiting tactic, trying to balance itself between the contestants. In July, it refused entry into its territories to papal troops on their way to attack Genoa, but at the same time rejected the French request to send troops north in order to help conquer the duchy of Urbino.

Florence understood that peace between Julius and Louis would be the best solution, but this needed to be accomplished before the eruption of armed hostilities. Deciding to play the French card first, the government opted to send an envoy to Louis, and the Ten entrusted the mission to Machiavelli. On June 2, Niccolò received a letter from the gonfalonier with instructions to assure Louis of Florence's friendship and suggest that he keep pressure on the Venetians with Maximilian's help—and, possibly, with the help of the king of Hungary; however, Soderini added that it was absolutely vital that the French should not break with Julius, "since having the pope as a friend may not be of much worth, but as an enemy he could be very damaging."

Despite the urgency of the matter, Machiavelli waited until the 24th before departing. We do not know the reasons for this delay, although it probably had to do with the presence of papal troops around Lucca under Marco Antonio Colonna: Colonna had left Florence's service, and the Ten were uncertain whether he intended to attack Genoa or move north into the Po Valley. Niccolò finally arrived at the French court in Blois on July 17, and he met with Louis the following day.

Although outwardly pleased with the arrival of Florence's envoy, the king clearly had no time for diplomatic niceties: "Secretary," he told Machiavelli in unequivocal terms, "I have no fight with the pope or with anyone else. But since alliances seem to be changing by the day, I want clear knowledge of what your Signoria intends to do to help me, in case the pontiff or someone else should decide to make some move against my Italian possessions. You must immediately get someone to come back as soon as possible with the reply, because I need to know who is a friend or an enemy of mine." In the face of such a request, Machiavelli could only answer that Florence had always respected the terms of its alliance with France, and was always prepared to help the king within reasonable terms: "I'm sure of that," Louis snapped back, "but need to be even surer." By now the French believed that war with the pope was practically inevitable, something Machiavelli considered "the worst misfortune that could befall our city."

The fear of a war that almost certainly would not leave his city unscathed prompted Machiavelli to offer Florence's mediation to try to end the dispute between the two powers—a step well beyond the limits of his mandate, but that Niccolò, urged on by Robertet, considered necessary for his country's preservation. Without waiting for the government's reply, Machiavelli plunged ahead, justifying himself in a letter of August 8 to the Ten with a clear rationale for his offer: "Should our attempts to get the two to agree be successful, it will be to our credit; otherwise, no one can blame us for having tried." Managing to get someone close to the king ("a person of great authority") on his side, he convinced him to go and speak to Louis about the perils of engaging in a struggle that could very well cause the king of Spain and the emperor to throw their lot with Julius, out of their fear of France's power, if nothing else.

The king answered that though all this may have been true, with his honor at stake he could not behave otherwise. He added, however, "I promise you that should the pope show me love the size of a fingertip, I shall give him an arm in return." The king also agreed to ask the Florentines to act as mediators, as the triumphant Niccolò informed the government. In his letter he included details about Louis's military preparations together with the more disturbing piece of news that the king intended to call a council of French prelates.

Machiavelli would not receive a reply from Florence until three weeks later, and in the meantime, the Italian situation had worsened considerably. In July, the pope had been repulsed at Genoa, but the Venetians' successes in retaking portions of their mainland possessions had more than compensated for this reverse. In mid-August a joint force occupied the Ferrarese city of Modena, and Reggio would have followed suit without the timely arrival of French reinforcements. Determined to teach Alfonso d'Este a lesson, Julius excommunicated him* for betraying his feudal overlord, and then moved to Bologna to prepare for a triumphal entry into the soon-to-be-conquered Ferrara.

The French had not been idle, but by hesitating to take incisive action had allowed their adversaries to gain the upper hand. Amboise's loss started to be felt more than ever, as Louis's plans got bogged down by innumerable details that the cardinal would have taken care of. "The king

---

* By then excommunication had become a blunt weapon, most Italians seeing it merely as a political tool in the pope's hands (the famous condottiere Niccolò Piccinino once compared it to being tickled). Some noble lineages even displayed a certain smug pride about past brushes with ecclesiastical censure. A Florentine aristocrat once told me: "If excommunications were bell-towers, our family would have more than the whole of Rome."

is not interested in minutiae, his advisers ignore them, and the sick man dies," would be Machiavelli's sullen comment. Louis, however, had already managed—through bribery—to convince the Swiss troops employed by the pope to return home. Nevertheless, he now needed every soldier he could get to fight in Lombardy, and the cheaper the better.

Florence had always been a money siphon for the French, and Louis decided once again to tap into this source. On August 13, he called Machiavelli and informed him that he wanted the Florentines to keep their troops at the ready for possible deployment to northern Italy. Niccolò then had a chat with Robertet about the problems with such a request, considering that in the event that the pope decided to attack Florence, the king would have to give the Republic military assistance, something difficult to accomplish given his many other commitments. Machiavelli was not far off the mark when mentioning a possible papal offensive: Julius, irritated with the Republic's fence-sitting policy, had told the Venetian ambassador that after dealing with Este his army might well march into Tuscany to restore the Medici in Florence.

By now, Louis's antipapal counteroffensive had moved to the spiritual front. In 1438, his predecessor, Charles VII, had issued the so-called "pragmatic Sanction of Bourges," by which, following the thesis of the "Conciliarist" movement within the church, the king of France became the superior authority regarding ecclesiastical matters within his domains. Not only did the French crown claim jurisdiction in matters such as episcopal appointments and church revenues, but it also maintained the superiority of general councils over the pope. By convening a council of French churchmen, plus a few other dissidents from other parts of Europe, Louis wanted nothing less than to have Julius deposed and another pontiff elected in his place, "and make these priests swallow a few bitter morsels." Louis's ecclesiastical policy would indeed produce some very sour food, but other people rather than the ones the king had in mind would end up eating it.

The Republic had decided to agree to act as mediator between France and the papacy, and selected a proper ambassador to do the job. At the beginning of September Machiavelli received notice of the imminent arrival of his old friend Roberto Acciaioli. Once Acciaioli was on the scene, Machiavelli departed, with no small relief and little money left. Pestering his stingy superiors for more cash, he warned them that "I may be coming back on foot, after being forced to sell the horses," a joke as well as a complaint, but at least this time the Ten proved more forthcoming, sending him 100 florins on September 13.

Machiavelli longed for Florence, having received little news from home except what was contained in official correspondence. Letters had been scarce even from the faithful Buonaccorsi, who was now totally overcome with grief because of his wife's terminal illness, and weighed down by medical expenses: "And so I'll end up without company or money," he wrote. Biagio would end his only missive to his friend during this period of time by adding the bitter comment, "Pray God to give you better fortune than what he has done with me, even if perhaps I deserve it more than you."

The distraught Buonaccorsi mentioned another sort of luck he heard Machiavelli had encountered at the French court. During this time Machiavelli had developed an affection for a woman by the name of Jeanne, and evidently an affair of some intensity had resulted, provoking Giovanni Girolami to tell Niccolò that "Jeanne is all yours." Some of his friends, however, were concerned about Machiavelli's womanizing. Roberto Acciaioli's ironic remark—"I believe you have arrived safe and sound in Florence, thanks to God and Jeanne, and maybe you've already paid La Riccia a visit"—could be an oblique reference to the perils of catching the "French pox," as syphilis was called, and thus warning Machiavelli to be careful in his philandering.

Luckily for him, Niccolò did not bring back any sort of venereal disease, and may have considered Jeanne one of the few good things he had found in France—at least this is how it sounds in the collection of impressions he recorded in "Ritratti delle Cose di Francia" (Description of French Affairs) after returning to Florence. In Machiavelli's descriptions, France appears as a rich and powerful country, with a strong central government but with serious weaknesses in its military and political organization and unable to properly handle its wealth. Despite Soderini's commitment to Louis XII's friendship, it is clear that Machiavelli had misgivings about Florence's alliance with France. Previous bitter experiences had taught him to treat the French with caution, and he considered them to be totally unreliable and lacking foresight. Sometimes Niccolò's mistrust verged on loathing. In some scattered notes that he did not include in the above-mentioned collection, he wrote:

> If they [the French] can't help you, they'll promise to do so; and if they can they'll do it with great difficulty or never. . . . They are miserly rather than careful. . . . They are humble in bad times and arrogant in good ones. . . . They weave their evil plans with force. . . . They are vain and superficial, always confident in success, enemies of the Roman tongue and of Rome's fame. . . . If you ask them for a favor, they first consider what advantage they may get from it.

This negative portrait notwithstanding, Machiavelli believed that the French would eventually prevail in the Italian struggle. France was the strongest country in Europe: "There is no ruler capable of confronting them," he wrote, "and Italy is not what it used to be in Roman times." But Machiavelli should have known that Fortune has a way of wrecking any human design, no matter how carefully and neatly it may be laid out.

10

~

THE NIGHT PIER
SODERINI DIED

The night Pier Soderini died,
At the mouth of Hell he showed his face
"Go to the baby's Limbo" Pluto cried
"Fools down here are out of place."
—NICCOLÒ MACHIAVELLI
ON PIERO SODERINI

"May cancer strike you all!" an exasperated Roberto Acciaioli would write to Machiavelli on October 10, 1510, about his embarrassment over the Florentines' behavior. Already under pressure from Louis XII's bribe-hungry ministers, Acciaioli had the right to wring his hands over the Signoria's infuriating wait-and-see policy, for which he considered Niccolò partly responsible. The king of France had withdrawn his original request that Florence send troops to Lombardy, and the Republic had then decided not to bother asking Louis for the authorization to hire the Milanese condottiere Teodoro Trivulzio.

Clearly the king had been banking on the Florentines footing some of his war expenses, and Acciaioli, lamenting that Louis had been left "high and dry," told Machiavelli that the French hotly resented the Florentines' duplicity (Niccolò may have been amused at this nice example of the pot calling the kettle black). Evoking a classical image of brawn and might, Acciaioli warned "mister Hercules" that "doing and not doing don't get along," and therefore the Florentines should not whine about the bitter consequences that could result from their two-faced action. "You would like to have a military leader unbound to France, the pope, Spain, Venice or the Emperor. In that case you better ask the Egyptian or the Ottoman Sultans to send you a pasha, or Tamerlane for that!"

Despite Acciaioli's raving, the financially stretched Florentines saw no reason to employ troops that might have to be recalled at the drop of a hat. The possibility of getting involved in a war between the pope and France worried the Florentine government: Vulnerable and weak, Florence could face massive destruction over all of its dominion. Nor did the Florentines wish to be left alone to face Julius's wrath, and possibly the revolt of subject cities, as had occurred in 1494 and 1502. Yet, unlike then, the Republic now had an army that was exclusively under its control, an infantry force that had seen extensive training in the field, even if not much action.

The cavalry remained the main weakness of Florence's military organization, with the city still having to depend on condottieri for its horsemen. Marco Antonio Colonna's recent defection had once again brought home the need to have reliable mounted units, but training a natural force of fully armored men-at-arms would have been impossible in the short run. Machiavelli, however, did not see this as too serious a handicap, given that he considered the cavalry auxiliary to the infantry: "In ancient Rome there were no more than six-hundred horsemen in every consular army," he would state in The Art of War. According to Niccolò, Italy's present condition was to be blamed on the reliance of the

Italian states on armies that were based on mercenary heavy cavalry. In any case, Machiavelli considered men-at-arms of limited tactical value, their function on the battlefield being restricted to working closely with infantry units.

Indeed, even the charge of the French heavy cavalry, which he considered the best in the world, could be repulsed, and France's reliance on its men-at-arms had resulted in more than one defeat. Armored horsemen were useful only when fighting dismounted against infantry, but even in this case the same job could be accomplished by foot soldiers. Light cavalrymen, however, were more versatile—and, by the way, less expensive—being able to execute a number of tasks: scouting, for example, or cowering the peasantry, and in a battle could stop enemy horsemen from attacking the side or rear of infantry squares.

The Ten, again, without asking for any official sanction to do so, decided to start raising horse units, and on November 7 dispatched Machiavelli to recruit men of the appropriate type. Niccolò departed from Florence for the Valdarno and the Valdichiana on the 13th, not returning until two weeks later, and went back to those regions several times in the following months. Unlike the infantrymen, the new recruits received ten gold ducats each to cover their expenses for keeping a mount, with orders to be ready by April. On the Sunday after Easter, one hundred light cavalrymen, armed with crossbows, paraded through the streets of Florence, and if anyone grumbled about this armed display, Machiavelli could at least console himself with the written support of his friend Alessandro Nasi. In the meantime, Machiavelli had also been busy inspecting fortresses across the Florentine domain, in Pisa availing himself of the help of the famous architects Giuliano and Antonio da Sangallo. The experience he gained during these visits would serve him well later on when he would happen to work with another, and more famous, artist.

The Republic's attention to its fortresses stemmed not just from a justifiable concern about contemporary events and external enemies, but also from the need to forestall internal rebellions. Domestic enemies could be as dangerous as external ones, and the government started becoming increasingly alarmed at the propaganda activities of the exiled Medici. Over the years Cardinal Giovanni had successfully wooed his fellow citizens living in Rome to his side through a generous display of patronage, and supporting, thanks to his closeness with Julius II, the business of Florentine bankers with the papal curia.

The Florentine mercantile community in Rome could not but watch with alarm as Soderini continued to pursue his pro-French policy, especially considering that the fiery pope had threatened to throw into jail any Florentine living in his domains, should the Republic openly side with Louis XII. Even if the law forbade consorting with rebels, both Cardinal Giovanni and his brother Giuliano having been declared such in the aftermath of the Strozzi-Medici affair, the government could do little to punish those living abroad who should decide to ignore this ruling. Worse still, Cardinal Giovanni's friends could influence their relatives living in Florence and thus create the conditions for a regime change.

It was in this climate that a plot to kill Soderini matured, the first step toward the restoration of the Medici in Florence. The kin of Prinzivalle della Stufa had enjoyed political favor at the time of "Lorenzo the Magnificent," and by frequenting the Rucellai gardens the young man had made no secret of his dislike for the Soderini. He had already fallen under the scrutiny of the gonfalonier some years before for allegedly paying a visit to Vitellozzo Vitelli, and because of the fact that his mother, the formidable Guglielmina Schianteschi da Montedoglio, came from a feudal family of the upper Tiber Valley (part of her dowry had been the castle of Calcione in the Valdichiana). Prinzivalle started looking for the best place and time to execute his plan and tried to enlist Filippo Strozzi's help.

Strozzi would have none of it and told della Stufa that he would inform the authorities on the morrow, thus allowing the would-be assassin to flee before the plot was reported. Robbed of its prey, the government had Prinzivalle's father, Luigi, questioned by the Eight of Watch, and despite the fact that he initially denied having any knowledge of his son's plans, upon further investigation it emerged that Luigi and his wife had helped Prinzivalle to escape. The two received a letter from Lucrezia de' Medici, wife of Jacopo Salviati, saying that she and her husband had learned of the plot from Matteo Strozzi, one of Filippo's brothers, who was married to one of Alamanno Salviati's daughters. Piero Soderini wanted Luigi della Stufa to be brought to justice, claiming that the conspiracy had been aimed at the Republican regime as well as his own person.

Prinzivalle had recently paid a visit to Julius II and Cardinal de' Medici in Bologna and had allegedly mentioned the pope's involvement in the plot. However, when the pontiff heard of this, he flew into a rage, accusing the gonfalonier and the other members of the Signoria of lying through their teeth. It is doubtful that Prinzivalle ever managed to get the Medici's support for what appeared from the very beginning to be a botched enterprise, although the eventual removal of Soderini could not have displeased them. In the end, the government declared Prinzivalle a rebel, removed Luigi from his post as governor of Pisa, and sentenced him to confinement in Empoli, thirty-five miles from Florence, for three years; the political pressure exerted by his friends saved Luigi from harsher consequences. Although apparently a compromise solution, the verdict represented a defeat for Soderini, as it demonstrated that he could not even rally enough support to adequately punish a declared enemy of the state.

We have no record of Machiavelli's thoughts on these events, and in any case, he had other things on his mind. Apart from recruiting militia cavalrymen, he had to travel to Siena to remind Petrucci that the truce between his city and Florence would soon expire—and at the same time negotiate another one, with a longer time span, on condition that the Sienese return the town of Montepulciano to the Florentines. On May 5, 1511, Niccolò left Florence for Monaco, his task to obtain the release of a Florentine ship captured by the local lord Luciano Grimaldi and try to reach an agreement with him for mutual assistance in the realm of shipping. While still on his way, the government had second thoughts, now finding it "dishonorable, not to say dangerous, to receive his

[Grimaldi's] vessels in our ports with stolen merchandise aboard." In fact, Luciano practiced the lucrative trade of piracy, and assisting him in any way could have raised diplomatic storms of the greatest magnitude. Machiavelli at least managed to obtain the release of the captured Florentine ship, and he arrived back in Florence by June 11.

During his absence, much had happened on the Italian chess board. The Venetian-papal offensive against France's allies in northern Italy had continued to be successful in the first months of 1511, Julius having managed to capture the strategically important fortified town of Mirandola at the end of January, thanks to the indecisiveness of the French governor of Lombardy, Charles d'Amboise, Lord of Chaumont (nephew of Cardinal d'Amboise). Matters altered dramatically in February, with Chaumont's untimely demise, and Louis XII choosing to replace him in the field with the aged but energetic Giangiacomo Trivulzio and the young and impetuous Gaston de Foix, Duke of Nemours. The change in the style of command became immediately apparent when, in the spring, the French army marched south toward Bologna, forcing the pope to flee to Ravenna.

Julius had entrusted the city's defense to Cardinal Francesco Alidiosi, but this unsavory prelate had managed to make himself so hated that as soon as the French army appeared, the Bolognese rose in revolt, expelling the papal garrison and welcoming back their former Bentivoglio rulers. Lacking Julius's presence in person, the elated citizenry exacted their revenge on the pope's bronze effigy, which had been made by Michelangelo, reducing it to pieces, and the duke of Ferrara used the broken metal to cast one of his famous artillery pieces. When the pontiff vented his fury on Alidiosi for losing Bologna, the cardinal tried to shift the blame onto the duke of Urbino, Francesco maria della Rovere, who, upon meeting the treacherous clergyman in Ravenna some time later, decided there and then to drill a dagger through his skull.

The Florentines could very well gloat about the pope's misfortunes, and indeed had been egging the French on to finish the job for good. As a result of Prinzivalle della Stufa's plot, the government had been taking a much harder line with Julius than before. When, in January 1511, Louis proposed holding a peace conference in Mantua, Florence tried to dissuade him, doubting the feasibility of such a plan, and warned the king that the pontiff and Spain were trying to get Venice to make peace with the emperor in order to isolate France. The Florentines had little to fear, since Julius, flushed by his earlier successes, declined the invitation, and at this point Louis countered by asking the Florentines to be allowed to move the council he had convened from Tours to Pisa.

The Republic waited until the French victories in May before giving its consent, and even then tried to keep the decision secret for fear of angering the pope. In any case, the king did not seem too keen to pursue his campaign *à outrance*, refusing to advance further into the papal territories and even withdrawing his troops from Bologna—clear indications of his desire to reach a negotiated settlement with Julius. The pope, however, appears to have been alarmed by the news of the Florentines' decision regarding Pisa (it would have been impossible to keep it secret, given the number of citizens involved, and, in any case, Cardinal de' Medici had his informers within the city), and probably for this reason he decided to try to sever Florence from her most powerful ally.

The reason Machiavelli had been sent to Siena in April to denounce the truce between Florence and Petrucci was that the Republic wanted to regain Montepulciano. The French were urging the Florentines to attack Siena, since it would give Louis an excuse to come to the aid of his friends and thus enable him to gain a foothold in Tuscany, which he could then use as a springboard, if need be, for a future advance on Rome. Julius had no intention of seeing this happen, and, with the backing of a number of Florentine ottimati, managed to broker a longer truce between Florence and Siena by convincing Petrucci to give up Montepulciano.

Louis XII remained uncertain about how to proceed with the "Gallican" (from the Latin term *Galli*, Gauls, used to indicate the French) council he had convened, since he appeared to be its only remaining patron. The emperor, once supportive of the idea, had become rather more lukewarm, although he still hoped that the French would help him gain what he had been promised at Cambrai. Besides, no one harbored any illusions about the participants really being intent on reforming the church; Robertet had told Roberto Acciaioli that the cardinals opposing Julius were more interested in getting bishoprics than anything else.

The pope also trumped Louis's schemes when, on July 18, he issued a bull for the convocation of a universal, ecumenical council to be held at the Lateran in Rome the following April, and at the same time denouncing the Gallican convention as illegal, heretical, and schismatic. Once the bull was published, Louis could only acknowledge it or decide to go ahead with his original project. He chose the latter, believing that Julius's rabid anti-French feelings precluded any possibility of a negotiated peace, and in August he renewed his request to the Signoria to concede Pisa as the seat of the Gallican council, asking for safe conduct for those prelates wishing to attend. Concerned with the spiritual censures and the damage to their trade that an affirmative reply would inevitably entail, the Florentines procrastinated as much as they could. In the end they had to give in to the pressure, taking care to inform the pope that they were only acting under duress; they themselves had refused to participate, were obedient to the Holy See, and were trying to convince Louis to reconsider his decision.

However, the Republic held little hope of appeasing Julius with simple words, and on September 10 the Ten dispatched Machiavelli to meet with three of the dissident cardinals making their way to Pisa and ask them to postpone their arrival. Furthermore, he had to proceed to the French court to request that the king move the Gallican council to some other place and try to make peace with the pope. The government took care to inform its ambassadors in Rome, Milan, and France about Niccolò's mission, to give it all the resonance possible. News had also arrived from Rome that Julius was seriously ill; if he died, the political cards on the Italian playing table would be completely reshuffled.

Machiavelli met the Gallican cardinals Caravajal, Borgia, Sanseverino, and Briçonnet on September 12 at Borgo S. Donnino, north of Lucca. He informed them about Julius's certain fury at the news of their procurators' having opened the council in Pisa on September 1 and the possible risks of this anger being directed against Florentine merchants residing in the papal territories, asking them to avoid passing through the Republic's domains. The prelates agreed to get to Pisa via Pontremoli but expressed surprise at Florence's unpreparedness for the hardly unforeseeable eventualities connected with agreeing to hold the council in one of their subject cities. Furthermore, the Florentines had agreed to hold a council in Pisa in 1409, and then in opposition to a "saintly pope"; in any case, they would be protected by Louis's powerful army, and the gathering of clergymen and doctors of divinity surely would be so great that anyone opposing it would be considered a heretic.

Machiavelli also learned that one of the cardinals' agents had been sent to Maximilian to seek his participation, with the promise that the council, once in session, would be moved to a place of the emperor's choice (Maximilian had been entertaining thoughts of being the next pope).* Machiavelli could do little but report these opinions before departing for France, and on September 24 he met with the king at Blois. The report of his discussion with Louis was drawn up, following proper diplomatic procedures, by the Florentine ambassador Roberto Acciaioli. Louis expressed his sympathy for the Republic's concerns and stated that peace, indeed, was the thing he most desired. However, he refused to dissolve the Gallican assembly, believing it to be the only way to bring Julius to the negotiating table. Machiavelli answered that, on the contrary, Julius's intransigence could only worsen if the king continued with his ecclesiastical policy. The king would not budge, but he nevertheless agreed to delay the official opening of the council until the beginning of November and promised to transfer it somewhere else as soon as possible. The pope's illness justified the delay, and the king was quite prepared to dissolve the council should the new pontiff prove more tractable.

---

* Not many people are aware that any adult Catholic male, *compos mentis* and not tainted with heresy, can be elected pope or, when the Holy Roman Empire existed, could become emperor.

Ailing Julius may have been, but he had enough strength remaining to prove once again what it meant to antagonize "the terrible pope." The papal nuncio left Florence on September 20, and three days later its archbishop published the pontifical decree of interdict against the city, to the chagrin of the authorities, since they had not been informed in advance. In response, the Republic ordered six of Florence's main churches to continue celebrating the Mass and threw the priest of Ognissanti into jail for refusing to comply. The government also prepared an appeal against the pope's decree to be presented to a future general council of the church, carefully avoiding specifying whether they intended the Pisan or the Lateran one.

As for the Florentines themselves, the observance of the interdict depended largely on individual political or ideological affiliations. Soderini's faction by and large continued to attend Mass, and so did some of the old *frateschi*, who saw the Pisan council as the fulfillment of Savonarola's prediction about the church's renewal. Others decided to comply with Julius's wishes out of hatred for the gonfalonier. The split became even more pronounced when Soderini suggested the imposition of a tax on the Florentine clergy. The proposal was rejected three times by the Great Council and the Eighty before a narrow two-thirds majority could be found. In this case, the motives of the opposition were in part religious but in part the result of fear of Julius's wrath and the fact that many members of great families enjoyed rich ecclesiastical benefices. Once again Soderini had proved unable to rally the citizens to the colors in times of need.

When the pope heard of Florence's appeal to the council, he proceeded to tighten the screws on the city even further. On September 23 he told the Republic's ambassador that he had ordered the sequestration of all Florentine movable property in the Marches region and the next day intended to arrest all the Florentine merchants in Rome and seize their goods. Julius now had a rather more substantial military force than before at his disposal to pressure Florence, having managed after months of negotiations to conclude an alliance with Venice and Spain called the

Holy League. with the objective of recovering Bologna, maintaining the Holy See's independence, and safeguarding the church against schism.

Also, predicting, quite correctly, that Maximilian was getting thoroughly fed up with the French, the league approved an article of the treaty that provided for the emperor's entrance into the pact at a later date. Six weeks later, Henry VIII of England joined the alliance, thus helping to distract French troops from the Italian theater. Julius had developed a hatred for Soderini nearly as strong as the one he had for the French, and made it clear that he intended to restore the Medici to power. Soderini's enemies received important positions, with Cardinal Giovanni de' Medici being made legate of Bologna (a nominal appointment for the time being) and Guglielmo Capponi going to Pisa as papal commissioner.

When the Gallican council finally convened in Pisa on November 1, the Florentines proved none too cooperative, refusing to provide any sort of armed or political support to the participants, and in general made their lives as uncomfortable as possible. Machiavelli, just back from France, arrived in Pisa on November 3 at the head of three hundred infantry who had been sent by the Republic to protect its interests in the city. Three days later he had a meeting with one of the cardinals, warmly suggesting that the assembly remove itself to a more comfortable location, and blaming the bad harvest of that year for the lack of victuals. The prelate answered that although bearable, living in Pisa could not be compared to what Milan and Rome could provide, and thus he agreed on the need to move the assembly. Niccolò remained in the city until all the conciliarists had departed for Milan, leaving detailed descriptions of the sessions he attended. By November 13, when everyone had left, the Florentines breathed a sigh of relief and started examining the possibility of reconciling themselves with Julius.

The pope made it known that he expected the Republic to send two ambassadors to Rome, one from the government and another from the clergy; he also wanted Florence to repeal the clergy tax and renounce its appeal to the council. Disagreement in the *pratiche* convened to discuss these terms caused the government to employ its usual delaying tactics, although at the same time it refused to make an official declaration in support of Louis XII. Concern about the city's dignity and honor was palpable in the mandate given by the Ten to Antonio Strozzi, Florence's new ambassador to Rome: In exchange for the renunciation of the appeal to the general council, the pope had to release the city from the interdict without any sort of public absolution; as for the clergy tax, since it had been approved by the Great Council it could be repealed only by the same body. Although the pope remained obdurate in his request, a bill allowing the government to abolish the controversial levy failed to pass the Great Council, as the legislators were unwilling to devolve to others some of their political power. By allowing the tax to be approved in the first place, the usually cautious Soderini had rashly backed himself into a corner and could not get out.

Events started to take a dramatic turn. At the beginning of February 1512, the Venetians managed to retake Brescia, putting a wedge into France's eastern front. But it was not for nothing that Gaston de Foix had earned the sobriquet of "the thunderbolt of Italy," and two weeks later he recaptured the city by storm, subjecting it to a horrific sacking. When news of this victory arrived in Florence, the government ordered bonfires to be lit in celebration, and the more rabid pro-French members of the citizenry clamored for the collection of the clerical tax. The Signoria turned down the request by a slim majority of five to four, but fiscal officials started collecting the tax all the same. The clergy put up a stiff resistance, and as soon as the new Signoria came to office on March 1, Soderini had the collection stopped. The move seemed to appease the pope to some extent, and thanks to the intervention of Florence's ecclesiastics, he agreed on April 10 to lift the interdict. In the meantime, Florence had been resisting pressures from France and the Holy League to declare itself. Buying time had paid before and could still turn out to be to the Republic's advantage as it waited to see which of the contenders would prevail.

The strategy seemed to work when, on April 11, the French army won a resounding victory at the battle of Ravenna. Florence rejoiced at the news—the pro-French party magnifying the victory. Francesco Guicciardini accused Machiavelli, "for passionate reasons," of having diminished Louis's losses while exaggerating the league's—and a *pratica* suggested, with a large majority, that the defensive alliance with France should be renewed. Having waited for such a long time to declare themselves, the Florentines now rushed to the winner's aid, when a bit more procrastination could have been beneficial. The battle had been bloody to the extreme, but a substantial portion of the Spanish infantry under the viceroy of Naples, Ramon de Cardona, had managed to retreat in a body, killing Gaston de Foix in the process. His successor, Jacque de La Palice, showed no interest in pursuing the Spaniards, preferring instead to enter and sack Ravenna.

The French had won a Pyrrhic victory, suffering thousands of casualties, including Foix. Worse still, a few days after the battle Maximilian ordered the German infantry in Louis's service to return home, while the Swiss came to the Holy League's aid by invading Lombardy. Forced to retreat, the French abandoned most of their recent conquests, including Bologna. On June 20, the league's troops entered Milan, and nine days later Genoa rebelled against the occupying French. By then La Palice had taken the road to the Alps at the head of a disorganized and demoralized army, leaving the Florentines and France's other allies in Italy to fend for themselves. Political opportunism could have saved the day for the Republic when, on July 11, the papal ambassador, Lorenzo Pucci, arrived in Florence to ask the Republic to join the Holy League and help finish the job of expelling the French from Italy. Various solutions were discussed in the pratiche, but none of them proved sufficient to satisfy the league's demands or feasible enough to do so without alienating the French (possible reprisals against the Florentine merchants in France loomed large). Once again the Florentines fell back onto their usual delaying policy, counting, as they had at other times, on time and fortune. But the first was running out fast, and the second had already chosen others on which to bestow her favors.

At the beginning of August the victors held a conference in Mantua with Maximilian's representative in attendance, although the emperor had never joined the league. It quickly became clear that mutual enmity for the French had been the only thing that had kept the coalition together; once that cement was gone, old rivalries and jealousies raised their heads once more. Despite getting Parma and Piacenza, the pope could not impose the eviction of the Este from Ferrara. Although one set of "barbarians" had been driven out of Italy, others had taken their place, and they had every intention of staying. The Sforza regained the duchy of Milan, but largely on Swiss sufferance, and the Spanish now were firmly entrenched in the kingdom of Naples.

The only thing the statesmen at Mantua managed to agree upon was to punish Florence for its pro-French policy and to evict Piero Soderini. The task fell on Ramon de Cardona, who received a generous offer of 10,000 ducats from Cardinal de' Medici to pay the Spanish troops, with promises of further rewards once he had finished the job. Florence proved unable to furnish equivalent recompenses, partly because, being ignorant of the discussions going on in Mantua, the government had no clear idea about what to do. At the eleventh hour, when Cardona's troops had already crossed the Appenines, the Florentines were certain of only two things: They were being attacked, and the diplomatic clock had stopped ticking.

According to one of his nineteenth-century biographers, Machiavelli had already seen the writing on the wall sometime before. The fact that he drew up of a will in November 1511 has been taken as evidence "that he saw very dark times ahead." But at the time, it would not have been unusual for a forty-two-year-old to consider the eventuality of death and his need for a will, particularly if he had children who were minors (Bernardo, Niccolò's eldest, was eight). In reality, from the time the Gallican council left Pisa until the following May, Machiavelli appears to have been doing his usual work for the Ten: raising and inspecting militia units, visiting fortresses, and handling other administrative tasks. There is no doubt, however, that he considered the times perilous. In a document of March 1512 formally authorizing the creation of militia cavalry units, there are clear references to the need for preservation of Florence's liberty and a concern about "those powers that at present run the states of Italy."

As news of the events following the battle of Ravenna started trickling in, Machiavelli's workload increased. The Republic made some timid efforts to guard its frontiers. At the end of June, following a trip in which he carried Florence's condolences for the death of Pandolfo Petrucci to Siena, Machiavelli went to San Giovanni in the Valdarno to confer with the local governor about the march of the papal troops going north. The Republic had authorized the passage of these soldiers but was concerned because they belonged to the Orsini. From there, Niccolò traveled to Montepulciano to organize the defenses around that area in case the papal forces should stray from their stated march.

Yet, the lack of strong political leadership made Niccolò's job more difficult, as did the proverbial Florentine stinginess and pride. At the end of July, Machiavelli, then busy raising troops in the Mugello, received notice that the Spanish army had assembled at Loiano, some six miles from the Florentine frontier. He immediately warned the government about the danger, but as an answer he received the order not to pay the troops until absolutely necessary and dismiss all but a couple of hundred infantrymen. The pratica convened to discuss this matter and the possibility of further negotiations with the league applauded the Ten's parsimony, decided to elect a commissioner to supervise Machiavelli's work, and voted to punish alarmists "who spread false news." The old and blind Antonio Giacomini immediately saw the folly of such behavior and begged the government to fortify the Futa pass, guessing—quite correctly—that the Spanish would choose that route to penetrate into the Republic's territory.

His appeal fell on deaf ears. The government instead opted to concentrate several thousand soldiers at Firenzuola, calculating that the Spanish intended to invade from that direction, and in any case would have to take that stronghold before continuing their advance, so as not to leave such a large concentration of troops at their rear. On August 22, the Republic's envoy to the viceroy of Naples, Baldassarre Carducci, reported that Machiavelli had gone to Firenzuola at the head of 2,000 infantrymen. Carducci was confident that "everything will go according to your Lordships' benefit and wishes."

His optimism proved misplaced, as the Spaniards marched through the Futa pass just as Giacomini had predicted. The viceroy remained adamant about his intention to push on toward Florence, requesting the removal of Soderini and the return of the Medici as private citizens. An offer of 30,000 ducats to induce him to withdraw dissatisfied Cardona, and he insisted on 100,000. He also chided the Florentines for their wavering attitude, pointing out that his sovereign could not trust the Republic to honor any sort of treaty. He suggested that since Cardinal Giovanni de' Medici happened to be in the camp, Carducci should have a word with him. The Florentine ambassador, mindful of the prohibition about consorting with rebels, politely refused. Carducci could do nothing more but inform the Ten that by the morrow the Spaniards would be in Barberino and that they probably intended the town of Prato as their next objective. "Keep Prato well guarded," he warned, "for here people are talking and saying that the inhabitants of that place are favorable to the cardinal."

In haste, the Ten ordered the governor of Prato to refurbish the local fortifications and prepare to defend the town, adding that they would be sending firearms, gunpowder, and other supplies. Little of this weaponry seems to have arrived in time, and although afterward some people would talk about treason and sabotage (a story circulated about a gang of Florentine youths attacking the ammunition train, scattering the drivers, and smashing the powder barrels), it makes much more sense to think that, whatever the orders, the Ten's attempts to come to Prato's aid were too little and too late.

The news of Cardona's advance created consternation in Florence. The invaders had begun to behave with the usual brutality of all sixteenth-century armies, killing at will, carrying off women and livestock, and in general terrorizing the countryside. Reportedly they amounted to 8,000 infantry and 800 horsemen ("most of them sick, but the hope of booty puts wings on their heels," noted Carducci), and two artillery pieces, although their real strength appears to have been little more than 5,000. But whatever their numbers or ailments, these soldiers were veterans of many a campaign, tough and fierce individuals from the bitter lands of Estremadura, the dry plains of Castille, and the harsh mountains of Aragon, quite a few being *moriscos*—indigenous Muslims.

At Ravenna they had seen scores of their comrades blown to pieces by the duke of Ferrara's artillery, trampled by the French heavy cavalry, and savaged by Louis XII's German infantry. They did not fear taking losses, especially from what they considered to be an army of amateurs. But they suffered from a serious lack of supplies—food in particular— having found few victuals on their road south. The prospect of his army dissolving for want of the most basic necessities clearly worried Cardona, and if forced to retreat he would have risked being caught between the main Florentine army and the forces concentrated at Firenzuola. Facing a do-or-die situation, the viceroy had no option but to press on.

In Florence, opinions were divided on the best way to respond to the Spanish threat. Machiavelli had been urgently recalled to Florence on the 24th, as the Signoria wanted him to supply an assessment of the situation. Niccolò believed, as he would later write in *The Art of War*, that "the heart and the vital parts of a body need to be protected, not the extremities, be- cause one can live without these; but once the heart is struck, death en- sues." Soderini thus opted to concentrate most of the army, 9,000 infantry and a few hundred horsemen, directly outside the walls of Florence, de- spite the opinion of some of the Ten that it would be better to concentrate all the forces in Prato, ignoring Commissioner Pierfrancesco Tosinghi's warning that unless this happened, "I see all our plans going to ruin."

Soderini would not listen, and with the benefit of hindsight it is easy to criticize his decision; yet both strategies had their merits, at least on paper. Besides, the gonfalonier feared that a defenseless Florence would be at the mercy of the Mediceans within the city. On August 27, Soderini scored a personal victory when both the Eighty and the Great Council passed a vote of confidence in his favor, rejecting both his resignation and the request to readmit the Medici. Strengthened by this display of popular favor, the government ordered the arrest of a number of suspected Medici sympathizers.

The Spaniards, in the meantime, had arrived in Campi, proceeding to sack and burn the town. From there they could either move north toward Prato, or south, to attack Florence. "You know who," wrote Buonaccorsi to Machiavelli on the evening of the 27th, "is very displeased and worried about the enemy taking up lodgings in Campi this evening, and wishes me to ask you to get something done. Do what you can and don't waste time in discussions." A decisive action could have turned the tables in Florence's favor. A Ferrarese agent with the Spanish, writing to Cardinal Ippolito d'Este, brother of the Duke of Ferrara, noted that "should the Florentines decide to do so, they could strike, bringing damage and shame to this camp." But whether out of indecisiveness, lack of confidence, or deliberate strategy, the Florentine army did not move, wasting the best chance they had to force the Spanish to retreat. However, the militia's poor training and lack of adequate leadership could easily have turned such an attack into a disaster, so the decision to stay put, whether made by Machiavelli or someone else, could be considered the most logical course of action.

The following day the invaders moved north, taking up a position in front of Prato. The city's garrison consisted of about 3,000 militia infantrymen, 1,000 local levies, and a few hundred cavalry units under the elderly and uninspiring Luca Savelli, the Republic's most senior officer, given Florence's lack of a proper commander in chief. In theory these forces should have been more than enough to contain the Spanish, but nothing had been done to update Prato's medieval wall circuit. Moreover, the city lacked adequate military supplies; in one instance, the soldiers had to remove the lead from the roof of a church in order to make bullets. In addition, the governor had received only 100 ducats to pay the troops, with instructions to economize as much as possible. A week before, the Florentine councils had agreed to raise some 50,000 ducats for war needs, but collecting this money would take time, and in the meantime, the lack of wages did nothing to boost the soldiers' already sagging morale. The citizens of Prato had been ordered to keep to their homes, but this convinced the militiamen from other parts of the Florentine domain that the Pratesi had no intention of helping with the defense.

On the morning of August 28, the Spanish opened fire against the walls with their two artillery pieces. One of them burst its barrel after a few shots, and the other was too small in caliber to damage the lower part of the masonry. An attempt to storm the battlements with scaling ladders similarly failed, with the Spanish losing about forty men against three of the defenders. Now in dire straits, Cardona sent an ambassador to Florence with the offer to retreat in exchange for 30,000 ducats and a hundred pack-loads of bread.

Despite his outward resolve, the viceroy had received instructions from the king of Spain to reach a negotiated settlement, if possible, the Medici being an expendable commodity at this point. The Holy League had already started to fall apart. Ferdinand of Aragon was displeased with Julius's acquisition of Parma and Piacenza and his attempts to evict the Este from Ferrara. Indeed, the viceroy told the Florentine ambassador Niccolò Valori that he would much prefer Florence as a free city than one under the pope's sway. Given the circumstances, it would have been sensible for the Florentines to accept Cardona's offer; instead, Soderini, his hopes raised, chose to procrastinate, calculating that hunger would be a cheaper way to get rid of the Spaniards. Ex post facto, Machiavelli would bitterly criticize the decision, which he attributed to arrogance on the part of his fellow citizens. By giving in, he argued, the Florentines would have preserved their liberty: "Prudent rulers and republics should be satisfied with winning; for in most cases this lack of satisfaction results in defeat." In truth, although nobody could deny Soderini's prudence, in his case the virtue had become a vice.

Getting no response from Florence, Cardona had to make a quick decision. On the morning of the 29th he moved his remaining artillery in front of a section of walls near the Serraglio gate, where rising ground allowed for easier access to the battlements. By eleven o'clock a breach about twelve feet in width had opened up in the upper segment of the walls, and the viceroy assembled his troops for the attack. He reminded them of their predicament and said that plenty of food could be found in Prato, and fed their spirit of revenge by recalling their comrades who had been killed by the poisoned wine they had found in deserted dwellings along the route. Whether true or not, it served the viceroy's purposes. Cardona also promised his men a free hand should the city be taken by storm and one hundred ducats for the first man into the breach. Nevertheless, wishing to avoid unnecessary bloodshed among his soldiers, he sent a herald to request the city's surrender, threatening to take it by force otherwise. Defiantly, Luca Savelli answered that if the wanted Prato they would have to take it at swords' point.

Around midday, the Spaniards charged the breach like "rabid dogs." The militia of San Miniato and the Valdinievole tried to resist, but after taking two losses recoiled under the fury of the onslaught. Other units rushed to plug the gap, but by now the assailants at the breach had stormed through as the rest of the Spanish poured over the unguarded battlements from their scaling ladders. The attackers could still have been repulsed, had a group of harquebusiers covering the breach from the cover of a garden wall not taken to their heels. Moving with the speed and experience of veterans, the Spanish swiftly occupied the main streets and the central square, ruthlessly slaying anyone who tried to resist.

Those militiamen lucky enough to find refuge in houses or cellars largely survived, once the attackers' adrenaline had subsided, the Spanish preferring ransom money to worthless blood. Luca Savelli and the Florentine governor of Prato were captured and the victorious Spanish abandoned themselves to an orgy of looting and violence, raping women of all ages, torturing men to force them to reveal hidden treasures, and taking children as hostages. The viceroy and Cardinal de' Medici had asked that women's honor be preserved, but even if they had wanted to they could not have stopped the battle-maddened soldiers. Cardona and the cardinal did manage to save a number of women who had sought their protection, but for the next three weeks the Spanish would systematically rob the inhabitants of Prato of their goods and virtue.

How many people died during the fighting and the sacking is difficult to say. Estimates ranged from as low as 500 to over 6,000. The truth probably lies somewhere in the middle, with perhaps 2,000 militiamen "who perished while running or pleading for mercy," as mentioned by Francesco Gucciardini, to which one should add scores of those Pratesi killed while trying to defend their families, property, or honor. The responsibility for these deaths must fall squarely on Soderini's shoulders, although, in all fairness, the whole Florentine political system should take its share of the blame.

As soon as news of the disaster reached Florence, panic swept through the city. The militia had failed in Prato, and there could be no guarantee that it would not do the same if the Spanish attacked Florence. Undecided about what to do, the government sent Baldassarre Carducci to negotiate with the viceroy. On his return, Carducci reported that Cardona wanted 150,000 ducats and the return of the Medici as private citizens. He also related what he had seen in Prato, magnifying the extent of the destruction there, which only increased the terror of his fellow citizens about the possibility that they might suffer the same fate. "Thus one can say for certain," Francesco Vettori would comment, "that an enemy of the Medici like Messer Baldassarre did more to help their return to Florence than any of their closest friends." On the evening of the 30th, the Eighty suggested to Soderini that the viceroy's demands be met. The gonfalonier wanted to resign, but the Signoria managed to dissuade him.

The situation took a dramatic turn the next day, when a group of four young ottimati, Antonfrancesco degli Albizzi, Paolo Vettori (Francesco's brother), Bartolomeo Valori, and Gino Capponi, broke into the government palace and threatened to kill Soderini unless he resigned from his post. The gonfalonier dithered, and Albizzi grabbed him by the robe demanding also the release of citizens who had been arrested and put into prison a few days before. Soderini, realizing that he was alone, quickly agreed to do so. He could hear angry crowds gathering outside the palace. Soderini called for Machiavelli and asked him to fetch Francesco Vettori.

He wanted to be permitted to leave the city without suffering harm, and Vettori, when he arrived, managed to convince the gonfalonier's opponents to let him depart unscathed. Vettori offered to escort Soderini home, and the two left the palace.

Some members of the government could hardly suppress their satisfaction at seeing him leave. At the Santa Trinita bridge he was so shaken that he asked to go to Vettori's home, which was nearby. The following night, Francesco smuggled Soderini out of Florence, traveling with him as far as Siena. In the meantime, the colleges and other important magistracies convened to decide the gonfalonier's political fate. Initially the motion to deprive him of his office was rejected, and the officials approved it only after Francesco Vettori warned those present that unless the motion passed, Soderini's life would be in danger.

On September 1, Giuliano de' Medici entered Florence, walking through the streets unescorted and dressed in traditional Florentine garb. This modest behavior was more than justified, given that many in the city detested the very name of the Medici; although the ranks of the *palleschi* were swelling by the hour, Giuliano and his brother, the cardinal, realized the weakness of their position. Apart from a small core of die-hard Mediceans, most Florentines had been content to go along with the Soderini regime, and their fealty to any new government would be dictated by expediency more than conviction. Once the Spanish took their leave nobody could guarantee the Medici's permanence in Florence, so Giuliano and the cardinal needed for the time being to appear favorable to the Republican constitution.

For this reason, once the viceroy arrived at the government palace, and, sitting on what had been Soderini's seat, had made his appeal in the Medici's favor, it was decided to convene a pratica, which would include Giuliano among its members, to discuss political reforms. The committee proposed reducing the gonfalonier's term of office from life to one year, augmenting the Eighty's numbers, and increasing the pay for officials. On the 6th, the Eighty approved the motion, and the Grand Council passed it the following day, both by slim majorities. Giovanbattista Ridolfi, considered a moderate fratesco but tied to the Medici by blood, became gonfalonier, and in appearance the Republican state structure had not been significantly altered. Yet nobody held any illusions that this situation would last or that the Medici would renounce making a bid for power. Ridolfi himself saw it coming all too clearly. Answering a group of citizens who had come to express their doubts about the Medici's real intentions, he said: "What do you think we should do? Our enemies have put us in a sealed barrel and can easily hit us through the cork-hole." Ridolfi and the rest of Florence could do nothing but wait.

The new law dissatisfied almost everybody, and most of all the rabid palleschi, who perceived it as little more than a political sop. Moreover, it was known that the viceroy had offered to restore Soderini to his place, which some believed a ruse to create violent divisions within the city and thus allow the Spanish to intervene. Both Florence's independence and the Medici position were in peril, and the most loyal of the Mediceans gathered around Cardinal Giovanni and convinced him to take action. On September 14, the cardinal entered the city at the head of several thousand professional soldiers, his progress applauded by the population. Two days later, Giuliano and his friends entered the government palace with weapons concealed under their robes while the cardinal's soldiers gathered in the nearby square. At a signal, those inside the building drew their arms and demanded the calling of a parliament.

In the face of such an overwhelming show of force, the government could do nothing but accept. Under threat of violence, the assembly of Florence's citizens voted for the establishment of a *balìa* to reform the constitution. The trick that the Medici had used many times before had worked again, but the cardinal took care to include as many moderates possible in the new body. He needed these men not just for their political experience but also because the consensus of the most prominent and wealthy citizens would be essential to guarantee the Medici's political survival.

The Great Council became the main victim of the political upheaval when, after some debate, the balìa decided to restore the constitution as it was in 1494. Although not disenfranchised, a large section of the population lost the power it had enjoyed since Piero de' Medici's eviction, while the frateschi saw the reforms of their beloved Savonarola brought to naught. But the Medici could not satisfy everyone, and in the end they calculated the support of the *uomini dabbene* (more or less, "men of quality") to be more important than that of the middle-class artisans who formed the bulk of the Republic's main assembly.

Machiavelli seems to have gone along with the flow. In a letter to a "gentlewoman" written sometime after September 16, he recounted the events leading up to the establishment of the balìa, concluding with the words: "And this city is very quiet indeed, and hopes to live with their [the Medici's] aid in the same honorable way as in the past, when the magnificent Lorenzo their father of most happy memory ruled." Not a particularly Republican statement, and indeed, Machiavelli, despite his many enemies, had little to fear, even if considered, by most, to be Soderini's man. Yet, starting on November 7, a series of orders of the Signoria deprived him of all offices and dignities, confined within the Florentine domain for a year, ordered him to pay a hefty bond in surety of good behavior, and forbade him from entering the government palace for twelve months. The same penalties were also imposed on Biagio Buonaccorsi. Since Biagio and Niccolò were the only two people in the chancery to lose their jobs, it is legitimate to ask what happened in the two months following the Medici coup d'état.

The answer can probably be found in two of Machiavelli's writings dating to that time. At the end of September, the balìa created a panel to oversee the recovery of all Medici property confiscated and sold after 1494. The buyers were to be compensated with a sum equivalent to the original purchase. Machiavelli wrote to Cardinal de' Medici asking him to scotch the whole operation, arguing that taking away something from someone who had not legitimately owned it would inevitably cause resentment:

> People resent losing a farm (*podere*) much more than having a brother or a father killed, for sometimes a death is forgotten, but never one's property. The reason is obvious. Everyone knows that a regime change will not resurrect one's brother, but could mean getting back a farm. And most of all the Florentines, who are usu-

ally more avaricious than generous. . . . Since I wish to make friends
for your family and not enemies, it would be better if the balìa discussed the possibility of the Commune of Florence giving you for
a certain time 4,000 or 5,000 ducats a year in compensation.

In writing this letter Machiavelli committed a serious political blunder. First, nobody had asked for his opinion (he had started with the
statement "May affection be an excuse for condescension"). Second,
coming from someone who had been close to Soderini, his words about
regime changes had some clear threatening overtones. Third, the Medici
had strategic and social interests in recovering their properties that far
outweighed any ill feelings this might have caused. Finally, Niccolò, as a
civil servant, should have known better than to openly meddle with affairs of state. Under Soderini, he had grown used to playing first violin
in the Florentine political orchestra. Unfortunately the musicians had
changed, and so had the tune.

Still, Machiavelli would likely have kept his position in the chancery
if he had only been able to lay low for a while, even after this misstep;
instead, his diva streak got the better of him. It did not take long for Julius
II to become disgruntled about the regime change in Florence, having
found out very soon that the Medici had no intention of becoming a pliable tool in his hands. The pontiff would have wanted Cardinal Giovanni
to send troops against Alfonso d'Este, but after paying the viceroy and
other postulants 150,000 ducats, in no way could the Florentine government ask the financially strapped city to foot another hefty war bill,
especially for a campaign that Ferdinand of Aragon opposed. Faced with
this refusal, the pope uttered bloody curses against the ungrateful
Medici and started to plot the restoration of Florence's former regime.
The Soderini, with the exclusion of Cardinal Francesco, had received
sentences exiling them to various places, Piero having settled in
Dubrovnik. Yet the ex-gonfalonier still had a large following in the city,
and unable to curb this group by force, Mediceans opted for a propaganda campaign to discredit Soderini and his rule. At this point, Machiavelli composed a memorandum to the Medici, usually known as "Il

Ricordo ai Palleschi" ("Memorandum for the Mediceans"), but entitled by Niccolò "Pay Good Heed to This Writing."

The didactic tone of that phrase was not the best way to produce among the document's readership a positive disposition toward its author, and the rest of the text could hardly have improved matters. Machiavelli argued that it was foolish and counterproductive to bad-mouth Soderini's rule, since any other regime in Florence would share its shortcomings. Those who so hotly criticized the former gonfalonier did not have the city's well-being in mind, but only their own private interests. The new rulers should be wary of individuals who "behave like whores, indifferent to the Medici and the popular faction," attempting to become the Medici's protectors by currying favor with the people after demonstrating how right they were to oppose Soderini. It would be in the Medici's best interest to create a rift between these evil men and the people, so that they would be forced to be loyal to the state.

For Machiavelli, writing this memorandum was a huge mistake. His targets were those aristocrats who had always opposed Soderini, and even more so the ottimati who had joined the Medici cause at the eleventh hour. Yet these were the same people the Medici needed to prop up their fledgling regime, and moreover, they included in their ranks quite a few of Niccolò's enemies. By defending Soderini's rule, Machiavelli had not only positioned himself as among the ranks of the former gonfalonier's followers, someone the new regime would not like to hold governmental positions, but had also indirectly admitted his contribution to fourteen years of anti-Medici policies. This ultimate foray into the public sphere had turned Machiavelli into political poison, arousing his enemies' call for his blood. *Pro bono pacis*, and for the sake of their own security, the Medici were quite happy to serve his head on a platter. Buonaccorsi suffered the same fate, largely because his known friendship with the secretary made him a political liability.

While leaving the chancery for the last time, Niccolò may well have recalled the adage "Always think what to say; do not always say what you think." But it would take time before Machiavelli managed to put these words of wisdom into practice.

11

~

SATAN'S PROGENY

But as Satan's progeny are everywhere,
intermingling with the sons of God, and will
continue to exist until he "whose fan is in his
hand will thoroughly clean his threshing-
floor," so this son of Satan, trained in all
forms of wickedness in the midst of the many
sons of God, was born in that noble city
[Florence] and has written things which stink
of Satan's every wickedness.
—CARDINAL REGINALD POLE ON
NICCOLÒ MACHIAVELLI

Post res perditas: "After everything was lost." Thus would Machiavelli often refer to the time following his forced removal from the chancery, for him a veritable psychological watershed. Out of a job, out of favor, with few friends left, and despised by Florence's new rulers, Niccolò would look back longingly at the days in which he had enjoyed power and honor, craving constantly to return to such a position of prestige. In the meantime, he had a family to tend to, and the income that he earned annually from his small country estate could barely cover his daily needs—provided he did not have to face extraordinary expenses such as a money-consuming illness. The future looked bleak.

But bad as things were, worse was in store. In February 1513, two young men, Pietropaolo Boscoli and Agostino Capponi, hatched a plot to murder Giuliano de' Medici, but one of them carelessly dropped a list with the names of the people they intended to make privy to their intentions, including Niccolò Machiavelli. The authorities moved swiftly, arresting Boscoli and Capponi and rounding up everyone else on the list. Not finding Machiavelli at home, the Eight of Watch issued a decree ordering anyone who knew of his whereabouts to report them within the hour, under penalty of banishment and confiscation. Niccolò turned himself in, and like the other suspects endured a few (four, he would later say six) pulls of the *strappado* inflicted to get him to confess.*

Nothing could be found involving him in the conspiracy, however, except for his friendship with Niccolò Valori and Giovanni Folchi, who were also on the list, plus an acquaintance with Boscoli. Folchi stated that during his conversations with Machiavelli the latter had been much more interested "in wars than the city," although he also worried about the new regime lacking a strong leader. Niccolò's greater attention to foreign rather than domestic politics is evidence that he still nourished the hope of being readmitted to the chancery. But just to be on the safe side, the authorities locked him up, pending further decisions about his fate.

The conspiracy had been the brainchild of two isolated intellectuals who had read too much classical history and figured themselves as a pair of Brutuses. The authorities recognized this quickly enough but

---

* The strappado (in Florence known as *la fune*—the rope) consisted in tying someone's arms behind his or her back and then using the same rope to raise the body from the ground. The victim sometimes would be dropped nearly to the floor, with the resulting suffering and physical damage depending on the height of the fall. However, in many cases the lifting and dropping would be limited to a few inches, enough to inflict suffering but little else.

nonetheless considered it expedient to make an example of them. Boscoli and Capponi were condemned to death by decapitation; Valori and Folchi were sentenced to two years imprisonment in Volterra; and others were given various lengths of confinement within the Florentine dominion. While waiting to know his fate, Machiavelli heard the funerary litanies of the "Blacks" that accompanied the two condemned men during their last night on earth.* With feet bound, his whole body hurting, lying in a stinking cell with lice crawling all along the walls, Machiavelli's Florentine spirit could stand it no longer. There and then he composed a sonnet to Giuliano de' Medici containing the cutting lines: "But what rankles me the most / that while sleeping in the early light / I started to hear the final post / 'Your hour has come.' So go they might."

Machiavelli had never had much patience for fools, and the case of Boscoli and Capponi only confirmed the Florentine saying "No heaven for suckers" (*Per i bischeri non c'è paradiso*). In the meantime, it could pay to amuse Giuliano, and in another sonnet to his would-be patron he savaged the poetaster Andrea Dazzi and his "trashable comedy." That Dazzi had as his mentor Niccolò's erstwhile boss Marcello Virgilio Adriani is hardly a coincidence; Machiavelli likely resented having been abandoned by his former colleagues in the chancery. But Machiavelli still had influential friends, and immediately after his arrest, his brother, Totto, sent a courier to Rome asking Francesco Vettori, now there in the capacity of Florentine ambassador, to intercede with Cardinal de' Medici for Niccolò's liberation. Freedom, however, would end up coming from an entirely different direction.

On February 21, 1513, Pope Julius II died. "The cause of Italy's ruin," would be the pontiff's epitaph composed by the Venetian diarist Marin Sanudo, who with glee added at the bottom of the entry a number of doggerels circulating in Rome against the late pope. The cardinals, gathered

---

* The "Blacks" (*i Neri*) were the members of the confraternity of Santa Maria della Croce al Tempio, whose duty consisted in assisting those condemned to death. The name derived from their somber garments and hood, which covered the entire face.

in conclave, initially had trouble electing a successor, until Francesco Soderini approached Giovanni de' Medici with an offer the latter could not refuse: amnesty for all his exiled relatives and a marriage agreement between the two families. Medici had until then received but one vote (presumably his own), but Soderini used his influence with the pro-French cardinals to sway the assembly in Giovanni's favor. On March 11, the announcement came that Cardinal Giovanni de' Medici had been elected pope, taking the name of Leo X. When the news reached Florence ten hours later, collective jubilation erupted.

For the first time in history, a Florentine would sit on Peter's chair. Everyone believed that having one of their citizens as pope meant good business opportunities for all. During the three days of festivities that followed the elections, the Florentine regime proclaimed a general amnesty for all those, with few exceptions, who had been detained for political reasons. Among them figured the still aching Machiavelli, thankful that the indult had saved him from having to find the extra money to pay yet another surety for good behavior.

It is possible that he composed "Il Canto degli Spiriti Beati" (The Song of Blessed Spirits) immediately after his release, a *canto carnascialesco* (poetic composition to be sung during Carnival—Leo X had been elected during Lent, but the rigors of that penitential season had been temporarily suspended to allow Florence to celebrate adequately) in which Niccolò imagined the spirits of Heaven descending on earth to bring peace and prosperity, as the Christian powers united to fight the Ottoman threat.* While adulatory toward the Medici, the poem contains some genuinely Christian *topoi* not usually associated with Machiavelli.

---

* Roberto Ridolfi assigned the poem to this period. Other commentators have moved it to 1522 or 1524, identifying the "new shepherd" mentioned by Machiavelli with Adrian VI or Clement VII and arguing that the Ottomans appeared to be much more menacing after sultan Selim I's conquest of Egypt in 1517 and his son Suleiman I's attack against Rhodes. Yet a crusade against the Turks had always been on Julius II's agenda and was an object of discussion during the sessions of the Lateran council. For this reason, and the circumstances of Machiavelli's life, I'm inclined to agree with Ridolfi's dating.

The brush with prison, torture, and—possibly—death* would have brought out the Catholic in almost anyone, including Niccolò.

Once home, he wrote a letter to Francesco Vettori thanking him and his brother Paolo for their efforts to get him freed, adding: "Fate had done everything it could to harm me, but thank God that's over. I hope not to suffer the same again, not only because I shall be more cautious, but also because the general atmosphere will be freer and less burdened with suspicion." He went on to recommend Totto for a position in the papal household, requesting Francesco to intervene with the pope in that regard. In addition, he asked Vettori to ask Giuliano de' Medici to take him into his service, "since I believe this will bring honor to me and gain for you." More than lofty ideas about statecraft, Machiavelli's main concern throughout his life would be to satisfy the two very Florentine and down-to-earth needs for *honore et utile*. In another letter to Francesco he repeated his request for aid, thanking his friend for the invitation to stay with him in Rome. He put his hopes in Vettori, since it had been he, together with two of Machiavelli's relatives, who had come up with the 1,000 florins Niccolò had been obliged to pay as a collateral for his good behavior after being evicted from the chancery. Furthermore, Paolo Vettori had established close links with Giuliano de' Medici, whom Machiavelli considered a sure source of patronage.

Vettori, however, could do little to help Machiavelli, or anyone else, for that matter. Droves of postulants had arrived in Rome seeking preferment, and Francesco, unlike the staunch Medicean Paolo, did not figure high on the pope's list of favorites. His behavior at the time of Soderini's eviction and his opinions on retaining some of the Republican institutions probably affected Leo's attitude toward him, and because of this he did not expect to remain ambassador for long. Vettori penned a reply to that effect on March 30, and received in return a rather peeved response from a very disappointed Machiavelli, singing himself "once a secretary" (*quondam secretarius*). If at all possible, Niccolò announced, he would

---

* People believed that all those arrested in connection with the Boscoli-Capponi plot would be executed.

come to Rome to ask the pope in person, but flatly stated "I shall wait until September," though wondering about the wisdom of writing to Cardinal Soderini for a recommendation. He also expressed a desire to exchange thoughts with Vettori about current events. Francesco, frustrated that he had not been able to predict Leo's election, had demurred, saying, "I do not wish to discuss things rationally, for I've been misled so many times," to which Machiavelli responded:

> You are right to tire of trying to reason about current affairs, since the outcome often goes against one's opinions and ideas—the same has happened to me. But if I were able to speak with you, I would fill your head with abstractions, Fortune having decided that, being unable to discuss the silk or wool trades, or profits or losses, I must stick to politics, and talk about that or take a vow of silence.

From this passage we can easily fathom the extent of Machiavelli's loneliness in a city like Florence, where even today the earthy attitude of its inhabitants makes intellectual conversation a rare commodity.* Besides, for fourteen years Niccolò had been immersed in statecraft by working in the chancery, and he longed for anything that somehow could take him back to those days.

As for employment, Machiavelli had no intention of giving up that easily. On April 16 he would again ask Vettori to press Giuliano de' Medici, "who is coming there," and Cardinal Soderini to find him a job, "for I cannot believe that with some adroit maneuvering my skills will not be put to use, if not for Florence's benefit at least for Rome's and the papacy." He also recounted some incidents involving mutual acquaintances: Donato dal Corno had opened another shop that had become a gathering place for sodomites; Girolamo del Guanto had lost his wife,

---

* That the Florentines, narrow-minded as they sometimes can be, could have over the centuries produced such wonderful art is something of a miracle. But then, one has to admit that, with all their faults, in general the Florentines have taste.

but after behaving for a few days like "a stunned fish" had decided to re-marry, becoming a source of gossip for Niccolò and his friends; Tommaso del Bene, "who has become eccentric, rude, irksome, and disheveled," had bought some seven pounds of veal, but then insisted that Niccolò and two other chums share the expense with him of a dinner costing fourteen *soldi* each: "I had only ten, and every day he asks me for the other four; even yesterday evening he pestered me for them on the Ponte Vecchio." He was driving home the point, just in case Vettori had not gotten the message, that he desperately needed a job.

Francesco answered a few days later, informing Machiavelli about the truce between France and Spain, and adding that approaching Cardinal Soderini on Niccolò's behalf would most likely produce an adverse effect: "For although he has fingers in many pies and outwardly enjoys the pope's favor, nevertheless many Florentines still dislike him and so it would be unwise for him to support you. Besides, I believe that he would not do so willingly, for you know with what caution he moves." As a matter of fact, Soderini happened not just to be careful, but most times downright stingy and avaricious, something both Machiavelli and Vettori must have known. But if the cardinal was unlikely to do something unless it was to his personal advantage, Francesco could offer his friend hospitality for free in Rome once his brother Paolo became one of the Eight of Watch (which would have meant the repeal of Machiavelli's confinement), with the added incentive "of passing some time with a girl who happens to be my neighbor."

Niccolò would constantly put off accepting Vettori's offer, the following December explaining that when in Rome, he would have to visit "those Soderini," and he feared that once back in Florence, he would end up in jail again, "because although this regime is solid and safe, new suspicions abound." Given what he had gone through, Machiavelli had every reason to be wary of behaving rashly, although Vettori would tell him not to worry, since he owed nothing to Soderini and, in any case, he doubted the former gonfalonier had any desire to see him.

Piero Soderini, meanwhile, had been forgiven by Leo X, and he had settled down in Rome with his brother the cardinal. The pope had in fact taken a liking to the honest, if inept, Piero, and in any case had every reason to try to keep the former gonfalonier's followers in check. The situation in Florence worried Leo, and in particular the question of Medici leadership there. He would have liked his brother Giuliano to run the show, being a man of age and experience; but immediately after the conclave Giuliano had departed Florence hoping to enjoy a much more comfortable and less stressful life in Rome. Leo's next choice would have been his illegitimate cousin Giulio, but the latter, being a cleric, also saw better opportunities in Rome than in Florence; in any case, the pope needed collaborators whom he could trust, and although he had made Giulio archbishop of Florence following the death of Cosimo de' Pazzi ("God receive his soul, and of all his kin," Machiavelli would comment— one can only guess how much with tongue in cheek), he preferred to keep him at his side in the Vatican.

Only Lorenzo de' Medici, son of the deceased Piero, remained, but he had the drawback of being only twenty years of age and not at all happy to leave Rome: He had seen the prestige enjoyed there by a pontiff's relatives, "and while in Florence he would have to behave with a thousand cautions, in Rome he needed not one," Francesco Vettori would comment in his *Sommario delle Istoria d'Italia* (Summary of Italy's Affairs). Furthermore, Lorenzo lived under his mother's thumb, the imperious Alfonsina Orsini, who put her own ambitions second to her desires for her son's aggrandizement, but just slightly. Forced to make virtue out of necessity, Leo took care to instruct his nephew in how to behave: Put trusted men in the principal positions, and if this is not possible, be sure that the men who are in those positions lack courage and intelligence; satisfy the ambitions of lesser people with minor offices; use the Eight of Watch to keep you informed; provide swift justice for the humbler folk; don't get involved in legal suits; and, most of all, see that the officials of the *Monte Comune* (the institution handling Florence's public debt) are all on your side, "for the heart of the city lies there." But Leo realized that the power of the Medici was closely tied to his papacy, and after his death no one could guarantee their permanence in Florence.

The election of Leo X had catapulted his family from being de facto rulers of a medium-sized Italian state to the stratosphere of European sovereigns. And the pope would do anything to see that this power became fixed, whether within or outside Florence.

Machiavelli had rather more mundane concerns, and he was still convinced that earning Giuliano de' Medici's favor would be the best card in the deck. It is probable that during this period Biagio Buonaccorsi, with Niccolò's complicity, transcribed and bound a series of poems written by people such as Lorenzo "the Magnificent" de' Medici (Giuliano's father), Agnolo Poliziano (Giuliano's tutor), and Niccolò Machiavelli, whose poetic compositions included references to a beautiful young lad to be identified with Giuliano himself. Given that the illustrations included in the volume have been attributed to Sandro Botticelli (one of the Medici's favorite painters before 1494), it is possible that Buonaccorsi and Machiavelli were trying to create for Machiavelli a history of intimacy with Florence's present rulers in the hope of sufficiently impressing Giuliano that he would consider employing Niccolò.*

This operation, like all others attempted by Machiavelli, appears to have met with little or no success, and by now Niccolò had really started to feel the money crunch, having little income and still needing to finish paying off some rather hefty debts. The fact that he, by his own admission, liked to spend money, "and can't go without spending," did nothing

---

* Mario Martelli, having established Buonaccorsi' handwriting, dated the volume to sometime before 1494, with the rationale that Biagio would never have transcribed Medicean poetry after that date. He also excluded the period after 1512, since Botticelli had died two years before. By this reasoning, Martelli maintained that (1) the young Machiavelli was part of the Medici circle of old; and (2) he and Buonaccorsi knew each other before both became part of the chancery. The main flaw in this reasoning is that drawings, unfinished manuscripts, and other papers were available on the market, and often the heirs of a deceased person would sell off some of the inherited chattels to *rigattieri* (secondhand dealers). It would make perfect sense for Buonaccorsi to acquire something formerly belonging to the late Botticelli for his own use.

to improve an already serious financial situation. Vettori's gripes about being taxed four florins, saying, "Since I do not practice any trade, my income barely allows me to live, and I have daughters who need dowries," only rubbed more salt into the wound. In addition, Niccolò had been ordered by the regime to justify his expenses during the time he had been in the chancery, and for that purpose had authorized him to return to the government palace a few times between April and July 1513. It would appear that he managed to justify himself in a satisfactory way, for we hear nothing more about this matter.

Amid all of these troubles, Machiavelli derived some solace from the reports about current events that Vettori would include in his letters, and send replies to his friend's political commentaries. Niccolò certainly did not have the privileged access to news enjoyed by Francesco, and he excused himself for "speaking out of ignorance, having based everything on the information you have provided." But the theorist in him could not refrain from building *castelluci* (fantasies) about the development of international affairs, and he and Vettori would spar about the various possibilities open to the European rulers.

Machiavelli still remained convinced of France's power, even after Louis XII's attempt to retake Milan in the spring of that year had been bloodily crushed on June 6 by a joint Swiss-Milanese force at the battle of Novara, and the French also had to face an attack from the English. But he considered the Swiss to be a greater problem for Italy than, as Vettori maintained, the Ottomans: After Novara the Swiss had taken virtual control of the duchy of Milan, and the battle itself proved that in the past the French had managed to win only because they had faced armies composed of mercenaries. Ancient history demonstrated that those who relied on citizen armies almost always won; the exceptions of Hannibal and Pyrrhus, who had managed to win with paid soldiers thanks to their own abilities and personalities, only confirmed the rule.

With the benefit of hindsight it is easy for us to lambast Niccolò's lack of foresight; however, it is also true that he had chosen to ignore the victories of the Spanish at Barletta, Cerignola, and the Garigliano against armies containing large numbers of Swiss; but then, of course, they had been operating as mercenaries under French command. Yet, intellectual honesty should have made him wonder why Florence's levied army had suffered such a serious defeat in Prato at the hands of the paid soldiers he so despised. But asking such a question would have brought Machiavelli's antiquity-based world crashing down; besides, he considered himself the militia's father, and, like many parents, turned a blind eye to his beloved offspring's limitations.

Machiavelli's obsession with citizen armies had only increased after the Prato debacle, and he viewed the new regime's plans to scupper the Florentine national army with alarm. The Nine had already been suppressed and all company commanders sacked, but the militia remained in a state of limbo while the government debated what to do with it. Machiavelli probably knew he could count on Francesco's support on this matter. Sometime between September and November 1512, Paolo Vettori had written a memorandum to Giovanni de' Medici, still a cardinal at the time, arguing, among other things, about the necessity of raising a force of professionals to guard Florence and the utility of keeping the militia in the *contado* and the *distretto*, employing it, if necessary, to quash dissent in the city. His brother Francesco agreed that he liked "the battalions, but one should keep them active and the city guard well disciplined." Echoing Paolo's comments, in chapters 12–14 of *The Prince* Machiavelli would stress the importance of a citizen army for a ruler's safety.

In reality, the Medici did need the militia, since hiring large numbers of mercenaries would have been an unbearable financial burden for Florence to carry and likely to cause disaffection among those whom the Medici wished to keep happy; besides, retaining the Florentine levies could outwardly be seen as evidence of the Medici's desire to preserve Florence's free institutions and not rule by martial law. In the wake of these considerations, the infantry branch of the militia was revived the following May under the jurisdiction of the Otto di Pratica, the magistracy that had taken the place of the Nine and the Ten. An efficient command structure would arrive the following year, and in a totally novel fashion.

On August 25, Machiavelli wrote to Vettori asking him to talk to Giuliano de' Medici about Donato dal Corno, who until then had tried in vain to have his name placed in the electoral bags. Giuliano's intervention had become necessary because the electoral officers were very "fastidious"—which could refer either to Donato's blatant homosexuality or his lack of social standing, despite being a rather affluent individual. Machiavelli was known for his generosity toward his friends, but by helping Donato's political career he could hope that the latter would one day be in a position to return the favor, perhaps from the upper echelons of power. He signed this letter as coming from Florence, but since the previous April he had moved to his country estate at Sant'Andrea in Percussina. There he would stay until the following February, intermittently going to Florence for business but otherwise "reduced to living in the country away from any human face."

Well, not exactly. For one thing, he had his family with him, his loyal wife and growing children joining him at some point in the spring. Besides, although immersed in the Tuscan rural landscape, at the time Sant'Andrea was hardly as remote a place as Machiavelli would have liked us to imagine. The road between Florence and Rome passed through the village, making it an ideal place for getting the latest news, since travelers along the route would inevitably stop there and talk about what was going on in the seats of power—as Niccolò himself would admit. Moreover, living in the countryside allowed Machiavelli to work on his writings away from the political turmoil of the capital.

Niccolò would give a detailed account of his rustic living in a letter of December 10, replying to one by Vettori written at the end of the previous month and describing Francesco's somewhat indolent existence in Rome. "I see how discreetly and tidily you fulfill that public office of yours," Machiavelli would quip in the opening paragraph, not being able to hide his envy at Vettori's late rising, consorting with ambassadors, and dining with cardinals, with a bit of sexual distraction on the side. He continued the missive by recounting his own pastimes: hunting for thrushes and the like. He told of a comedic incident involving an altercation with a woodcutter, and another involving certain stacks of firewood that he had promised to his friends; having second thoughts, he had claimed to have no more timber, "and they are all miffed, in particular Battista [Guicciardini], who adds this to the other calamities of Prato."*

In the morning he would take a walk in the woods carrying with him the works of Dante Alighieri, Petrarch, "or one of those minor poets like Tibullus or Ovid," which he would read as a form of consolation, and after that would go to the nearby inn to get the latest from any traveler who might be stopping there. After lunching with his family, "eating what this poor place and my miserable patrimony allows," he would travel once more to the inn and spend the rest of the day playing cards and backgammon with some of the locals. These gambling sessions more often than not ended in heated discussions, "and by consorting with this lice I ease my brain from its rot, and vent the evilness of my fate, to see if she is ashamed of having trodden me to the ground." Once home, he would take off his dirty and muddy clothes to don his robes of office and then, adequately dressed, hold imaginary conversations with the great men of the past, imbibing their wisdom and counsel.

On the strength of these inputs he had started writing a booklet entitled *De Principatibus*, which he intended to dedicate to Giuliano de' Medici, discussing the nature and running of princedoms. "And if you ever liked any of my fantasies," he wrote to Vettori, "you should appreciate this one." He thought it would be "well received by a ruler, in particular if new to the job." He added that he had talked with Filippo Casavecchia about seeking an opportunity to present his work in person to Giuliano. They had evaluated the pros and the cons of doing so, but in any case, he hoped that the Medici would employ him, "if only to roll a stone." However, he believed that once the booklet was read, "people would see that I have not slept or loafed during the fifteen years spent studying statecraft, and everyone should cherish employing someone

---

* Giovanbattista Guicciardini had been the governor of Prato when the Spaniards took the city. Taken prisoner, he had to pay a stiff ransom for his release, and here Machiavelli is implying that Guicciardini held him responsible for his misfortunes.

who has gathered so much experience at the expense of others." Whatever the case may have been with his employment, Machiavelli never doubted his intellectual abilities.

Machiavelli wrote again to Vettori ten days later, once more to plead Donato dal Corno's case, since it appeared to have foundered against the rocks of Florentine politics. In his answer, Vettori assured his friend that he had already moved to solve this matter in a satisfactory manner, and that he had also been on the lookout for any possible job opening for Niccolò. He added that he would be happy to receive Machiavelli's work, and once he'd read it would give his opinion about presenting it or not to Giuliano. Niccolò, however, could not wait, and it is possible that during this period he sent to Giuliano a sonnet entitled "The Thrushes," possibly with the accompaniment of a gift of such birds. This may have been meant to indicate his intention of soon providing his would-be patron with something more substantial:

> *I'm sending you Giuliano, if I might,*
> *Several thrushes—a small gift I guess*
> *But good to make your Lordship think a bit*
> *Of your poor Machiavello in distress*
>
> *And if you have around you men who bite,*
> *Into their throats you may soon force all this,*
> *So that, while eating of these birds, who knows!*
> *They may stop rending some man's name and right*
>
> *But you will say: "How can these birds achieve*
> *All this being neither good nor fat at all?*
> *Of touching them my men would not conceive"*
>
> *Then let me tell you this: As they recall*
> *I am too thin, yet of my flesh they leave*
> *No inch untried by their teeth's hungry fall*

Oh, answer not the call
Of empty words, my Lord and judge and see,
Not with your eyes but with your hands, my plea.

Even this time Machiavelli would be disappointed in his hopes, and probably even more so not to get any answer from Vettori except gossip, amusing tales, and lamentations about losing his manly prowess. Niccolò had no time for such self-deprecation and answered Vettori that, evidently, he, "since I like screwing women," needed to come to Rome to correct his friend's ascetic disposition: "For as soon as I had assessed the situation I would have said 'Ambassador, you shall wither away if you don't get some discretion: In this place there are neither young boys nor women. What the fuck of a household is this?'"

Machiavelli at least did not have to worry about his own virility. With the arrival of the winter chills he had returned to Florence, spending most of his time in Donato dal Corno's shop or at La Riccia's home, even if his constant presence had started to irritate people: His friend had nicknamed him "shop-bug," and the courtesan "house-bug."* Nevertheless, he had found both to be willing to ask his advice, which allowed him to enjoy the heat of Donato's brazier,† and sometimes La Riccia would provide some sexual diversion. The woman, a down-to-earth and streetwise individual, had difficulty understanding Machiavelli's lofty arguments: "These thinkers, these thinkers: where do they live?" she once uttered in frustration. "It seems to me that they turn everything upside down."

Machiavelli's thoughts were not the only thing gone topsy-turvy. During his months of seclusion, Lorenzo de' Medici had taken control of the

---

* *Impacciabottega* and *impacciacasa* in the original. The verb *impacciare* in this context mean to obstruct or to clutter.

† *Focone*, which I have translated as "brazier," could also mean the touch-hole of a harquebus or artillery piece. Giorgio Inglese wonders if Machiavelli was intending this as a double entendre with sexual overtones.

city, and Giuliano had gone to Rome for good. The process of reviving the Medicean constitution had been progressing steadily, as the balìa re-created the old magistracies that had allowed the Medici to keep the city under control before the revolution of 1494. Yet the ruling family had not always had a smooth run; even the balìa had opposed the more extreme proposals to tighten the Medici grip on the city, turning down, for instance, the scheme to give Giuliano extraordinary powers in fiscal matters and hire condottieri at will. Moreover, even those closest to the regime felt that after acquiring the papacy the Medici had little time for Florence. The constant absence of a member of the ruling family had not gone down at all well with the Florentines.

This situation not only harmed the Medici's leadership but also left the door open for all sorts of infighting among the members of the regime. Giuliano had to intervene personally, if only by letter, to secure the nomination of his protégé Giovanni Berardi as gonfalonier after the latter's enemies tried to prevent him from gaining that position. That Berardi also happened to be a friend of Soderini is proof of the complicated power-mongering game played by the Medici to bring as many Florentines possible into their fold. But despite these attempts, the abolition of the Great Council had deprived a lot of people—too many for the Medici to compensate for adequately—of the political power they had enjoyed uninterruptedly for eighteen years.

In addition, the political revolution of 1512 had caused the frateschi, who under Soderini appear to have been a rather loose group, to close ranks, and on a number of occasions the regime had to take measures against friars for their apocalyptic preaching and defense of the late Savonarola (true to type, Machiavelli would scoff at these sorts of sermons). In an effort to quell dissent, the electoral scrutiny of 1513 for the major offices was done so as to include everyone who had been vetted for the minor ones, kindling the hopes of people like Donato dal Corno. It had become clear that the Medici could not adequately control the Florentine ship of state without one of the family members personally steering it.

Lorenzo de' Medici arrived in Florence on August 10, having dragged his heels up to the very last moment. Compared to Rome, his native city had little to offer except a lot of headaches with little monetary comfort attached. Already in October he would lament Florence's financial exhaustion to convince the pope not to raise funds there for his own international necessities (Leo X, despite all his protests of neutrality, had given the Swiss 42,000 ducats just before the battle of Novara). To Cardinal Giulio he said, "You know how difficult and burdensome it is trying to get money out of these people, in particular when no peril is in sight."

His efforts to impose family strategies favorable to the Medici on the Florentines met with similar resistance: The prospective marriage between a member of the Saviati with a girl from the Alamanni, for example, had encountered the opposition of Jacopo Salviati, who went around saying, "Should Lorenzo try to force me into this, I shall go to the pope and Giuliano, who never have failed me." Clearly, certain *uomini dabbene* considered Lorenzo to be of little consequence compared to other members of his family, and if this were not enough the young Medici faced a personal shortage of cash. His mother would pester the pope to raise Lorenzo's monthly allowance of 400 ducats, and eventually, through the papal datary Silvio Passerini, managed to get for him the revenues of four pontifical venal offices worth around 10,000 ducats a year.

Alfonsina Orsini had less luck trying to convince her son to moderate expenses, Lorenzo flatly stating that as long as youth and a pope in the family permitted him, he intended to have a good time. His grandfather and namesake had come to power more or less at Lorenzo's age, but thanks to his intelligence, training, and youth in Florence, had turned into a very smooth operator. His grandson instead showed a singular ham-fisted approach to politics, alienating those he most needed to woo.

In February 1514, Alfonsina would write to her son about a rupture existing in the Medici extended family, with some members aligning with Jacopo and Lucrezia Salviati and others with Lorenzo and herself. Jacopo had been miffed because, despite his opposition, the Salviati-Alamanni match had been concluded; moreover, the pope had reneged on his promise to his sister Lucrezia about giving some lucrative benefices to her kin by marriage. Lucrezia had begged Leo to allow Jacopo to come to Rome to avoid being subjected to further humiliation. Lorenzo shrugged his shoulders, stating that he would be happy to get rid of such a troublesome pest. Undiplomatic as his handling of the Salviati might have been, Lorenzo managed to anger the rest of his supporters by spending long periods in Rome, often without informing anyone of his departure and leaving those who needed to consult with him before making a decision in a quandary about what to do.

At the beginning, Lorenzo's behavior could not have been more appealing. He rose early, gave audiences, and took a keen interest in the city's politics and in the reform efforts of the regime. Machiavelli seems to have been initially struck by Lorenzo's modest and generous attitude, writing to Vettori that "he incites love and reverence, rather than fear; a most difficult thing to obtain, and therefore more than laudable." Around this time he may have started to consider dedicating his booklet to Lorenzo instead of Giuliano, perceiving the former as the most likely for employment. Besides, he could be sure that Vettori would be circulating his name in Rome, and could possibly convince the pope and Giuliano of his loyalty. He may not have known about the squabble going on among the various members of the Medici family, and therefore not realized that by favoring one side, he would have automatically displeased the other. Whatever the outcome of the struggle might have been, small fry like Machiavelli would be easily expendable.

Nevertheless, Niccolò still hoped that his pamphlet would help him win favor with the Medici. He had managed to get Vettori to help him convince the Florentine fiscal board to lower his taxes, with Francesco writing to the competent officials that Niccolò was "without income, penniless and burdened with children." At some point he must have solicited Vettori for an answer about his employment and his literary composition—but the response he received must have been a negative one, as can be inferred from the pervasive bitterness of the letter he wrote to Francesco on June 10:

I received two letters of yours, sent to me by Donato through Brancaccio since I am in the country with my family. I replied in an appropriate manner about my own personal matters, your love affair and other things. But having forgotten them when I came to Florence two days ago, and considering the effort involved in rewriting them I shall send them at a later date. In the meantime I'm penning you this one, so that you may know yours arrived safely. And briefly I shall explain my motives for not coming to Rome, held back by those reasons you elucidate now, which I had already understood on my own accord.

I shall remain as now among my lice, unable to find anyone mindful of my services or who believes I could be good for something. But for me it is impossible to remain in such a state for long, for I am wasting away, and if God does not help me I shall be forced to leave home and, if nothing better, find work as a tutor or as secretary to a captain; or end up in some wasteland teaching children to read, and leave my family here to treat me as if I were dead— better actually, for I am a loss, being used to spend and not being able to avoid doing so. I'm not writing this to you so that you may trouble yourself or worry for me: I'm only venting my frustration, so that I may not write anymore about this odious matter.

In his answer, Vettori, while recognizing his friend's affliction, could not but offer kind words as consolation. He, in turn, had been having trouble satisfying Donato dal Corno's political ambitions. Although he had managed to convince Cardinal Giulio to order the appropriate officials to settle the matter, and induced Donato to pay a bribe of one hundred ducats to the papal secretary, Piero Ardinghelli—sarcastically described as "that friend"—to grease the wheels further, things had not gone as planned, because Ardinghelli had wanted the money on the spot. Vettori was trying to convey to Machiavelli his difficulties in exercising pressure on influential people in Rome, for if the rich Donato had up to then been stifled in his desires, the poor Niccolò could not hope for better treatment. That Francesco repeated the invitation for Machiavelli to come to Rome was more than a simple manifestation of friendship. Vettori understood that unless Niccolò showed his face and established friendly contacts with the Medici circle, he would never get the employment he needed so badly.

Even if Machiavelli had wished to go to Rome, he had in the meantime gone down with a fever against which there could be no remedy: love. In his next letter to Vettori he would tell his friend about being smitten with one of his neighbors. He had taken to visiting her at all times of day and night. "I have left behind," he announced, "grave and great matters; I get no pleasure from reading the ancients, no debating about modern affairs: everything has been transformed in sweet thoughts." Caught in this whirlwind of passion he failed to answer Vettori's letters again until December 4, when he asked for his intervention with the ecclesiastical authorities to solve the marital problems of Niccolò Tafani's sister, who had been abandoned by her husband (the man was by then living in Rome). He once more bemoaned his own misfortune as well.

Francesco, rather peeved at his friend's silence, had already written to him with a juicy proposal: The pope had been seeking advice about the best foreign policy to follow "in order to keep the Church's spiritual, temporal, and political status as he has found it, or even increase it." Francesco warned Niccolò that he would present the opinion to the pope as coming from Machiavelli, dropping a number of hints about how to word an appropriate response: "Evaluate everything; and since I know your fine brain, I do not believe that you have forgotten the trade even after two years of absence from the shop [the chancery]."

As a matter of fact, the pope had already decided to throw in his lot with France's enemies, but at the same time had been conducting negotiations and even signed a treaty with the French. Did Machiavelli or Vettori know that in September Leo had finalized a secret anti-French accord with Ferdinand of Aragon? Rumors of such an agreement had started circulating in Florence in November, and in any case, prudence would dictate that Niccolò should have been wary about giving a blunt reply.

Machiavelli may not have forgotten "the trade," but he should have remembered how his way of handling "business" had gotten him into his present troubles.

Machiavelli could not have been more undiplomatic in his answer of December 10. Having laid out in detail all the possible scenarios, he concluded that the pontiff should side with the French, unless the Venetians decided to abandon their alliance with Louis XII. This could have been acceptable to the pope and Cardinal Giulio, the person who had asked Vettori for Machiavelli's opinion in the first place, had not Niccolò included the phrase: "No matter who should win, I see the Church being at someone's mercy, so I judge it would be better to be at the mercy of those who are the more reasonable and known of old, rather than some unknown quantity whose intentions are unknown."

Machiavelli evidently realized that he had probably been too direct for his own good, and on December 20 he wrote again to Vettori expanding on some of the points included in the previous letter. After describing the perils in store for Leo, should he choose neutrality, or the wrong side, he passionately defended his point about France, stating that it resulted from "sound judgment" (*giudizio saldo*) rather than "love" (*affectione*) for the French. Vettori answered ten days later telling Machiavelli that Leo, Cardinal Giulio, and Cardinal Dovizzi had read both letters, "and all were impressed by your intelligence and praised your judgment." Francesco, however, immediately after that added, "Although I have received nothing but words, being unlucky and not knowing how to help friends, nonetheless the friendship of important people may come useful to you sometime." That the pope and Cardinal Giulio in reality had not at all appreciated Machiavelli's opinion is evident from the next line: "I have been wishing to confute some of your arguments, to kill time and give you something to write about, but being busy, as I have already told you, I have laid the work I had begun aside; maybe I'll finish it and send it to you sometime."

Machiavelli may have been right, but he should have learned by now that, as the Florentines would say, "Telling the truth will get you stoned"

(*Le verità attirano le sassate*). The Medici did not want a French alliance, nor did they want to hear anything that smacked of Florentine republicanism, and Niccolò's partiality to France was a reminder of the "affections" still held by many Florentines. Moreover, as we shall see later, Lorenzo de' Medici had started to express a desire to free himself from the pope's tutelage by pursuing his own pro-French foreign policy, and therefore Machiavelli's memorandum landed directly in the midst of the Medici family squabble. Niccolò had reasons to blame his misfortunes on ill luck.

Machiavelli once again had ruined his chances. Vettori, on a previous occasion, had mentioned that his brother Paolo would be returning to Florence, and that he held him in high esteem—a hint that something could be in store for him. Everyone knew of Paolo Vettori's closeness with Giuliano de' Medici, and it was possibly for Paolo that, in the first months of 1515, he wrote *I Ghiribizzi d'Ordinanza* (roughly, Thoughts on the Military), a small treatise about the reorganization of the militia. Moreover, the pope had decided to carve a state out of a region that included Parma, Piacenza, Reggio, and Modena (courtesy of the emperor, in exchange for a substantial sum). Everyone predicted that Paolo would play a large role in the new polity, and Machiavelli hoped to get something out of this turn of events.

His elation is palpable in the letter he wrote to Francesco Vettori on January 31, 1515, as he recounted all the advice he had given to Giuliano, through Paolo, about running his domain. Moreover, he was still in love, and opened his missive with a sonnet about Cupid's power. He then proceeded to joke about his correspondence with Vettori, quipping that anyone who read their letters in the future might think that they were people who were at one and the same time "grave, all bent on great things," and "light, fickle, lustful, only interested in trifles," adding, "But we only imitate nature, which is variable." (This alone tells us more about Machiavelli than any of his literary works.) But some men, evidently, did not share the same feelings and were not disposed to condone Niccolò's defects.

On February 15, Cardinal Giulio ordered Piero Ardinghelli to write to Giuliano about rumors that he intended to employ Machiavelli, stating flatly that it would not "serve his [Giuliano's] needs or ours." The cardinal thought the tale had originated with Paolo Vettori, and he urged Giuliano "not to get mixed up with Niccolò." With his memorandum Machiavelli had proved himself a major political liability, and besides, Paolo Vettori was persona non grata both with the cardinal and with Lorenzo de' Medici. It did not help that Ardinghelli happened to be a friend of Machiavelli's old enemy Jacopo Salviati.

His hopes once again dashed, Niccolò had only one card left to play. In May, Lorenzo de' Medici returned to Florence, in the company of Francesco Vettori, with plans to exercise power by freeing himself from the pope's suffocating embrace. Machiavelli jumped on the opportunity to ingratiate himself with the city's ruler and wrote an introductory letter to accompany the booklet he had written two years before, switching the dedication from Giuliano to Lorenzo. Possibly with Francesco's help (although Niccolò may have taken the initiative on his own accord, against his friend's advice and his own better judgment), he managed to secure an audience with Lorenzo to give him the *opuscolo* (pamphlet or booklet) in person.

But adverse fortune had not yet abandoned him, for when Niccolò presented his work, Lorenzo showed no interest in it, being taken instead by a brace of dogs being offered by another postulant. Machiavelli stormed out in a rage and afterward allegedly told his friends "that he was the kind of man who could make conspiracies against the prince, but all the same if [the Medici] observed his methods [in the book], they would see that conspiracies resulted from it, as if he meant to say that his book would give him his revenge." On a previous occasion Machiavelli had expressed the fear that his work might be ignored, and now, at Lady Luck's dinner table, the only things left for him to eat were sour grapes.

The piece of writing on which Machiavelli had staked his remaining chances of earning favor with the Medici would later become his most famous work, and one that would inscribe his name among the wicked for centuries to come. Oceans of ink have been spilled on *The Prince*, and thus going over it in detail once more would be superfluous. Nevertheless, given the book's fame, a few comments are warranted, and to do so one should take in consideration the following elements: (1) the genesis of the work in the context of Machiavelli's life and what he wished to accomplish with it; (2) Niccolò's character, in particular the mixture of gravitas and flippancy; (3) his faith in the experience he had acquired over the years and in his own intellectual capacities; (4) his belief that history, ancient history in particular, could provide answers for contemporary events; (5) his obsession with citizen armies; and (6) his habit of telling people what they ought to do, often in a most undiplomatic manner.

Many of the ideas found in *The Prince* were also themes appearing in correspondence between Machiavelli and Vettori during the summer of 1513 and in a hodgepodge of other sources. For instance, the question of whether it is better for a ruler to be loved or feared already appeared in the *Del Felice Progresso di Borso d'Este* written by Michele Savonarola (uncle of the more famous Girolamo) some sixty years before Machiavelli composed *The Prince*. However, while Savonarola opted for love, Niccolò preferred fear, since men are, with few exceptions, riddled with vices, promising to do everything for their leader when peril is far away, "but revolting when it is close."

By keeping historical examples in mind, a prince could avoid the pitfalls present in the exercise of power, a brutal and lonely job. There is an echo of Machiavelli's own personal experience his these words, and a reminder of how the Florentines had treated their own governors in the past. And yet, the examples he provides are so extreme or twisted that one is left wondering if Niccolò is being serious or pulling the reader's leg, to the point that some commentators have considered *The Prince* to be little more than a satire. With his emphasis on deception, Machiavelli mocks the lofty, often moralistic treatises about good state keeping. Being a Florentine, he possessed his fellow citizens' cutting and often cruel way of making fun of people and situations, and his smirk can be detected in some of the treatise's most brutal pages.

There is no doubt, however, about Niccolò being completely serious in chapters 12–14, the ones dedicated to a polity's military organization. Having one's "own arms" (*armi proprie*) had become a veritable bee in Machiavelli's bonnet, especially at a time when it appeared that the Florentine government wanted to get rid of the city's militia, so much so that under the guise of giving advice first to Giuliano and then Lorenzo de' Medici, Niccolò is really defending his own work; indeed, one may say that *The Prince* revolves around the above-mentioned chapters.

In essence, the book is a skillful and beautifully written collection of different thoughts, put together in some haste and often in contradiction with each other. For example, Machiavelli states that in order to survive, a polity needs "good laws and good arms," but he justifies in the name of political opportunism Valentino's extrajudiciary execution of Ramiro de Lorqua. Likewise, if Chapter 15 is a hymn to the goddess Fortune, in the following chapter the Christian God is very much present. *The Prince*'s unsystematic construction made it prone to misinterpretation, as proven by the endless attempts over the centuries to pull it in one direction or another according to ideology, intellect, or whim. Besides, Machiavelli's rather haughty professorial way of laying down the law, combined with a thinly disguised, schoolboyish desire to shock, was not likely to be well accepted in some quarters, and not exactly the right way to get a job—the primary reason given by Niccolò for writing the book in the first place. Machiavelli can be accused of a lot, but not of being a politician.

It would appear that copies of *The Prince* started circulating soon after its official presentation, possibly with Machiavelli's help. Sometime between 1515 and 1516, Biagio Buonaccorsi sent an example of the book "by our [*nostro*, which could stand for mutual friendship as well as common citizenship] Niccolò Machiavelli" to his friend Pandolfo Bellaci, describing it as "recently composed." Buonaccorsi went on to describe and praise the work, warning Bellacci "to be prepared to utterly defend it against those who, out of malice or envy, might desire, according to what happens these days, to rip and tear it apart."

The lack of any form of correspondence between Machiavelli and Buonaccorsi after 1512 has led some scholars to hypothesize some sort of fallout between the two. However, Buonaccorsi appears to have been among the first to receive Machiavelli's new works, as in the case of *The Art of War*, and since Biagio made a living by working as a copyist, it makes sense that "our" Niccolò would send him anything he wished to have reproduced and distributed. Buonaccorsi's caveat to Bellacci about those ready to thrash *The Prince* is a sufficient indication that this had already happened, with people starting to judge the work by concentrating on its most egregious parts.

In July 1517, the Florentine commissioner general in Arezzo, Luigi Guicciardini, received a letter from his son Niccolò, who jokingly suggested that his father behave toward local dissidents "in the same way Machiavelli, in his book *De Principatibus*, describes Iuriotto da Fermo acting when he wanted to become lord of Fermo; but even so, one could never entirely trust those who should survive." Liverotto ("Iuriotto" in the young Guicciardini's rendering) had become the ruler of his native city by massacring his whole family, and Niccolò's apparent admiration for the deed (Niccolò Guicciardini, however, being an intelligent Florentine, seems to have understood the extent of Machiavelli's cynical sense of humor in his description of the events) would for centuries be held against him.

It is more than probable that Niccolò expected neither the book's success nor the ruckus associated with it. In the winter of 1538, Machiavelli now dead for eleven years, Cardinal Reginald Pole traveled to Florence in an effort to understand the reasons behind the composition of such a godless book like *The Prince*, on which Pole blamed all the evils that had befallen England following Henry VIII's 1534 Act of Supremacy, including the persecution against those English Catholics who had opted to obey the church rather than their king, masterminded by the Lord Chancellor Thomas Cromwell—the person who had told Pole of Machiavelli's work in the first place. Pole talked to people who had known Machiavelli:

> These Florentines replied with what they said Machiavelli himself had answered when they had previously confronted him: that indeed he had observed not only his own judgment in that book, but also that of the man for whom he was writing. And since he knew him [Lorenzo de' Medici] to be of tyrannical nature, he inserted things that could not most greatly please such a nature. Nevertheless, [Machiavelli] judged, as have all of the other writers who have written concerning how to make a man into a king or a prince, and as experience teaches, that if the prince did put these things into effect, his rule would be brief. This he greatly hoped for, since inwardly he burned with hatred toward that prince for whom he wrote. Nor did he expect from that book anything other than, by writing for the tyrant the things that please a tyrant, to give him, if he could, a ruinous downfall by his own action.

These words, if they were really uttered in that way, smell as if Machiavelli had been "attempting to close the stable after the oxen have run out" (*chiudere la stalla dopo che son fuggiti i bovi*)—as goes a Florentine maxim. One of his greatest faults, in the eyes of many of *The Prince's* readers, lay in having reduced religion to a mere *instrumentum regni*, while his emphasis on man's ability to bend Fortune to his will smacked of Pelagianism (the belief that man can save himself without any need of God's grace). To the casual reader, *The Prince* appears to reduce everything to human will, even if Niccolò's thinking can be fuzzy on this matter: Moses is put on the same level as other great figures of ancient times who possessed "spiritual virtue" and luck, but at the same time Moses had been but a mere agent of God's will.

As a result, Machiavelli managed to anger nearly everyone, his disorganized thinking allowing people to pick his work apart, if for different reasons, and extrapolate from *The Prince* only the negative bits that affected them directly. As Giovanni Battista Busini put it, "the rich considered his *Prince* a manual to teach the duke [Lorenzo de' Medici] how to deprive them of their property; the poor, all their liberty. To the Savonarolans he appeared a heretic; the good considered him dishonest; the wicked thought him more wicked, or more effective, than they were; and so everyone hated him." Busini wrote this damning epitaph long after Machiavelli had died, and by then his work had gone through a number of runs in the printing press. But criticism of *The Prince* had started to mount during Machiavelli's lifetime.

Concerns about his reputation may have caused Machiavelli to accept the idea of having the philosopher Agostino Nifo rewrite his book in a sanitized form, possibly thanks to the help of Cardinal Giulio de' Medici. The revised work appeared in print in 1523 under the title *De Regnandi Perita* (On the Skill of Statecraft), curiously enough at a time when both Nifo and Machiavelli, who at last had managed to get back into the Medici's graces, were both employed by the University of Pisa. Although this may be seen as a mere coincidence, Niccolò, always rather jealous of his intellectual property, had the backing of powerful patrons who could easily have stopped Nifo's plagiarism, if that had been the case.

Overall, Nifo did a skillful job. He kept most of Machiavelli's examples and added a few of his own, but arranged them in such a way as to give the work an appearance of propriety. He also eliminated altogether some politically or religiously sensitive matters—for instance, Niccolò's admiring opinion of Cesare Borgia. Moreover, *De Regnandi Perita* appeared in Latin, thus giving it an academic aura that *The Prince* did not possess. In essence, Nifo tried to provide the "correct" way of reading *The Prince*, but since bad currencies push out good ones, this attempt would eventually fail in the face of Machiavelli's notorious work. Probably unaware of what he was doing, Machiavelli had exposed the rules of the political game, always followed in practice, but their existence seldom admitted. For Machiavelli, his attempt to get employment had produced unforeseen results, and ones he would have been happy to do without.

12

~

THE BYSTANDER'S GRIN

And the only hope for a reward
Is that all the bystanders shall grin
Speaking ill of what they saw and heard
　　　　—NICCOLÒ MACHIAVELLI, *THE*
　　　　　　　　　　　　MANDRAKE

"I have become useless to myself, my relatives, and my friends, for so has my unhappy fate decreed." Thus a very downcast Machiavelli would write on February 16, 1516, to his nephew Giovanni Vernacci, then engaging in trade in Pera (now part of Istanbul). He had written fairly regularly to Vernacci in the past two years, mostly about family business matters. At one point he had suggested that Vernacci marry one of the daughters of his cousin Lorenzo Machiavelli, "a bit lame, but nevertheless handsome, good natured, and intelligent," with the proviso that his prospective father-in-law give him 2,000 sealed florins and the possibility of opening a shop for trading wool. Now Vernacci told him that he had never received any of his uncle's letters, news that Machiavelli compared to "being stabbed with a knife." Everything seemed to conspire against him, and Machiavelli could only watch with dismay his world falling apart, while other people prospered.

A lot had changed in the previous year. Louis XII had died, but his successor, the twenty-one-year-old Francis I, showed every intention of continuing the late king's expansionist policy. The possibility of a French inroad into Italy precipitated a clash between the pope and Lorenzo de' Medici over Florence's foreign policy. Leo wanted the city to side with the Spanish and the Swiss, whereas Lorenzo, also pressured by his followers, who feared possible negative repercussions for Florentine merchants in Lyon, had shown a marked preference for an alliance with France. Things were not going well in Florence for Lorenzo. He had chosen his cousin Galeotto de' Medici to serve as deputy during his absence from the city, but Galeotto had neither the age nor the stature to fulfill such a difficult task. This, combined with a general resentment for high taxation, had created disaffection within the regime, and the Medici suffered a number of political setbacks in various matters of state. Moreover, Lorenzo's aspirations in Rome had been thwarted, and he seethed watching his uncle Giuliano becoming the head of a quasi-independent state and contracting a marriage with Philiberta of Savoy, while in the meantime, the pope had refused to raise his own allowance. Rome had become a dead end for his ambitions, and his presence in Florence was badly needed. But Lorenzo wanted to be his own boss and had been looking for a chance to claim an autonomous policy-making role.

The chance arrived when Leo ordered Florence to raise seven hundred men-at-arms to fight alongside the Spanish and the Swiss against the French. The Florentines ranted and raved but nevertheless complied with the pope's wishes. The question remained who would command these troops. According to Francesco Vettori, Giuliano de' Medici had promised the job, with a large salary, to his brother-in-law, the count of Geneva. Lorenzo, however, wishing to save the Florentines this extra burden, asked that he be given the title of captain general of the Florentine forces, though without any soldiers or pay for himself. The pope acquiesced, on condition that his nephew obtain the approval of the Council of the Seventy (now the main legislative body of the city), sure that it would be refused. The council, instead, gave Lorenzo what he sought, and at that point Leo could do nothing but entrust his nephew with an appropriate command.

Vettori's account is to a point disingenuous, given that Lorenzo had for some time been scheming to get the title, the troops, and the salary. With some maneuvering, Galeotto managed to get the balìa first, and then the Seventy, to allow the Eight of Watch to raise up to five hundred men-at-arms, and once Lorenzo returned to Florence the magistracy had no difficulty or legal preclusion in hiring Lorenzo as commander in chief. Moreover, his condotta contained the extraordinary clause forbidding the city's officers and magistrate to try and punish anyone serving under Lorenzo—a privilege reserved to the captain general and the commissioner general of the army—except in the case of high treason. Needless to say, a lot of young Florentines of good family flocked under Lorenzo's banner, attracted by the pay and judicial privileges. As luck would have it, Giuliano de' Medici, whom Leo had chosen to lead his own forces, fell ill, and the pope had no alternative but to reluctantly entrust Lorenzo with leadership of the papal army.

In August the captain general departed with his troops toward Lombardy with Francesco Vettori at his side as commissioner general. By now Leo, Giuliano, and Cardinal Giulio had become seriously worried about Lorenzo's behavior. They were old-style Medici, born and raised in the Florence of "Lorenzo the Magnificent": Although they desired to exercise control over the city, they wanted to do so according to the constitution they had known in their youth and were aghast at Lorenzo's semi-princely and nontraditional behavior, coupled with his pro-French stance. Yet, Lorenzo and his mother had reasons to fear that if the French were victorious, Florence would be at their mercy and the Medici forced to resume a life of exile.

Their analysis had some merit, since from the previous July the pope had received intelligence about Francis I having contacted the anti-Medici elements in Florence. With the specter of a revolt similar to that of 1494 looming large, it is understandable that Lorenzo, despite the pope urging him not to get obsessed with the French, should have preferred to tread with caution on the international stage. His pro-French stance thus can be seen as both an attempt to avoid the same troubles faced by his father, Piero, by catering to the Florentines' wishes, and at the same time as an effort to shape a foreign policy for Florence quite different from the one hatched in Rome. Interestingly enough, in Machiavelli's exhortation to Lorenzo in the final chapter of *The Prince*—which Niccolò probably added to the original text soon after Lorenzo had become captain general—in a somewhat oblique way the Spanish and the Swiss "barbarians" are made out to be a greater menace than the French, with Niccolò, true to style, providing advice on how to defeat both. In this way Machiavelli was expressing not only his own opinion about who Lorenzo should choose as an ally but also the desires of the Florentines at large.

Francis I had crossed the Alps through an unexpected and unprotected route, bypassing the papal-Spanish contingents in Piedmont and marching on toward Lombardy. Lorenzo had assembled his forces in Piacenza and was under pressure from both the pope and the viceroy of Naples to cross the Po River and advance on Milan, with Cardona telling him that he would hold him responsible if the city was lost. Lorenzo may have been willing to move, but Vettori told him bluntly that in this case, the Florentines would stay behind because in Florence, nobody wanted to anger the French. However, Cardona himself did not seem too keen to throw his troops into the fray, and as a result the Swiss were left alone to face the French, also having to contend with the Venetians attacking from the east.

Battle was joined on September 13 at Marignano. It was a struggle of giants, as Francesco Guicciardini would later describe it, and after two days of bitter fighting the French forced the surviving Swiss off the field. Francis entered Milan a few days later. Seeing the turn of events, Leo hurriedly agreed to discuss peace terms in person with the king of France. Machiavelli may have felt vindicated when he heard the news of Marignano, even if his military analysis had not been totally correct: The French had won because of their nearly two-to-one advantage in terms of manpower, but the Swiss had come close to success on a number of occasions during the battle; still, the pope now stood at the victor's mercy, just as Niccolò had predicted.

On his journey north toward Bologna, the place selected for his meeting with Francis, the pope stopped in Florence, where the government gave him a triumphal entry worthy of a victorious Roman general. As he passed through the temporary archway outside one of the city's gates, he was greeted with an image of his father, Lorenzo the Magnificent, underneath of which lay the inscription: "This is my beloved Son, in whom I am well pleased"—a nearly blasphemous use of the words uttered by God about Jesus in the Gospel of Matthew. Savonarola had wished Florence to become the new Jerusalem, but by comparing the Almighty with a human being, and his son with Christ, the Florentine regime had gone a bit too far in adulation.

Machiavelli has been labeled as impious, but he seems to have been in good company. We have no record of Niccolò watching the papal procession passing through Florence, however, and most likely he preferred to stay in Sant'Andrea sulking and bemoaning his fate—justified by the circumstances, perhaps, but nonetheless showing that Machiavelli may not have been ready to admit how much he had contributed to his own ill luck. Fortune, however, was about to change her attitude toward Machiavelli, bringing an end to his voluntary confinement among the "lice" of the countryside.

It is not known when Niccolò started frequenting the Rucellai Gardens, which had become the favorite meeting place for young brainy Florentines. Bernardo Rucellai had died in 1514, but his sons Giovanni and Palla and their nephew Cosimo had continued the family tradition of hosting intellectual debates on various topics. Socially and politically the Rucellai group was a mixed bag, going from the rich and aristocratic types, such as the Strozzi brothers, to people of more modest means and class, such as Machiavelli himself, and including, at least initially, moderate

Mediceans—in particular those coming from the ranks of the ottimati and advocates of a governo stretto. Although we do not know who introduced Machiavelli to the gardens, circumstantial evidence would point to Filippo and Lorenzo Strozzi.

It may seem strange that the Strozzi should have befriended Machiavelli, given the latter's reputed opposition to Filippo's marriage to Clarice de' Medici, but one may argue that at the time Niccolò had acted according to his political superiors' wishes. Besides, his brother-in-law Francesco del Nero happened to be one of Filippo's close collaborators, and both he and Machiavelli's wife, Marietta, came from families of known Medicean sympathies. It is possible that del Nero first introduced Niccolò to the Strozzi, and Filippo must have found in Machiavelli a kindred spirit of sorts, both enjoying the pleasures of life and of women. Be that as it may, Niccolò appears to have started frequenting the Rucellai Gardens sometime in the spring of 1516, for in the introduction to *The Art of War* he mentions that the dialogue making up the book took place in April of that year. For Machiavelli becoming part of the Rucellai group would prove beneficial in many ways. The intellectual talks held in the gardens stimulated his literary output, while the young Florentines who gathered there enjoyed both his writings and his company, and also saw fit to alleviate his financial problems by providing him with some small monetary relief. Machiavelli at last had found the right sort of influential people he had sought all along, and being considered a *maître à penser* boosted his ego.

Evidence of Machiavelli's influence can be found in Lodovico Alamanni's memorandums of 1516 to Lorenzo de' Medici and Alberto Pio di Carpi, Imperial ambassador to Rome. Lodovico, together with his brother Luigi, was a member of the Rucellai group and a friend and correspondent of Machiavelli, so it is not surprising to find echoes of Niccolò's thoughts in his writings. In the first document Alamanni gives Lorenzo advice on how to keep Florence in his grip, in some cases paraphrasing in a succinct manner passages of *The Prince*; in the second, he stresses the importance of a state having *armi proprie* by raising an efficient militia. At the time the question of military organization had become a hot topic among Florentine thinkers, yet not everyone agreed with Machiavelli's belief that one could re-create a militia along the lines of ancient Rome's citizen army. Francesco Guicciardini, for one, had deep misgivings about following such a model, astutely and accurately pointing out that the past could hardly be used as an example for the present, and, in any case, the passage of time always distorted and clouded historical memory.

At the time of Alamanni's memo, Lorenzo de' Medici had other things on his mind than listening to intellectual debates. In March of the same year, Giuliano de' Medici died, much to Leo's pain and displeasure. He had concentrated most of his hopes toward establishing a Medici dynasty on his brother, and now only Lorenzo remained to fulfill his ambitions. Moreover, the peace terms he had agreed upon with Francis I included the restitution of Parma and Piacenza to the emperor, and Modena and Reggio to the Este. The Medici state in northern Italy had melted away like snow in the sun, and Leo, desperate to find a permanent sovereignty for his family, turned his greedy eyes on the duchy of Urbino.

Leo had reasons to hold a grudge against the present duke, Francesco Maria della Rovere, who had systematically avoided providing the military aid requested by the pope at the time of the French invasion the previous summer. A bull stripping Francesco Maria of his title and possessions was duly prepared, and in the meantime, Leo tried to get Francis I's approval by verbally promising that he would not oppose the former's occupation of Naples upon the death of Ferdinand of Aragon. Francis did not trust the pope, but he nevertheless acquiesced to his wishes, fearing that otherwise Leo could decide to ally himself with Maximilian and become a major nuisance for the Venetians. Lorenzo de' Medici took Urbino with ease, but the Florentines were most unhappy about the whole operation, since they had been forced to foot most of the war bill. Moreover, Lorenzo and his mother soon departed for Rome, having no interest in staying in Florence now that Giuliano had died and Lorenzo had acquired his own state and the title of duke of Urbino.

The Florentines would have breathed a sigh of relief to see the pair go—Alfonsina Orsini, in particular, had made herself very unpopular for her high-handed attitude—had Lorenzo shown greater acumen in choosing his deputy. Unfortunately his choice fell on Goro Gheri, a decision that the Florentines found deeply insulting, since Gheri came from the subject city of Pistoia and displayed no tact whatsoever in dealing with those he had been sent to govern. He disliked and distrusted the Florentine patriciate, being more or less cordially hated in return. To make things worse, Alfonsina continued from Rome to meddle with Florentine politics, causing even greater resentment among the city's elite against the Medici's rule. However, with the memory of the Republic still fresh in their minds, the ottimati could do little except seethe and attempt to block, in the voting chambers, some of Gheri's most egregious attempts to run the show alone, but otherwise opt for the devil they knew rather than the one (Alfonsina) they had known.

Lorenzo would return to Florence, but only to collect money to finance another war. After losing his duchy, Francesco Maria della Rovere had sought refuge with his father-in-law, the Marquis of Mantua, and had been actively working to reclaim his former domain with the backing of the Venetians and Ferrara. In mid-January 1517 he launched his campaign against Lorenzo, quickly conquering the whole of Urbino except for the nearly impregnable fortress of San Leo. The pope needed money to help his nephew, since Francis I, seeing that Leo had not returned Modena and Reggio, declined to intervene. As luck would have it, in April a conspiracy to murder the pope was uncovered in Rome. Among the plotters figured a number of cardinals, including Francesco Soderini. The pope could not have hoped for a better opportunity to raise cash, not only by extorting colossal fines from the guilty prelates to buy his pardon, but also through the creation of new cardinals in exchange for huge sums.

Lorenzo, however, had already started to milk Florence dry in January, and further taxation approved by the regime in the spring emptied the Florentines' purses even more. Eventually the Medici weathered the storm, as Francesco Maria did not have enough funds to continue the war, and Venice and Ferrara refrained from supporting him in the field. But for Leo and Lorenzo the cost of the conflict had been colossal both financially and politically. In Florence, anger against the Medici was but thinly concealed, and many were just waiting for Francis's next descent into Italy in the hope of seeing a repeat of what had been done in 1494. However, at this point the Medici, opting for an if-you-can't-lick-'em-join-'em policy, played their trump card, proposing a French bride for Lorenzo. With this move, the pope not only left his opponents in Florence orphaned of their potential patron, but also reassured the Florentine business community that their interests in France would be safeguarded from now on. Francis agreed, and on May 2, 1518, Lorenzo wedded at the castle of Amboise Madeline de La Tour d'Auvergne, rich and connected by blood with the French royal family. In a stroke of ability worthy of his father, Leo had managed to disarm both Francis and the Florentine anti-Medici.

There is no doubt that Florence's political situation was discussed in the Rucellai Gardens. Machiavelli's original contribution to the debate can be found in his unfinished satirical poem "L'Asino" (The Jackass), a parody of both Dante Alighieri's *Divine Comedy* and Lucius Apuleius's *Metamorphoses*. Machiavelli imagines his descent into Hell in the company of a woman—with whom he manages to sleep—where he beholds a number of beasts, each representing a well-known public figure. The poem is filled with inside jokes that would have been easily understandable by his companions in the gardens. He certainly intended to read the composition to his friends, as witnessed by his letter of December 17, 1517, to Lodovico Alamanni, in which he grumbles about Ludovico Ariosto forgetting to include him among Italy's poets in his *Orlando Furioso*. Machiavelli notes: "And what he has done in his *Orlando*, I shall not do in my *Jackass*."

Machiavelli probably knew Ariosto in person, since he tells Alamanni: "Should he [Ariosto] be there, give him my regards," and the lighthearted treatment of the poet displays humor rather than resentment.* In any

---

* In the same letter Machiavelli talks about a trip to Flanders, or at least to Venice for Carnival, that he and his friends of the Rucellai Gardens had been planning. The reason for choosing Flanders is one of the many tantalizing mysteries of Niccolò's life.

case, Niccolò never had a chance to hit back, as his poem stops after eight chapters and before the protagonist changes, Apuleius style, into a donkey. The reasons for this interruption are unknown, but most likely have to do with Machiavelli shifting his attention to other writings nearer to his heart.

Around the time he composed *The Prince*, Niccolò had started working on another book on the nature of Republics. He interrupted the writing various times—fatigue, disappointment, and love getting in the way—until the conversations in the gardens stimulated him to resume the task. Significantly, he dedicated the finished manuscript of *The Discourses on the First Ten Books of Titus Livius* (*Discorsi sopra la prima deca di Tito Livio* or *The Discourses* for short) to his conversation partners Zanobi Buondelmonti and Cosimo Rucellai, and his satisfaction in finding a qualified audience after years of slights is evident in the introduction:

> Believe me, that in one thing only I am satisfied, namely, that while knowing that I may have made mistakes in many matters, I have not erred at least in choosing you before all others as the dedicatees of these Discourses. By doing so I believe to be showing a little gratitude for the kindness received, and at the same time departing from the trite habit of many authors to bestow their work on some ruler, whom they praise as possessor of every virtue, blinded as they are by ambition and avarice, while they should instead lambast him for all his vices. Thus, to avoid this mistake I have not chosen rulers, but instead those who for their infinite merits would deserve to be such; not those with the power to load me with titles, honors and riches, but those who would do the same if they could. For men with the right judgment esteem those who are generous, rather than the ones who have that potential; and likewise the people who know how to run a polity, instead of those who don't.

Much has been written on *The Discourses*, and so it is not necessary to examine the work in detail. In essence, Machiavelli once again looked back to the golden past of an imaginary Roman Republic to compare it with the leaden situation in Florence. In his work Niccolò hammers on familiar themes: the need for a militia, good laws, and civic virtue. Otherwise, the book is unsystematically organized, being, like *The Prince*, a collection of thoughts rather than an organic whole, the result of the various conversations held in the gardens. Niccolò himself admitted as much when in the dedication he told Buondelmonti and Rucellai, "You have forced me to write what otherwise I alone would not have written." In *The Discourses* Machiavelli shows his unlimited trust in ancient history, convinced that it is there that one may find every remedy for political maladies.

In doing so, he often twists historical examples to prove his thesis, and Francesco Guicciardini had a field day tearing *The Discourses* apart by stressing these incongruities. Machiavelli, he intimated, failed to understand how the past seldom provides useful examples for a completely different political and psychological environment. Moreover, the book reflected the current Florentine situation rather than accurately describing ancient Rome, as Machiavelli's concept of "liberty," lined with the necessary historical and humanistic trappings, was closely tied to the institutions under which he had served at a time when a large section of Florence had enjoyed *honore et utile*. Lorenzo de' Medici's quasi-despotic rule had alienated many Florentines, and the intellectual young toffs frequenting the Rucellai Gardens had started to look back with nostalgia at the days of the Republic, when the Florentines, despite the defects of their political system, had handled their own affairs. In this sense, in *The Discourses* Machiavelli was singing to the choir.

The gardens proved a rich stimulus for Niccolò's literary output. Between 1516 and 1520, he produced not only *The Discourses*, *Belfagor*, and an incomplete version of the second part of his *Decennali*, but also one of the greatest theatrical masterpieces of all times, *The Mandrake*. Machiavelli had long been interested in theater, as witnessed by his lost *Maschere*, and around 1517 had translated Terence's play *Andria* (*The Woman from Andros*), updating it with the use of current-day bawdy language and references to contemporary events easily understandable for a Florentine audience. *The Mandrake*, while relying on the structure and *topoi* typical of ancient Greek and Roman theater, is entirely Niccolò's creation and possibly the best example of his attitude toward life.

The story is set in Florence in around 1504 and figures a young man, Callimaco Guadagni, just back from France (the Guadagni, incidentally, were important bankers in Lyon) to seek the love of a local beauty, the childless Lucrezia, married to a suspicious, crusty, miserly, haughty doctor-at-law by the name of Nicia Calfucci. To fulfill his desire, Callimaco, with the help of the parasite Ligurio, dresses up as a medical doctor and convinces Nicia that in order to have children his wife needs to sleep with someone after she has drunk an infusion of mandrake root. There is only one unfortunate snag, namely, that after she takes the concoction the first person with whom she has sex will die soon thereafter; but Callimaco quickly comes up with a plan: They should kidnap a young loafer and make him drink the potion before putting him in Lucrezia's bed. After some hesitation Nicia agrees, and Lucrezia also acquiesces, bending to her mother's pressure and the honeyed arguments of the corrupt Fra Timoteo. The latter, however, is forced to join the kidnapping gang in disguise, since Callimaco has in the meantime dressed up as the given victim. Thanks to this ruse, he manages to sleep with Lucrezia, who in turn, miffed by all the stupidity, selfishness, and hypocrisy surrounding her, promises him eternal love.

The protagonists of the play are types and at the same time typically Florentine. People like Nicia, moderately affluent, close-minded, and with an exaggerated sense of their importance, could be seen every day walking the streets of Florence, and so could scoundrels like Fra Timoteo be found in the city's convents and monasteries. In reality, the play contains not one positive character, for even Lucrezia falls short of exercising the virtue her name implies: The historical Lucrece, wife of Lucius Tarquinius Collatinus, had committed suicide after being raped by Sextus Tarquinius, and wickedly, Machiavelli has Fra Timoteo convince Lucrezia to commit adultery by stating that "it is the will that sins, not the body," therefore twisting the words used by Collatinus to console his violated wife: "The body sins, not the mind."

Being an avid and wide-ranging reader, it is not surprising to find that Niccolò used references from a number of sources, ancient and more recent, plus elements of everyday life that he had witnessed or gossiped about. The picture that emerges is not different from that found in *The Prince*, but this time with a negative slant. Far from being the praise of infidelity and dissimulation, *The Mandrake* is a bitter indictment against the Florentines' lack of *virtus*, and at the same time a denunciation of the narrow-mindedness, verging on gullibility, that had reduced them to their present state. Nicia is not just a Florentine; he is Florence itself.

It is unclear when or where the first production of *The Mandrake* took place. The original manuscript has the date 1519, but since in Florence the year started on March 25, the first three months of 1520 should be included. It is possible that the staging took place during the Carnival of 1520, but in any case, it turned out a success. *The Mandrake* would enjoy numerous productions during Machiavelli's lifetime, being put to print soon after, and parts of it were set to music in 1525. Its immediate fame caused the pope himself to bring the play to Rome for his own entertainment, and a skeptic individual like Leo X, who had labeled the beginning of the Protestant Reformation as "monkish squabbles," most likely rolled with laughter at the depiction of Fra Timoteo. On April 26 of that year, Battista della Palla, a member of the Rucellai group, wrote to Machiavelli that he had found Leo "very well disposed toward you," adding that the pontiff was looking forward to watching the play. Della Palla also added that he and his friends were trying to convince Leo and Cardinal Giulio to entrust Niccolò with some sort of literary undertaking "or other."

The "other" had already started to come about. In the spring of 1518, Machiavelli had traveled to Genoa to recover the goods of a group of Florentine merchants from a bankruptcy; it did not involve much of a commission, but at least it allowed him to ride somewhere different from Sant'Andrea in Percussina and also make a bit of money. Carlo Strozzi, one of the businessmen involved, was a kinsman and protégé of Filippo Strozzi, and it is possible that the latter got Machiavelli the job in the first place. Given his closeness not only to Lorenzo de' Medici but also the pope and Cardinal Giulio, Filippo could help Machiavelli, bypassing the omnipresent Goro Gheri. Apparently Gheri even approved sending Machiavelli to Lucca on a minor diplomatic mission. The wheel of Fortune had slowly started to turn in Niccolò's favor, while for others it had started to take a reverse direction.

On May 4, 1519, Lorenzo de' Medici died, three weeks after the birth of his daughter Caterina, the future queen of France, and the passing of his wife due to postpartum infection. There is some inconclusive evidence that in the last year of his life he tried unsuccessfully to get the pope to make him prince of Florence, but in any case, he had seen his pro-French policy thwarted by those closest to Leo—in particular Jacopo Salviati and his wife, who detested Lorenzo and his mother. When in January 1519 the news arrived of Emperor Maximilian's death, Lorenzo had wanted the pope to back Francis I's candidacy to the Imperial throne, but instead Leo opted to back Charles of Habsburg, Maximilian's grandson, who in 1516 had succeeded his other grandfather, Ferdinand of Aragon, as king of Spain.

Charles was duly elected with the financial help of German bankers, placing France between the thongs of Spain and the empire. Leo had been right in his ultimate political choice, for Charles V (as he had become) knew perfectly well how much the Florentines resented the Medici regime. Defeated and out of favor, during his last illness Lorenzo refused the assistance of doctors, wanting at his bedside only his two close friends, Filippo Strozzi and Francesco Vettori. He had fallen out with his mother, the possessive Alfonsina, who was rabidly jealous of her daughter-in-law; he also quarrelled with Cardinal Giulio, who had come to Florence to relieve his ailing cousin of the city's leadership. When the news of Lorenzo's death became public, few mourned his passing. The man whom Machiavelli had once hailed as Italy's savior had not even managed to salvage the respect of those he had been sent to govern.

13

~

A HISTORY OF LIES

For some time I have never been saying what I
believe, nor do I ever believe what I say; and if
it happens that I should utter the truth, I
cover it with so many lies that it is difficult to
find it.
—NICCOLÒ MACHIAVELLI TO
FRANCESCO GUICCIARDINI

"I am pleased to know that you have taken Machiavelli to the Medici's
home, for he is someone who will go a long way when he acquires
a bit of the master's trust," wrote Filippo Strozzi to his brother Lorenzo
on March 17, 1520. The Strozzi understood that Niccolò's best chances
lay in Cardinal Giulio's patronage. The prelate had taken over the de facto
rule of Florence after the death of Lorenzo de' Medici, inheriting a very
fractured and sullen city. At least the death of Alfonsina Orsini in February 1520 removed one source of contention, and it may be more than
coincidental that Machiavelli's introduction to Cardinal Giulio took
place the following month.

Unfortunately, the nature of the conversation between the two is unknown, but something in Niccolò must have struck Giulio, who soon after the meeting asked Machiavelli to write an opinion for him on how to reform the Florentine state, alleging it to be the pope's wish. By mentality and education the cardinal belonged to the fifteenth rather than the sixteenth century, and, like his cousin Leo, was a believer in the Florentine constitution as it had been before 1494. Indeed, by looking back at Florence's "golden age" of their youth, the two Medici and those closest to them had imbued the political settlement under Lorenzo the Magnificent with a nearly mythical aura—in the same way the Republicans had for the Savonarolan constitution. In 1512, the Medici had not attempted something new, but only revived those institutions that in their eyes had worked so well in the past. Yet, nobody could fail to notice the substantial failure of this archaeological experiment, and it makes sense that someone as intelligent as Cardinal Giulio would look about to find a way to combine political stability with Medici leadership.

The document that Machiavelli produced is a curious mixture of republicanism and princely rule, seemingly a rather clumsy attempt to please everyone. Niccolò started by saying that Florence's main problem was that it could not be called either a republic or a principate. He went on to recount the city's political history from the end of the fourteenth century, blaming its maladies on the fact that only a few individuals were the policymakers, "while the people did not have any part in it." Only the wars against the visconti of Milan, and later, the governing abilities of Cosimo de' Medici and Lorenzo the Magnificent, had allowed this situation to continue, although the Medici had forced their rule on the city through parliaments and proscriptions. However, the Republic had not done much better, since the settlement of 1494 had dissatisfied many, and the gonfalonier, in office for life, had at one and the same time too much power and too little.

Machiavelli argued that Florence could not go back to the way it was preceding the Medici's eviction. The international situation had changed, for one thing, and the Medici themselves had gone from being the first citizens of a medium-sized Italian city to being rulers of a state that played an important role throughout Europe. Nor was the *governo largo* the answer, if it meant simply enlarging the legislative body. Niccolò then went to the core of the argument. Every polity had three types of citizens—great, middle, and lower—and all of these needed to be satisfied. First, Machiavelli argued, Florence needed to abolish the Priorate and other senior magistracies and in their place create a body of sixty-four citizens selected from the major and minor guilds with the same ratio as the present-day Priorate (three-fourths being from the major guilds, and the rest from the minor ones). This body would do the work of the Signoria and the pratiche and be headed by a gonfalonier elected either for life or for two or three years. Similarly, the various councils had to go, to be replaced by a new body of two hundred citizens, also from the upper and middle political classes. For the small businessmen and artisans, Niccolò proposed the re-creation of the Great Council, which would have the power to elect all the city magistrates except for the gonfalonier, the sixty-four, the two hundred, and the Eight of Watch, the choice for these being reserved to the pope and Cardinal Giulio.

The document would seem to be a veritable political pie in the sky, and one is left wondering whether Machiavelli really ever considered his scheme to be a feasible solution to the city's problems. Clearly he was trying to keep a balance between the Mediceans, his friends at the Rucellai Gardens—who were by now ever more critical of the city's regime—and his own classical-minded republicanism. Sometime later, Alessandro de' Pazzi would call Niccolò's proposal "unusual and eccentric for this city"; yet Pazzi's own plan for reform in many ways reflected Machiavelli's, with the primary difference being that he foresaw the Medici as constitutional heads of state and the Great Council's competences limited to the election of lesser magistracies. It should be noted, however, that some parts of Niccolò's proposal, such as an assembly of two hundred people, would eventually be incorporated into the constitutional changes of 1532, although by then historical events had buried the Great Council forever.

Both the pope and Cardinal Giulio refrained from implementing any sort of reform, possibly for reasons of political conservatism. But this time Machiavelli did not suffer the consequences of his actions; indeed, the cardinal, while ignoring his political suggestions, had come to recognize Niccolò's talents and decided to put them to use—albeit with all the necessary prudence. Michele Guinigi of Lucca had debts with some Florentine citizens worth 1,600 florins but had refused to pay back the money with the excuse that his patrimony had been entailed to his children. Machiavelli duly received the assignment to go to Lucca and convince that government to allow an arbitration on the matter. The commission had evidently been given to Niccolò at Giulio's wish, and the cardinal used Machiavelli for some extra political work while he was in Lucca.

On July 20, Giulio wrote to him in cordial terms, addressing Machiavelli with "Most respectable gentleman and my dearest friend," asking him to request the local authorities to banish from their territory three Sicilians, who were once students in Pisa, since they had been thrown out of the university there but had been harassing their former colleagues. "Be prudent and thoroughly informed about everything," added Giulio, "but we do not need to give you further instructions since we know you'll do the job with all the necessary diligence and care." Machiavelli must have felt thoroughly satisfied, especially when, after months of negotiations, he convinced the local government to grant the requested arbitration. He also managed to put together some intelligence notes, not always precise, about the polity itself, the *Sommario delle Cose della Città di Lucca* (Notes on Lucca's Affairs), laced with his usual comments about well-ordered republics. Lucca, in essence, had some strong points compared to Florence, such as a better judicial system, as well as some weak ones—for instance, the fact that a lot of those in government were not qualified for the job—and Niccolò used the examples of ancient Rome and modern-day Venice to make his point.

More important, during his stay in the city Machiavelli had the time to write a short biography of one of the former lords of Lucca, the celebrated Castruccio Castracani. As a source he used the work in Latin *Cas-*

trucci Antelminelli Vita by Niccolò Tegrini, reelaborated according to templates found in the works of certain classical authors. The parallels between Machiavelli's work and Diodorus Siculus's biographical narrative of Agathocles, once tyrant of Syracuse, are unmistakable; moreover, he attributed to Castracani sayings that instead could be found in Plutarch and Diogenes Laertius. The friends to whom he sent the book noticed the latter immediately, while praising Machiavelli's effort otherwise. Niccolò's *Vita di Castruccio Castracani*, however, is hardly history, being instead a largely fictional biography with a political angle.

For Machiavelli, Castruccio was an example of the model ruler, and in some ways the *Vita* is a spinoff of *The Prince*. Castracani, according to Machiavelli, used deception against his enemies: "He never won by force what he could win by deceit; for he used to say that victory brought glory, not the way in which it was obtained." The book is at the same time a hymn to Fortune and to Machiavelli's military ideas: Castracani won against the Florentines because he preferred infantry to cavalry—a nice example of Niccolò's taste for historical anachronisms. Putting together the *Vita* and Machiavelli's memorandum to Cardinal Giulio, one is left wondering what Machiavelli really believed to be the best political system: a republic, or a monarchy of sorts?

Given the many similarities existing between Castracani's biography and *The Prince*, the simplest answer to this riddle is that the *Vita* is an attempt to rewrite and tone down the most extreme elements of *The Prince*: Castracani is presented as a ruthless individual, yet he is "generous with his friends, ferocious with his enemies, just with his subjects, and disloyal with all others." Here realpolitik and nobility go hand in hand, and for the same reason in the biography Niccolò even managed to find something nice to say about the adulators he had so thoroughly condemned earlier on—one may rightly suspect that Machiavelli had learned through bitter experience that sucking up to the powerful could be more rewarding than antagonizing them. Nifo a few years later may have attempted to make *The Prince* more palatable to the educated classes, but with the *Vita* Machiavelli was trying to do the same thing.

Be that as it may, the biography of Castracani was favorably received by Machiavelli's friends and established his reputation as a historian in Medici circles. On November 17, Filippo de' Nerli, one of the Rucellai Garden chums, wrote to Niccolò about a treatise on the life of Alexander the Great composed by an "imbecile" (*nuovo pesce*) for Lucrezia Salviati. It had not met with either the lady's or Nerli's favor, and Filippo asked Machiavelli to tart the work up, "adding certain parts according to her desires, as you see fit." Lucrezia had very high standards, having been taught to read and write by the great humanist Angelo Poliziano, and therefore knew her classical authors. Incidentally, Cardinal Giovanni Salviati, her son, also frequented the gardens, and he apparently had helped to soften the Salviati's hostility toward Machiavelli. Nerli also begged his friend to get Zanobi Buondelmonti to send him a copy of Niccolò's new book *De re Militari*, since Cardinal Giulio had been wanting to read it and otherwise would "hold me to be a liar."

The book was none other than *The Art of War*, which Machiavelli had finished writing sometime that summer, since Biagio Buonaccorsi already had a copy in his possession by the beginning of September. To compile it Niccolò used the works of the classical authors Vegetius, Frontinus, Polybius, and Livy, as well as the more recent *De re Militari* by Roberto Valturio, and indeed he appears to have drawn quite a bit from the latter source. The work is constructed as an imaginary dialogue held in the Rucellai Gardens in the summer of 1516 between the renowned captain Fabrizio Colonna and a few of Niccolò's friends. Again, it is a contradictory piece of work, given that Machiavelli imagines the condottiere, Colonna, defending the idea of a civic militia and the value of ancient methods of warfare as opposed to the modern ones. Colonna also swings from one extreme to the other, defending his own trade as a mercenary commander in some passages and exalting citizen armies in others.

Speculation has been rife about why Machiavelli decided to make Fabrizio the main interlocutor in the dialogue, with some people finding rather elaborate solutions to what could be a simple problem. Colonna may in fact have met with the Rucellai group when in Florence during the summer of 1516; besides, he had the reputation of being one of the foremost military leaders in Italy and at one time Piero Soderini's candidate as Florence's captain general. He also had the advantage of having died in March 1520, and so could not give Machiavelli the lie. By choosing Colonna, Niccolò simply used a person with a lot of martial cache who was not in a position to contradict him. Yet there is another factor worthy of consideration, one that goes beyond the *Art of War*'s merits or shortcomings.

The book itself demonstrates Machiavelli's ignorance about military matters, despite his experience in administrating soldiers. He never witnessed a battle in person and had only limited experience in obsidional operations. The protracted siege of Pisa was hardly enough to make him an expert. What he knew about warfare derived from his readings and conversations with professional soldiers. As a result, he had some pretty fuzzy ideas about the use of artillery and firearms in general, and his obsession with antiquity brought him to favor some drill and tactical schemes of dubious value. That people considered Machiavelli an armchair strategist is evident from a story recounted·by the Dominican friar Matteo Bandello about an incident that had occurred in 1526 when Niccolò was with the army of the League of Cognac. The renowned commander Giovanni de' Medici, the son of Caterina Sforza and every bit a chip off his mother's block, having discussed military affairs with Niccolò, offered him—with that evil Florentine sense of humor—his own company to drill according to what he had written in *The Art of War*. Bandello, who happened to be present, thus recounted the incident to Giovanni himself:

> Messer Niccolò that day kept us occupied for more than two hours in the sun to organize three thousand infantrymen in the way he had described, and never managed to accomplish anything. . . . Seeing that Messer Niccolò had no intention of stopping any time soon, you said to me: "Bandello, I shall get all of us out of this mess so that we may have lunch." So you told Messer Niccolò to step

aside and let you handle the situation, and in a twinkling, with the help of the drummers, you maneuvered those troops in various ways and manners, provoking the admiration of all those who witnessed it. You then asked me to eat with you and also invited Machiavelli. After we had finished, you requested Messer Niccolò to entertain us with one of his amusing stories. Being an urbane and polite man he agreed to recount a pleasant tale that you enjoyed quite a bit, and then asked me to write it down.

Though some have doubted the authenticity of Bandello's account (failing to provide evidence to back their claim), nonetheless it is *se non vero, ben trovato* ("if not true, well thought"), for it gives us the measure of Machiavelli's reputation with his contemporaries as an abstract theorist also known for his great company. To be fair, Niccolò did not possess a crystal ball allowing him to see the future, and many people during that period were trying to find workable formulas for warfare during a time of rapid evolution. Indeed, quite a number of treatises had been written on the topic starting in the second half of the fifteenth century. Machiavelli was simply inserting himself in an established editorial market, and that *The Art of War* was put to print in 1521 is testimony to the public's interest in the subject.

The book got a warm reception, at least from Machiavelli's friends. Cardinal Giovanni Salviati praised the work's originality and the way that it combined ancient wisdom with modern knowledge, adding that the type of military described by Niccolò would make an army invincible. Salviati's enthusiasm may have been motivated by courtesy, rather than conviction, but there is no doubt that military affairs were very much on everybody's agenda. The Pisa war had helped Florence to develop its own military tradition, which received an added boost during the time of Lorenzo de' Medici's expedition in northern Italy and against Urbino. Quite a number of Florentines had undertaken a career in the military, and the aforementioned company of Giovanni de' Medici would include more than a few of his fellow citizens. Thus, Machiavelli's *Art of War* should be seen not just as a treatise on warfare, but an attempt to establish an effective civil-military relationship within Florence itself: Professional soldiers could be acceptable, provided they possessed the necessary civic sense of duty. Seen from this angle, the choice of the mercenary captain Colonna as the advocate of a citizen army makes perfect sense, even if Niccolò had to fictionalize Fabrizio's character in order to do so.

Niccolò's foray into history paid dividends. His friends encouraged him to continue on the same track and had already taken the necessary steps with Cardinal Giulio to allow him to do so. Zanobi Buondelmonti wrote to Machiavelli in Lucca saying that they needed to talk about "that project of ours you know about." When he returned to Florence in the first half of September, he probably found a rather welcome surprise: the proposal that he write the history of Florence, a work commissioned by the University of Pisa, where his brother-in-law Francesco del Nero happened to be the *provveditore*.

Machiavelli evidently had high hopes that, together with the prestige that this commission carried, he would receive adequate financial rewards for his work. Sometime later he wrote to del Nero setting down his conditions: a fixed number of years with a determined salary, covering a time period chosen at his discretion, and permission to write in Italian or Latin as he should see fit. Poor Niccolò once again saw his hopes dashed, if only partially: The university would employ him for one year, with the possible extension of another one, and pay him one hundred florins *di studio*—a debased account currency worth a little more than half the value of the broad florin. Yet it was a job, and Machiavelli now could breathe a bit.

The problem, of course, was that Niccolò could not write as freely as he would have liked. He had to be especially careful when describing the previous century of Florentine history, since this had coincided with the Medici's rise to power. It was not easy to keep a balance between factual accuracy and the necessary glossing over of unpalatable facts. Quite often he found himself in a quandary, and on August 30, 1524, he wrote to

Francesco Guicciardini, whose diplomatic ability he had come to respect: "I'm in the country busy writing the history, and I would pay ten *soldi*, I dare not say more, for you to be here so I could show you where I've got to. For having to deal with a few facts, I would like to have your opinion if I'm being offensive by exalting or diminishing certain things. In any case I shall go on meditating, and find a way so that I may tell the truth without insulting anyone."

A very laudable desire, no doubt; unfortunately, as became apparent when he was writing Castracani's biography, Machiavelli had the tendency to treat historical facts in a rather cavalier fashion, twisting and modifying them as it suited him best. Among his sources figured the solid works of Flavius Blondus and Leonardo Bruni, but he would unfairly berate the latter, as well as Poggio Bracciolini, for not adequately covering the "civil discords" that had characterized Florence over the years, "either because they considered them unworthy of being recorded, or because they feared offending the descendants of those participants who could be damaged by these events being recalled. And these two reasons (with due respect to their memory) I consider unworthy of great people." With this attempt at character assassination Machiavelli not only was trying to belittle other people's work but also hiding the fact that, in essence, his *Florentine Histories* is a skillful piece of pro-Medici propaganda. Niccolò, of course, justified his attitude by considering history as ancillary to politics (and in this case, also in the service of his own interests), with factual truth becoming an expendable commodity. This attitude would later provoke an irate comment from the historian Scipione Ammirato:

> [Machiavelli] mixes up the years, changes names, twists facts, muddles the causes, adds, removes, reduces and in an unbridled manner does everything according to his imagination, or without respect for any rule. And what's more irritating, in many cases he appears to do so on purpose, either because mistaken or ignorant about the reality of events; perhaps for the sake of a better and less

arid style of writing. . . . As if one should adapt facts to style and
not the other way round.

Ammirato had gotten it right on two accounts: *Florentine Histories* is
a totally unreliable and fraudulent piece of work, yet brilliantly constructed and written. Some of the most notorious cases of Machiavelli's
fact-twisting regard his treatment of professional soldiers as disloyal, devious, useless, and cowardly people, which he attempts to prove by reference to a number of fifteenth-century battles: Zagonara (1425), where
only three people died because they drowned in the mud; Anghiari
(1440), where just one was killed, trampled by the horses; and La Molinella (1467), which had no fatalities at all. (In reality, contemporary
accounts of these encounters, which Niccolò certainly knew, gave a
rather different and higher casualty rate.) Machiavelli had never digested
the licking taken by the Florentine militia at Prato, and he now used the
pen to get his revenge against mercenaries, under the guise, once more,
of exalting those civic duties that allowed the creation of citizen armies.
At La Molinella, in fact, there were a lot of fatalities, but they had been
caused by field artillery, and admitting this would have undermined what
Niccolò had said about guns in *The Art of War*.

That said, there is no doubt that Machiavelli often managed to brilliantly capture the atmosphere and emotions surrounding the events he
described. A good example of this is the depiction of the fate of Luca
Pitti, a top Medici partisan until his involvement in the conspiracy of
1466. Machiavelli, of course, knew very well what it meant to fall from
power and thus could relate all too well to Pitti's condition:

> One could see in his houses the greatest solitude, where once many
> citizens had gathered. In the street his friends and relatives feared
> not just to accompany, but even to greet him, since some had lost
> their honorable position, some their property, and all were under
> the threat of the authorities. The proud edifices he had started were
> abandoned by the builders, the favors he had formerly received
> turned into insults, the honors into shame. Thus many who had

given him expensive things in return for some favor received now demanded it back as if they had been loaned; others who had praised him to the heavens now berated him as an ungrateful and violent individual.

It took Niccolò some years to write the *Histories*, and the work stops in 1492 with the death of Lorenzo the Magnificent. From some fragments found among his papers, including excerpts from chancery documents, we can assume that at one time he intended to continue the narrative up to at least the return of the Medici in 1512, but significantly, and despite an increase in salary, he dragged his heels in completing the work: Dealing with the Florentine Republic could have led him into a historical and political minefield, potentially very damaging for his reputation and his standing with his Medici patrons. He had already had to perform logical somersaults to explain the Medici's system of governance after 1434, something he felt compelled to justify to the young Donato Giannotti, who later would make a name for himself as an advocate of the Republican system:

> Donato, I cannot write this history from the time that Cosimo [de' Medici] came to power until the death of Lorenzo [the Magnificent] as I would if completely free from all restraints. The actions shall be truthful and I shall not leave out anything, only avoid discussing the general causes of what happened. Thus I shall describe the events surrounding Cosimo's becoming the city's leader, but not the way and the means such greatness was achieved. And those who wish to understand this should be careful what I shall put in the mouth of his [Cosimo's] adversaries, for what I do not wish to say myself I'll get his enemies to say.

We can speculate about whether Giannotti was bragging, trying to protect his friend's memory among Florentine Republicans (Machiavelli being dead when Donato penned this testimony), or Machiavelli had once again acted disingenuously. One should not be surprised if it was the latter: Niccolò had struggled for long enough to regain some *honore et utile*, and he had no intention of forsaking them now.

Machiavelli made steady if slow progress in winning the Medici's favor. On May 11, 1521, he received an unusual commission from the Otto di Pratica: to go to the chapter general of the Friars Minor (Franciscans) in Carpi, near Modena, and attempt to obtain their agreement to a proposal to group the friars in the Florentine territory into a separate administrative province, ostensibly because in this way their behavior and morality could be kept under better surveillance. The operation had the backing of both the Signoria and Cardinal Giulio, who evidently wished to keep a potential hotbed of anti-Medici sentiment under control. A few days later Niccolò received another commission as well, this one from the Wool Guild in Florence, asking him to find a preacher for the cathedral, preferably one Giovanni Gualberto, known as *il Rovaio*: a term used to denote the Tramontane wind.

Machiavelli could well have considered the irony of being given such a task, and not just because of his well-known dislike for friars in general: In Florence, "to kick the *rovaio*" meant being hanged. The comedic element, however, was not lost on the papal governor of Modena, Francesco Guicciardini. He and Machiavelli had known each other for a long time, although apparently with little intimacy, living as they had next door to each other in Florence. But everyone knew about Niccolò's anticlerical attitude, and in a letter of May 17 Guicciardini commented that giving him the job of finding a preacher equaled asking Pachierotto and Ser Sano—two notorious sodomites—to seek a good and gracious wife for a friend. He also warned Niccolò about thinking of his soul at his age, "because you've always lived in the opposite way, people would think that it would be due to senility rather than conversion," and noted that he faced two perils: first, that consorting with the friars could turn him into a hypocrite; and second, that, since the air of Carpi made people into liars, "if by chance you should lodge with one of the citizens your case would be beyond hope."

An evidently amused Machiavelli answered the same day. "I was on the crapper when your messenger arrived," he started, "meditating about the preacher I would choose for Florence." He went on to state that "in truth, I think the opposite of my fellow citizens: They would like a preacher that could teach them the way to heaven; I instead one that would send them to the Devil." He thought that, given the times, the right person would have to be crazier than Ponzo, more cunning than Savonarola, and a hypocrite greater than brother Alberto, "so that what we have experimented with in many friars we could find in one," and so learn that the best way to reach Heaven would be "to learn about the road to Hell and avoid it." Evil friars enjoyed much credit, but a good one, "who spoke the truth and not falsehoods, following Saint Francis's footsteps," he said, would enjoy more.

Machiavelli disliked hypocrisy in men of religion, yet was quite prepared to recognize his own shortcomings in this field: "These friars say that when one is confirmed in a state of grace the Devil has no power to tempt him. Thus I do not fear they will make me into a hypocrite, for I believe nobody can teach me anything in this matter." As for the citizens of Carpi, he could beat them all at the lying game, since "I have been a doctor in that field for quite some time." In this vein he asked a favor of Guicciardini: In order to enhance his reputation among his hosts, could Francesco please send letters in abundance? When the messenger had arrived with Guicciardini's missives, everyone in the house who knew they had come would gape in surprise, while Machiavelli could enjoy dishing out a stream of utterly invented information.

Guicciardini was happy to oblige; for although he could be cold and calculating, he shared with Niccolò a very Florentine taste for practical jokes. He immediately wrote to Sigismondo Santi, Machiavelli's host and secretary to the local ruler, Alberto Pio, describing Niccolò as a "very special person." Santi, evidently somewhat of a snob, replied eagerly, asking for further details, but Guicciardini avoided answering to keep him salivating. However, he warned Machiavelli to exploit the situation as much as possible for his own gain, turning on its head a biblical quotation: "You'll not always have the poor with you." He also, ironically, exhorted Niccolò to stir dissent among the friars, or at least plant some seeds that could blossom later, "something I do not judge difficult given their ambition and evilness."

Machiavelli had found someone who could match his anticlericalism, as Guicciardini told Niccolò about the benefits he would reap in his work as a historian, he who had negotiated with sovereigns and rulers, by staying with "the Clog Republic" (the Franciscan chapter general), at the same time poking fun at Machiavelli's mania for finding historical precedents for everything. On a more practical note, since he wanted Niccolò to be adequately wined and dined, he had dispatched a messenger to him with a bundle of letters, including some news sheets (*avvisi*) from Zurich, sure that Santi would notice the bulky package. Santi was "mean and used to gossip," and Guicciardini intended to pull as much wool over his eyes as possible "for the sake of keeping the meals going." As for *il Rovaio*, Francesco thought it a poor choice, believing that the consuls of the Wool Guild expected Machiavelli—given his reputation as an eccentric with a knack for novelties—to find the right friar for their needs: the one that did not exist.

Guicciardini's ruse worked, for on May 18 Machiavelli could write that Santi had swallowed everything hook, line, and sinker, although he was puzzled about the whole situation and a bit suspicious about the authenticity of the information he was being fed. However, in the meantime, Niccolò had been enjoying his hospitality, "guzzling food like six dogs and three wolves," and saving a considerable amount of money in the process. He actually felt a bit sorry for fooling Santi and had been thinking of returning the hospitality if his host ever happened to be in Florence. Sigismondo, however, soon understood he had been tricked, as Machiavelli wrote to Gucciardini the following day:

> *Fuckus*! One needs to be clever when dealing with that fellow, for he is as crafty as thirty thousand devils. And I believe he suspects you are dicking him, for when the courier came he exclaimed: "Show me. This must be a big affair: The messenger arrived in haste"; then, after reading your letter he said: "I think the governor

is fooling both of us." I feigned ignorance, Messere, answering that, since you and I had some matters in common left unresolved in Florence, I had asked you to keep me informed should there be any news, and that was the reason for your missive. However, I feel my arse is going throb, throb, since I fear sooner or later he will take a broom and kick me back to the inn. So I beg you to go on holiday tomorrow, and not turn this joke sour, though the pleasure I have received up to now cannot be taken away: wonderful meals, glorious beds, and the like, so that for the last three days I have felt rejuvenated.*

As for the rest, things were not going too well. The preacher, *il Rovaio*, had proved to be unwilling to come to Florence, disgruntled that the city had failed to impose a dress code on the local prostitutes and, in any case, feared that if he preached the wrong stuff he would be sent to the galleys, as had happened to one "pope Angelico"—a notorious impostor. The chapter general had been taking time to decide about the creation of a Florentine province, and Machiavelli feared his lack of success would be held against him. At least he had learned a few things about the Franciscan Order's organization, "so that when I shall discuss silence I'll be able to say: 'quieter than friars eating.'" Around May 20 he wrote to Cardinal Giulio about the situation, stating that the friars had asked for some extra letters on the matter of the province from the Otto di Pratica and the cardinal himself. He took care to praise Santi's work: a small token of appreciation for having eaten Sigismondo out of house and home. But by then Machiavelli had left Carpi for Modena with the excuse of coming down with "a certain ailment"; in reality, he was seeking in Francesco Guicciardini's company that intellectual stimulus he had not found among the friars.

---

* The allusions to the "thirty thousand devils" and the throbbing "arse" come from *Il Morgante* by Luigi Pulci, a satire on chivalric poems and one of Machiavelli's favorites.

14

~

FORTUNE'S FICKLENESS

*Those who know they have good fortune may
take greater courage in their enterprises.
Nevertheless, one should remember that luck
not only is fickle in time, but may vary
according to different matters. Thus, we can
sometimes observe someone being fortunate in
some things and unlucky in others.*
—FRANCESCO GUICCIARDINI

Pope Leo X died suddenly on December 1, 1521, and his demise
left the Medici in a difficult situation. Without papal support the
Medici's position in the city of Florence could be in peril, and so Cardinal
Giulio entered the conclave on December 27 with a firm determination
to get elected. He found his way barred by the equally determined Cardinal Francesco Soderini, who, while not aspiring himself to the papal
crown, intended to do everything he could to stop Giulio from getting

it. Although Soderini played his hand badly, he had on his side the fact that Leo had overstayed his welcome by overspending and making an outrageous display of nepotism. As a result, and quite unexpectedly, on January 9, 1522, the conclave chose the relatively unknown cardinal bishop of Tortosa, Adrian Florensz, from Utrecht, who decided to keep his name, thus becoming Pope Adrian VI.

In some ways this election benefited the Medici, as the new pope was firmly in the Habsburg camp and had once served as Charles V's viceroy in Spain. The rulers of Florence could breathe in relief, since a pro-French pontiff could have boosted the confidence of the anti-Medici elements within the city. Yet with war between France and the empire having erupted once more in northern Italy, Cardinal Giulio had to be on the watch, so as not to be caught unawares by the turn of international events.

The death of Leo freed the hand of those who wished for a regime change in Florence, bringing together Francis I, his allies in the papal curia, and a number of those Florentines disaffected with the Medici rule. Cardinal Giulio was literally flooded with proposals about constitutional reform, and although he may have been inclined to enact some changes, the extremism of certain schemes alarmed him. Caught in a quandary, Giulio used a well-known Medici tactic: Bide for time and take advantage of events. He did not have to wait long. Cardinal Soderini had been actively plotting to overthrow the Medici with French backing, and in March 1522 organized, with the condottiere Renzo di Ceri, a military expedition against Florence, counting on the support of the local dissenters.

Ceri went only as far as Siena, intending first to reinstate the Petrucci leadership there, before his army dissolved owing to lack of funds and victuals. On April 7, the Imperialist army inflicted a crushing defeat on the French at La Bicocca, a battle in which firearms proved crucial, forcing Francis I to abandon Lombardy and depriving the anti-Medici of their most important military support. Even worse, the Florentines captured a French courier and from him discovered the existence of a plan to murder Cardinal Giulio and restore the Republic.

Giulio may have been shocked to learn that the plot had been hatched within the Rucellai Gardens, the culprits all being Machiavelli's friends and people who wished to restore Florence's "liberty" by imitating examples found in ancient histories. Jacopo Nardi, one of the members of the garden group, actually held Machiavelli to be partly responsible for the plot, as he had planted conspiratorial ideas in the heads of the would-be murderers. "They held all his works in high regard," Nardi wrote, "so that Niccolò cannot be held blameless for the thoughts and actions of these youngsters." Filippo de' Nerli, another member of the group, admitted as much but added an important observation: "They did not consider what Machiavelli had written in his Discourses about conspiracies; for if they had done so, either they would have avoided plotting altogether, or moved more cautiously."

In his book Niccolò had warned against such schemes, considering them difficult to execute and uncertain in their results. In any case, Machiavelli appears not to have been part of the plan, although, according to the confession of one of the conspirators, his possible involvement had been considered, "but not being a friend of that illustrious family [Medici] and poor, [it was thought that] his actions would draw attention." The statement is interesting, since it would imply that people considered Niccolò a staunch enemy of the regime despite all his efforts to prove himself faithful. However, one should be wary about accepting this account at face value, since the person giving it was trying both to save his skin and at the same time ingratiate himself with the Medici. Despite his theoretically strong Republican leanings, like most of his fellow citizens Machiavelli placed *honore et utile* above ideology.

Machiavelli may well have smelled trouble brewing already a year before, when he had received a letter from Rome written by Piero Soderini. The former gonfalonier had proposed to Prospero Colonna that he employ Niccolò as his administrator in chief with a yearly salary of 200 gold ducats plus expenses, "something I consider much better than staying where you are now writing histories for sealed florins," he told Niccolò. Yet Soderini also suggested that Machiavelli depart in secret "and arrive here before people in Florence realize you have left." Machiavelli might have been tempted by the considerable wage, but evidently suspected mischief: Colonna not only happened to be a close friend of Cardinal Soderini but at the time was also at odds with Leo X (things changed the following June, when the pope made Colonna commander in chief of his army). Accepting such an invitation would have ruined the years of work Niccolò had spent trying to get back into the Medici's graces, turning him instead into another pawn in Cardinal Soderini's power game, with potentially disastrous results.

Wisely, Machiavelli steered clear of Soderini and the plotters of 1522, and as a result he did not suffer in the aftermath of the failed conspiracy. But a lot of his friends did: Zanobi Buondelmonti, Battista della Palla, Luigi di Piero Alamanni, and others had to flee for their lives, while Jacopo da Diacceto and Luigi di Tommaso Alamanni lost their heads on the block. And buried with the conspirators were also the projects of constitutional change, Cardinal Giulio now having the perfect excuse to postpone indefinitely any decision about possible reforms of Florentine institutions. Niccolò could not but watch in sadness and dismay as the members of the Rucellai Garden group dispersed, ending what had been six years of intellectual stimulus. Once again, the Soderini, with their political incompetence, had been responsible for his misfortunes. But he must have gotten little relief from Piero Soderini's death on June 13 and the damnation of his memory by the Florentine authorities. However, his cutting epitaph for the former gonfalonier, quoted above, is sufficient testimony of his feelings.

His sadness can only have increased with the death of his brother, Totto, one of the victims of the plague epidemic that struck Florence that year. On June 8, Niccolò received a letter from the gonfalonier Roberto Pucci informing him that Totto was on death's door and telling him that he would take care of the younger Machiavelli's ecclesiastical livings. Niccolò had struggled to get his brother some sort of position in the church, and only after some difficulty had managed to get for Totto the parishes near San Casciano, which were under the family's patronage. Indeed, one of them happened to be occupied illegally by a priest, and this situation persisted, prompting Lodovico, Niccolò's second son, three years later, to threaten to take matters into his own hands and exact revenge on the ribald cleric. By then Lodovico had already built a reputation for being a hot-blooded individual with a record for violence, but other aspects of his behavior worried Machiavelli far more. Niccolò may have been a womanizer, a whoremonger, and in many ways a not very moral individual, but he nevertheless had a sense of propriety. He grumbled about his son's attitude with Francesco Vettori, getting an interesting answer in return:

> In via San Gallo, near the gate, there is a nunnery, known as Saint Clement. Francesco [del Nero], a devout man, had become very friendly with them, and since the plague had invaded the neighborhood he often told the nuns that he had an estate—I don't recall if Paterno or Villamagna—where the youngest of them could comfortably go to escape the now approaching epidemic. The plague had become so virulent that fifteen of the nuns, remembering the promise, went to del Nero's estate, got the keys from the agent, milled the grain, drank the wine, and treated the house furnishings and all the rest as if their own. Having relinquished the keys to the nuns, the agent came to Florence, met Francesco, and informed him of what had happened. By chance he was walking through the government square, and no sooner had he heard the agent's tale—you can visualize him running with his cloak flapping behind his back and shouting without restraint to his brother Agostino. Once he caught him he told him to hitch six horses to a cart, go to the country, and evict the nuns, by force if necessary, and send them back to their convent on horseback. The brother obeyed and threw them out, despite some resistance on their part, and the story has "reached the Heavens." Thus, why is it so strange, considering that Francesco has had the nuns on his estate, if Lodovico, the sister's son, wishes to bring his confessor to the country, inspired in this, if not by his father Aeneas, at least by his

uncle Hector?* But in our old age we have become too timid and choosy, forgetting what we did in our youth.

Vettori's answer, written in elegant Latin, is actually a string of jokes.†
The "nuns" in reality were ladies of negotiable affections, among the loveliest in Florence, who used to bestow their favors on important citizens, including del Nero and Filippo Strozzi. Needless to say, Lodovico Machiavelli's "confessor" happened to be a young lad, and Vettori quipped that probably he had brought him along "to avoid the contagion." More than Lodovico's ephebic love affair, apparently what bothered Niccolò was his son sleeping with his paramour in the family's country home; besides, one wonders if, by his reference to "what we did in our youth," Vettori is not attempting to make it a *mal comune, mezzo gaudio* (a shared evil is half a good) situation. In any case, propriety demanded that illicit sex of whatever kind be conducted outside of one's house, or even *extra moenia*, and by berating his son for his behavior Machiavelli appears to have been exhibiting a very middle-class concern for *bella figura* that we would not expect from someone whose deportment could otherwise be pretty outrageous.

Machiavelli had become more conservative over the years, the schools of hard knocks and penury having turned the once outspoken secretary into a cautious, even deceitful, individual. Financial worries were always on his mind, and more than once he would ask Francesco del Nero to get the University of Pisa to raise his salary. Finally, thanks to his connections with the Medici, his wage was doubled, and on July

---

* Vettori is quoting from Virgil's *Aeneid* (XII, 440): "*Tu facito, mox cum matura adoleuerit aetas sis memor et te animo repetentem exempla tuorum et pater Aeneas et auunculus excitet Hector*" ("When you grow up remember and recall the deeds of your forebears, and be inspired by your father Aeneas and your uncle Hector").

† Two versions of this letter exist, one being a draft (never sent) containing some very personal remarks on Niccolò's and Vettori's personal lives, which Francesco may have considered unwise to include in the final version quoted here.

27, 1525, del Nero wrote to him that "your happiness is multiplying," adding that with the one hundred gold ducats he had received for continuing to write the *Histories*, he could at last create a dowry fund for his daughter Bartolomea ("Baccina").

The "happiness" mentioned by del Nero had a lot to do with the changes occurring in Florence and Rome. On September 14, 1523, Pope Adrian VI died, much to the rejoicing of the Romans, who had never taken a liking to the austere Netherlander. Cardinal Giulio de' Medici played a skillful hand in the conclave that followed, exploiting the rivalries within the college of cardinals and bringing some of his enemies to his side. He managed to convince Cardinal Colonna to vote for him with the promise of pardoning Francesco Soderini, whom Adrian had locked up in Castel Sant'Angelo after discovering his involvement in yet another conspiracy. On November 18, Giulio received the papal tiara, taking the name of Clement VII.

For the Florentines, his election, while well received by supporters of the Medici, represented a return to the days of Goro Gheri. The new pope sent Cardinal Silvio Passerini to govern the city—ostensibly as an aid to the young and illegitimate Ippolito and Alessandro de' Medici. Like Gheri, Passerini came from one of Florence's subject cities, Cortona, and his presence could only alienate the proud Florentines. In vain, and seeing the writing on the wall, did staunch Mediceans such as Francesco Vettori, Lorenzo Strozzi, Roberto Acciaioli, and Jacopo Salviati plead with Clement to let the Florentines run their own business until Ippolito and Alessandro should gain the right age and experience to allow them to handle the city's affairs. The pope also immediately started to display a worrying trait: hesitancy. He believed time to be his greatest ally and would ponder a decision endlessly before making up his mind. A more genuinely devout and moral individual than his cousin Leo X, he nevertheless lacked the latter's political instincts, showing himself incapable of taking speedy action when necessary.

As much as he had become guarded in some of his attitudes, Niccolò never hesitated when his enthusiasm was aroused. With another Medici on the papal throne, he held high hopes for his own future and busily set himself to the task of polishing what he had written of the *Histories*, desiring to present the work in person to the pontiff. Some of his friends did not share his enthusiasm. In March 1524, the ever-wary Francesco Vettori wrote to Francesco del Nero saying that although he believed the pope would receive Niccolò and his book favorably, and maybe even read some bits of the latter, Machiavelli risked departing from Rome "with less cash than when he arrived." Clement was not famous for dispensing monetary rewards and indeed led a relatively frugal life. Machiavelli, in contrast, liked good food, pleasant company, and beautiful women. He had started frequenting the house of a *nouveau riche*: one Iacopo Falconetti, known as *il Fornaciaio* (the Kilnman) because of his ownership of a brick-producing furnace. Falconetti had been on the board of the *Twelve Buonomini*, but for some unexplained reason had been removed from office and confined to his property outside the Porta San Frediano. He enjoyed the company of his social betters, including intellectuals and artists, providing in exchange some very gracious hospitality: In Florence, as Roberto Ridolfi aptly stated, "prejudices are swallowed with tasty morsels."

In any case, Machiavelli had never refused a free meal, and since the Fornaciaio's house happened to be a fifteen- to twenty-minute walk from his own, he often would consort with Falconetti and his company. But it was not just the food and the environment that attracted Machiavelli. A young widow also enjoyed il Fornaciaio's generosity: Barbara (or Barbera) Raffacani, a beauty and a talented singer and actress. Niccolò quickly fell under her spell and appeared to be completely smitten with love. Francesco Vettori saw this as a positive development, believing that it would help to take Machiavelli's mind off his quest to obtain favors in Rome. Writing to Francesco del Nero, he told him to relay a message to Niccolò: "I believe it far better to dine sometimes with Barbera at the Fornaciaio's expense, rather than staying here [in Rome] at dinner time, standing near a door that, even after a long wait, does not open."

Others took a different stance. On March 1, 1525, a rather worried Filippo de' Nerli wrote to Francesco del Nero about the gossip surrounding Machiavelli's amorous relationship, considering it highly improper that a paterfamilias like Niccolò should have bolted with Barbera—"*Non c'è cosa peggiore che in membra vecchie il pizzico d'amore*" (there is nothing worse than in old bones the itch of love), the Florentines would have said. Some individuals saw all this as a reflection of Machiavelli's character. In the summer of 1525, Francesco Guicciardini asked Machiavelli to inspect two properties he had recently bought. Of one, *il Finocchieto*, Niccolò produced a rather somber report, comparing the house to a dungeon placed in the middle of an Arabian desert, and suggested Guicciardini sell the property after revamping it a bit. On August 7, 1525, a somewhat peeved yet amused Francesco wrote a long letter to Machiavelli in which he made it seem as if the Finocchieto estate itself were speaking, but in a female voice. In this way he gave Niccolò both a stinging reply and some very serious advice about his love life.

The "house" starts off by chiding Machiavelli for his unkind comments, believing he is mistaken, "even if I cannot but detest your error since it is caused by a woman, and always a woman although raised in an immoral way." Guicciardini then gets to the core of the argument: "You consort with your Barbara, who attempts, as do those of her kind, to please everyone and appear rather than be," while instead Machiavelli, who had "read and written so many histories and seen so much of the world," should be wary of a woman "who lives with everybody and loves no one," instead of cherishing virtue and good behavior. The "house" continues by praising exactly those things that Machiavelli had decried, for "asperity and rigidness" is what makes her lovely to those, like her master, who can see beyond appearances.

Guicciardini then delivered a parting shot: "You see, Machiavelli, how much praise I deserve, and the more dear I should be held for those reasons that so displeased you. And the next time learn not to trust so much in yourself and in your opinion, and consider with greater care before passing judgment, because one can find excuses for others that in a person of your prudence and experience are unacceptable." In one blow Guicciardini had taken both Niccolò's affection for Barbera and his critical capacity to task: Far from being the acute judge of people and events he may have thought he was, Niccolò had a pronounced tendency to be guided by his emotions and by his readings, not to mention a tendency to let himself be struck by power, riches, and appearances.

Machiavelli had found, to some extent, all three of the above in il Fornaciaio, who not only appreciated Niccolò's talents but also had the necessary cash to act as a Maecenas. Sometime in the fall of 1524, another wealthy individual, Bernardino di Giordano, organized a performance of *The Mandrake* at his house, employing artists of the caliber of Andrea del Sarto and Bastiano da Sangallo to create the scenery. Wishing to emulate the munificence and magnificence of his fellow citizen, il Fornaciaio asked Machiavelli to write a play to be staged during a party he intended to give on January 13, 1525, to celebrate the end of his confinement. Niccolò set to work with enthusiasm, probably also spurred on by a desire to please Barbera, and by the given date had managed to complete his third known comedy, *La Clizia*, based on Plautus's *Casina*, but like *The Mandrake* set in contemporary Florence.

The performance—with the backdrops painted once again by Bastiano da Sangallo, and the music composed by the madrigalist Philippe Verdelot—was a huge hit (despite, according to Giannotti, the unruly behavior of some Florentine youngsters). A large crowd containing people of all social classes, including Ippolito and Alessandro de' Medici, gathered to watch it and gave it a standing ovation. On February 22, Filippo de' Nerli, then in Modena, wrote to Machiavelli that the news of his comedy's success had been spreading far and wide. He asked him for a copy of the text, but Machiavelli, true to form, failed to oblige him.

La Clizia differs significantly from *The Mandrake*, although the two plays do have some features in common. Both deal with lust and deception, but *La Clizia* delivers a moral message lacking in the other play. The plot is fairly straightforward. The old Nicomaco has fallen in love with his young protégée, Clizia, and plans to marry her to his domestic servant Pirro, in order to gain access to her bed. His wife, Sofronia, despite some resistance, seems resigned to the fact; but then having organized a bogus wedding she places another servant, Siro, in Clizia's alcove. Siro proceeds to beat up the husband, and the next morning a thoroughly bruised and humiliated Nicomaco is completely cured of his passion, realizing that should the story go out he would lose both standing and reputation in Florence. Clizia can now marry his son, Cleandro, who also has a burning passion for the girl.

Nicomaco is a thinly disguised parody of Machiavelli himself, starting with the character's name—Nic[colò]mac[chiavelli]o—while one is tempted to see in the long-suffering, astute Sofronia a portrait of Marietta Corsini. With typically Florentine self-mockery, Niccolò pokes fun at his own senile love affair with a younger woman, thumbing his nose at those who disapprove of it. Yet, he is perfectly aware that without the necessary display of prudence, such behavior could be very damaging. Unlike the successful adultery in *The Mandrake*, the planned one in *La Clizia* could lead to the disruption of domestic and social order. In both plays the victims are old fools driven by insane desires—Nicia for offspring, and Nicomaco for Clizia's body—that lead them to behave without that "political" savvy necessary to avoid being duped. In this sense, *La Clizia* reflects Machiavelli's belief that entrusting power, whether over a polity or a household, to inept individuals who lack a sense of civic morality is a recipe for disaster.

La Clizia's fame must have boosted Machiavelli's reputation, for when he asked Francesco Vettori about an opportunity to present his *Histories* in person to the pope, Vettori answered that Clement had stated: "He should come, and I believe that his book will be readable and enjoyable." Vettori, however, displaying his usual prudence, warned Machiavelli not to be too hopeful about receiving any monetary rewards, "lest you find yourself with empty hands," the current political situation being "unfavorable both to reading and giving."

Indeed, the times appeared to be grim for Clement, who in order to stem the Imperial advance in Italy had made an alliance with Francis I. On February 24, however, the French had been thoroughly trounced under Pavia, and the king of France himself had fallen prisoner to Charles V. The pope had hastily struck a deal with the emperor, agreeing to defend the duchy of Milan, now once more ruled by a member of the Sforza family. In return Charles promised to safeguard the church's lands and the rule of the Medici in Florence. However, the emperor also asked for 100,000 ducats, and a cash-strapped Clement had to milk the Florentine cow to find the necessary sum. In Florence, burdensome taxation, combined with the unpopularity of Cardinal Passerini, had started to become an explosive mixture.

Charles did not display undue desire to honor his side of the accord. One of the articles of the treaty compelled the duke of Ferrara to restore Reggio to the papacy, but in reality the emperor had already agreed with Alfonso d'Este to maintain the status quo, and he apparently had no intention of ratifying that part of the deal. A deeply concerned Clement decided to send an embassy to the emperor, headed by Cardinal Giovanni Salviati. Rather surprisingly, his father, Jacopo, then suggested Niccolò Machiavelli as secretary of the delegation. Although Clement ultimately rejected it, Jacopo's proposal was significant. Together with people such as Roberto Acciaioli and Lorenzo Strozzi, Jacopo made up what may be called the "constitutional" part of the Medicean faction; that is, he sided with those who, while content with hegemony of the Medici in Florence, nevertheless wished this leadership to be exercised within the boundaries of the traditional Florentine constitution, and who thus resented the pope's decision to rule by proxy through Cardinal Passerini. By now Machiavelli had gained a reputation for loyalty to the Medici, but at the same time he had made no mystery of his moderate republicanism. Jacopo's proposal appears to have been an attempt to bring Machiavelli within the sphere of the Salviati patronage system, turning him into a useful ally in the political struggle to establish a more acceptable form of government in Florence. Besides, no one doubted Niccolò's experience in diplomatic matters, which had been confirmed by the memorandum he had written some time before to Raffaello Girolami on the eve of the latter's departure as ambassador in Spain.

That document itself is interesting, since it represents a distillation of Niccolò's practice in the field, yet a mixture of what he had done with what he would have liked to do. His advice is certainly spot-on when he tells how an ambassador ought to behave, how he should gather news, how he should convey his government's desires, and how he should go about writing his reports; it is less so when he advises about the necessity of entertaining in order to obtain information. Not that he was wrong, in principle; however, the Florentine government had a notorious record of stinginess, and only someone personally well endowed with cash could hope to fete people adequately. Even so, Francesco Vettori saw little use in such activities, finding informal conversations with fellow diplomats rather less expensive and more profitable.

Machiavelli probably did not know about the maneuvers going on behind his back at the papal court, and in any case, had other priorities. At the end of May he traveled to Rome to present his *Histories* to Clement, now in a somewhat better mood despite his difficulties with the emperor. The pope must have liked the book, since he donated 120 gold ducats to Niccolò from his own purse. But Niccolò also received a more significant reward, departing from Rome to Faenza with a papal brief in his pocket for the local governor, none other than Francesco Guicciardini, instructing him to hear what Machiavelli had to say and give his opinion on the matter.

The topic under discussion happened to be right up Niccolò's alley: raising and training a militia force in the Romagna to protect the church's territories. The idea may have been suggested by Machiavelli himself, but one should also remember that his *Art of War* had given him a reputation as an expert in military affairs; in any case, it cost Clement little to explore the possibility of getting an inexpensive army. Guicciardini listened carefully but unequivocally rejected the idea. While raising a militia could be, in theory, feasible, he believed that practical considerations did not allow for the successful implementation of such a scheme. The people of Romagna were poor, politically divided, unruly, untrustworthy, and hostile to the ecclesiastical government; it would be far better if the pope considered instead doing something to ameliorate the fiscal pressures in the region. Clement took notice of these objections, for in a letter to Machiavelli written on July 6 the papal secretary, Jacopo

Sadoleto, informed him that the pope "wishes to consider the matter further." Anyone aware of the pontiff's character would have realized that this meant a *sine die* postponement.

Machiavelli waited in Faenza until July 26, when, with the excuse "of some business," he returned to Florence empty-handed—maybe also with a few ducats less, since in Faenza he had been consorting with a courtesan called La Mariscotta, who, as Guicciardini wrote to him, "greatly praised your manners and company." Niccolò's roving eye never allowed him to concentrate on just one woman, whether wife, mistress, or prostitute.

After inspecting Guicciardini's country estates for him, he departed once more, this time for Venice on behalf of the Wool Guild, to recover the merchandise of some Florentine merchants that was being illegally held by a Venetian subject. There he met the papal nuntio, Ludovico Canossa, who told Francesco Vettori in a letter: "I offered him my help, beseeching him to make use of it. I saw him no more: I believe that my advice was not of the type you suggested, and content with his own judgment he had no further use of me."

We do not know if he managed to fulfill his mission, but in the meantime, he enjoyed a successful gambling spree. Or at least that was what people believed, for on September 6 Filippo de' Nerli wrote from Florence to compliment him on the "two or three thousand ducats" he had won at the lottery, lamenting, however, that he had failed to inform his friends, relatives, and loved ones about it. Nerli added some rather welcome news: Machiavelli had been declared eligible for public office and could very well be selected, since the Accoppiatori had decided to ignore any *divieto* Niccolò may have had. Somewhat maliciously, Filippo said this turn of fortune must have originated "in Barbary" (clearly referring to Barbera's influence) or from "some other favor of yours." Yet, Nerli warned Machiavelli that if he neglected his friends this good fate could turn bad once more, and that once the news of the lottery win became public knowledge, without the influence of those in power he could be hit with a huge tax bill.

It is doubtful that Niccolò ever truly won or pocketed such a large sum, although if he did his silence on the matter would have been more than justified. Nerli's concerns, however, went beyond the realm of advice, for he regretted Niccolò's absence: "Now that you are not here, there is no gambling, going to taverns and other such trifles . . . and because you are away nobody will bring the gang together." More than all his erudite work on politics, or even his satirical writings, what his cronies most appreciated about Machiavelli was his ability to make a party out of life.

Back in Florence, he continued his correspondence with Guicciardini, discussing politics, the language of *The Mandrake*, and matrimonial projects in Florence, everything intermixed with a good dose of humor. Guicciardini intended to have *The Mandrake* performed in Faenza, and Niccolò had been discussing the matter with Lodovico Alamanni and Barbera. He was even considering rewriting some lines to suit the Faenza audience. Alamanni had offered lodgings with some friends of his to Barbera and her troupe, but Niccolò suggested instead that Guicciardini put her up in a male convent: "And if they [the friars] don't go crazy," he said, "I'll want no money." In the end, due to the "lack of brains" of the locals, another play got staged instead of *The Mandrake*, although Guicciardini asked Machiavelli to put together another piece and come to Faenza for its staging, "for in truth I would never have gotten into this mess unless I was certain of your arrival." Francesco's despondency stemmed also from the troubles of Italy and the wavering papal policies: "For I have never seen anyone who as ill weather approaches does not seek refuge somewhere, except for us that wait for it without cover in the middle of the road."

It is possible that not even an astute man like Guicciardini could have foreseen the storm about to break over Italy.

15

—

LOST OPPORTUNITIES

You know how many opportunities have been
lost: do not forsake this one, or rely on
waiting, trusting in Fortune and time; for
time does not always bring the same results,
and Fortune is never the same.
— NICCOLÒ MACHIAVELLI TO
FRANCESCO GUICCIARDINI

It took some time for Francesco Guicciardini's letter about *The Man-*
drake's cancellation to reach Machiavelli, who on January 3, 1526, still
worried that "certain lovers" of Barbera's would try to dissuade her from
going to Faenza and one needed to induce her by offering adequate monetary compensation. Niccolò must have been disappointed with Guicciardini's decision, considering that he had written and set to music five
new songs to be performed between the acts. But if Faenza failed to deliver, Venice did not. On February 28, Giovanni Manetti wrote to Machiavelli from the Lagoon that *The Mandrake* had opened to a rapturous

reception, beating, hands down, a rendition in Italian of Plautus's *Menecmi*, "which despite being an ancient and fine comedy, and with very good actors, nevertheless was held as completely defunct compared to yours." Such had been the success that Manetti wanted Niccolò to send him something else, "already written or hatched in your head," to be performed in Venice the next May.

As much as he enjoyed his reputation as a playwright, Niccolò had been focusing once more on international politics. In Francesco Guicciardini he had found an intellectual sparring partner akin to Francesco Vettori, but with much better political connections. Against his father's wishes—the elder Guicciardini had opposed his son's desire for a match above his station, and without a large dowry at that—he had married one of Alamanno Salviati's daughters, thus becoming part of the select group of Piero Soderini's opponents, and upon the return of the Medici had made a rapid career within the papal administration.

A lawyer by training, Francesco possessed a sharp, critical mind that went hand in hand with a determination verging on ruthlessness. When governor of Modena he had mercilessly put down a conspiracy through torture, banishments, and executions. Yet Guicciardini also had a wicked and very Florentine sense of humor along with a talent for understanding people and situations. He and Machiavelli shared a similar cultural background (Francesco having been the pupil of the celebrated humanist Marsilio Ficino), a taste for history, and a keen interest in statecraft. However, in contrast to Niccolò, who was primarily a theorist, Guicciardini had a very practical approach to politics as well as a killer instinct absent in Machiavelli. Time after time, with relentless logic, Francesco would demolish Niccolò's castles in the air. Nonetheless, he appreciated Machiavelli's talents and experience. Moreover, he would prove to be a good friend, and someone who would not hesitate to promote Niccolò with his political superiors. Indeed, Machiavelli's activities in the last two years of his life would be closely connected with Guicciardini's.

In mid-January 1526, Charles V and the captive Francis I signed the Treaty of Madrid, by which, in exchange for his freedom, the king of

France formally renounced his claims to Milan, Naples, and Burgundy and agreed to pardon and restore Charles, Duke of Bourbon, to his confiscated lands (constable of France and governor of Milan, Bourbon had fallen out with Francis over inheritance and territorial disputes). The news of the treaty caught many by surprise, including Machiavelli. To Guicciardini he had predicted that Charles would never release Francis, and even after learning about the French-Imperial accord, he adamantly maintained that the emperor would never set the king free, only to state immediately afterward that Charles could behave like a fool and act otherwise. In any case, Francis would have to adhere to the treaty's terms, for fear of losing his kingdom after having lost Italy. So now it was up to the Italians to reassert their own independence—possibly with French help—and at this point Niccolò came up with his master plan: The pope should employ Giovanni de' Medici, a bold, imaginative soldier very much feared by the Spanish. In this way, Clement could build a decent army and maybe get the king of France on his side.

Machiavelli had written as much to Filippo Strozzi, who on April 26 replied that he had shown Niccolò's letter to the pope. Clement, however, had objected to the employment of Giovanni de' Medici on the grounds that once Francis was freed, he would honor the treaty; moreover, Giovanni could not raise an army without money, and once the pope provided him with the necessary cash everyone would see through the ruse—de' Medici happened to be in France's pay and financing him would be tantamount to declaring war on the emperor. Clement had good reasons to be cautious, given that when, a few months before, the duke of Milan, Francesco Sforza, had tried to switch his allegiance from Charles to Francis through his secretary, Girolamo Morone (who also attempted to get the Imperial commander, Fernando d'Avalos, Marquis of Pescara, to change sides), it had resulted in Morone's arrest and the Spanish occupation of Sforza's fortresses in Lombardy. On that occasion Machiavelli had compared Sforza to a tamed falcon, saying, "and now that he's got his hood, all the other [Italian] princes will get it. There is no remedy: It has been decided from above." Significantly, Niccolò had added to his signature the semi-jocular, semi-serious titles "historian, comedian and tragedian."

Machiavelli would prove correct about the Habsburgs eventually dominating Italy, although, given his mixed success as a political analyst, one could attribute the accurate prediction to luck rather than acumen. He got it completely wrong in the case of Francis's liberation, and he was even more incorrect about whether the king would honor his word once free. No sooner had he crossed the French frontier than Francis denounced the Treaty of Madrid, asserting that he had signed it under duress, despite having left his sons as hostages in Spain. On hearing the news, Clement saw a chance to play the age-old Medici game of "divide and rule," and on May 22, France, Venice, the Duke of Milan, the papacy, and, reluctantly, Florence signed the Treaty of Cognac, creating a league with the intention of expelling the Habsburgs from Italy. On paper the treaty's articles called for the return to the status quo before the battle of Pavia, the liberation of the French princes, and a prohibition against Charles entering Italy with anything more than a modest retinue. Should the emperor refuse to accept these terms, the allies swore to wage war and expel him from the kingdom of Naples.

Nobody had any illusions about the emperor accepting such humiliating conditions, and Clement had already started to plan for the inevitable Habsburg onslaught. On April 3, Machiavelli received a letter in the pope's name from Francesco Guicciardini instructing him to go with the celebrated engineer Pedro Navarro—a onetime military architect, siege expert, turncoat, and pirate—on an inspection tour of the walls of Florence in preparation for a possible siege of the city. Niccolò's reputation as a military expert played a part in this choice: The seventh book of his *Art of War* dealt specifically with siege operations—by far the soundest part of the whole work. However, Guicciardini's and Filippo Strozzi's sponsorships played their part, both having the pope' ear.

Machiavelli replied the next day to Guicciardini about the discussions he had held with Cardinal Passerini on the various possibilities Clement had put forward for improving Florence's defenses. Niccolò, without hesitation, threw out the idea of extending the walled circuit to the south, so as to include the hill and monastery of San Miniato: One would need too large a garrison to man it. As for the second idea, reducing the ring of fortifications and demolishing the whole district of Santo Spirito, Machiavelli maintained that it would be "difficult and unusual"; in other words, the inhabitants of the quarter, including some of the staunchest Medici supporters, would not passively accept their houses being torn down. Niccolò instead proposed a compromise plan: On the south side of the river Arno, to partly contract, partly extend, and partly demolish the existing fortifications. But he would wait for Navarro's arrival before forwarding his official report to the pontiff.

The next day Machiavelli walked the walls of Florence with Navarro, producing a detailed account of his findings. Essentially, Navarro suggested lowering the towers above the city's doors, building redoubts, and demolishing a small section of the city from the San Niccolò to the San Miniato gates. The report had the double advantage of being both militarily and politically feasible: The stones of the towers could be used to reinforce the walls, and the district to be raised was—and still is to some extent—a working-class area, and thus of little consequence for Clement. Machiavelli went to Rome a few days later to present his conclusions in person to the pope, returning to Florence around the end of the month with some very good news for himself. On May 9, on Clement's orders, the Council of the One Hundred authorized the creation of a new magistracy, the *Procuratori delle Mura* (Officials of the Walls), and Niccolò was to become its secretary.

In this capacity he managed to get his son Bernardo employed as one of his assistants, for the young man the first step in what would become a distinguished career in the service of the Florentine polity. For Machiavelli it was a red-letter day: Years and years of efforts, pleadings, letter-writing, penury, and temporary jobs had at last borne fruit. The office itself carried little power or prestige, but Niccolò once more could set foot in the government palace as a state employee and in fact could handle affairs without having to answer to anyone except the pope himself.

Francesco Guicciardini would write as much to his brother Luigi, stressing that "it is up to you to treat him properly in this enterprise, and for anything else he may need, for he has indeed earned his dessert."

But Machiavelli would have to work hard to earn every meal, for dealing with such a wavering character like Clement was no easy task. On May 17 Niccolò would write to Guicciardini about having his head "filled with bastions," remarking that certain delays he had encountered made him wonder about the pope's full commitment to the scheme. Francesco answered a few days later reassuring his friend that the pontiff had every intention to proceed as planned, as could be proven by the rapid replacement of one of the *procuratori* who had been incapacitated by a stroke. Still, Machiavelli went on having problems, not least because Clement had the habit of changing his mind according to the latest piece of advice.

On June 2, Niccolò wrote again to Guicciardini lamenting that the pope had reverted to his previous idea of including San Miniato in the circuit of walls. Niccolò bewailed the whole scheme as costly, impractical, and ridiculous. Yet, in another missive of the same day, he did not exclude the possibility that incorporating the monastery into the Florentine defense system might be beneficial, arguing that it could easily be fortified by friend or foe alike—though God forbid the latter: "For if any powerful individual should ever come to Florence because of some turmoil, as happened in 1494 with the king of France, you would most surely be made into his servants." Interestingly, in both *The Prince* and *The Discourses*, Machiavelli had argued against the usefulness of fortresses to keep a city under control; the realities of warfare had evidently caused him to change his mind on this matter. As a matter of fact, during the siege of Florence of 1529–1530, San Miniato would prove a key element in the city's defense, being turned into a powerful fortress by none other than Michelangelo Buonarroti. Indeed, although never mentioned by Machiavelli in his report, some of Michelangelo's existing drawings of fortifications could lead to the conclusion that somehow he had been made privy to Navarro and Machiavelli's report on Florence's walls. (Incidentally, Niccolò had become acquainted with Michelangelo during the time he had served as secretary of the Ten.)

In the letter to Guicciardini of May 17, Niccolò had also argued forcefully that the pope should not dither or come to an agreement with the emperor, for there could not be a better moment to stop Charles. Niccolò had even gone to the extent of paraphrasing Livy with the invocation: "Free Italy from this long lasting torment, evict these fierce beasts that have nothing human except the look and the voice."* Guicciardini had answered not to worry since things were under way, although, when one had to deal with so many players, it was normal for matters to proceed at a somewhat slower pace. Still, Francesco, knowing all too well the vagaries of politics, had his doubts about the commitment of the league's members: "I hope that everyone shall pay his dues, if not as soon as we may wish, at least not so late that we could end up with no time left."

With the benefit of hindsight, Clement would probably have been wise to keep the door open for a rapprochement with Charles. The emperor was willing to make peace in exchange for 150,000 ducats from the pope and the promise from Francesco Sforza to pay 4,000 ducats a month to Bourbon in exchange for the duchy of Milan. Charles, however, who also had other cards up his sleeve, instructed his commanders in Italy to secretly get in touch with Cardinal Pompeo Colonna—one of Clement's electors, but thoroughly pro-Imperial and scion of one of the most warlike families of Italy—should the pope prove intractable. The pontiff at the time appeared for once to be determined to press on, having united his forces with the Venetians and invaded Lombardy. The allied army had been placed under the de facto leadership of Francesco

---

* We should not consider this as an example of nationalistic outrage, despite what some of Machiavelli's biographers would like us to believe. For Machiavelli and his contemporaries, the concept of Italy had more to do with the cultural and spiritual heritage of ancient Rome than with a united political entity. The "barbarians" from beyond the Alps were simply the enemies of the Italian civilization, and of the independence of the various Italian states.

Maria della Rovere, who in the meantime had managed to recover the duchy of Urbino, with Francesco Guicciardini as lieutenant general and Giovanni de' Medici in charge of the papal contingent.*

Della Rovere could not be described as the best of choices, having developed into a very—some would say excessively—prudent commander. He also harbored a grudge against the Medici for the treatment he had received at the hands of Leo X. The Florentines' reluctance to take part in the enterprise was reflected in the low quality of their troops, and Machiavelli—following the orders of the Otto di Pratica—duly traveled north in around the middle of June to attempt to instill a bit of order in the ranks. He found a very grim situation rife with disorder and indecision, which he described in detail to a friend.

Guicciardini had been nearly driven insane by the duke of Urbino's indecision, and to Roberto Acciaioli he expressed little hope that Niccolò could accomplish anything useful, given the circumstances: "Machiavelli is here. He had come to discipline this soldiery, but having seen how rebellious it is, he despairs about getting any honor out of the task. So he shall remain to laugh at men's mistakes, since he can't do anything to redress them." Acciaioli, however, did not believe that the theorist Niccolò could have done much in any case: "I'm happy that Machiavelli has been ordered to put the infantry in order," he wrote, "and would God allow him to execute what he has in mind. But I doubt this to be Plato's Republic, and it has not been possible to reorganize or create one according to his intentions. I believe it would be better if he returned to Florence to do his business regarding the strengthening of the walls, much more useful given the times." Others would have agreed, since it had become clear that Machiavelli was more of a thinker than a doer After the above-mentioned episode where Machiavelli had made a mess of Giovanni de'

---

* Francesco Maria della Rovere in reality was just the captain general of the Venetian army, but he found himself in command by default because he was the most senior, the most experienced, and the most socially elevated leader present. In fact, his constant dithering throughout the campaign could also be the consequence of this state of uncertainty.

Medici's company, Giovanni had commented that "Niccolò could write well, and he could do well."

Machiavelli had personal matters on his mind as well. Barbera had not been in touch, and this troubled his soul more than any military debacle. Although he knew her to behave in a somewhat loose and wonton manner, her apparent lack of care nevertheless pained him: "She gives me more worries than the Emperor," he had written to Guicciardini a few months before. Unable to resist any longer, he wrote to Jacopo Falconetti about his concerns, and il Fornaciaio replied on August 5 that he had visited Barbera and spoken to her about her callousness. The singer promised to write and excused her long silence by saying that she had been away, admitting that occasionally she ran circles around Niccolò to see if he really loved her.

Love pains aside, keeping in contact with Barbera served a practical purpose for Machiavelli, since she held the key of the ciphered code that he and some of his friends used in their correspondence. Francesco Vettori used it in a number of letters that he wrote to Machiavelli that summer updating him on current domestic and international affairs, including the news that a papal/Florentine army had been repulsed by an inferior force when attempting to bring about a change of government in Siena: "You know that I have difficulty believing in supernatural intervention, but this matter is so extraordinary, not to say miraculous, as any incident that has happened in war since 1494; similar to one of those biblical stories, where men were struck with fear and ran from the unknown." Vettori also warned Machiavelli that the league needed to win the war, or at least show some consistent success, by the end of November; otherwise, "the pope will have to accept the Emperor's terms, and no one doubts how harsh they shall be."

But victory had eluded the league's army, more thanks to its own inactivity than to enemy action. The duke of Urbino had abandoned the siege of Milan and pitched camp in front of Cremona, but seeing no result, in September Guicciardini dispatched Machiavelli to della Rovere to convince him to either take some resolute action or send his forces to aid the Genoese under Andrea Doria. Machiavelli accomplished little and later would vent his frustration in a letter to his friend Bartolomeo Cavalcanti. On September 13, in a general meeting of the army's commanders, he pushed for an assault on Cremona, even drawing up a battle plan for taking the city. The duke and the other commanders refused to budge, and although Cremona surrendered ten days later, the coming of winter made it impossible to start any new operation on a grand scale. Moreover, like a thunderbolt in a clear sky, news arrived from Rome of the dramatic events that had occurred there, which had forced the pope to agree to a truce with the emperor.

While Francesco Maria della Rovere had been busy dithering, Charles V had not been idle. Cardinal Pompeo Colonna had retreated to his estates outside Rome, quietly building up his forces, having as his guest Don Ugo de Moncada, one of the emperor's trusted commanders in Italy. True to style, Clement had been having misgivings about the league, largely because Francis I appeared to be giving but a token contribution to the war effort. Clement's already despondent mood did not improve when a French envoy arrived at the papal court requesting for his king one-tenth of the church's revenues in France and a cardinal's hat for the royal chancellor Antoine ·Duprat. Seeing their chance, the Colonna occupied Anagni and then requested negotiations with Clement. A treaty was duly signed on August 26, compelling the pope to pardon Cardinal Pompeo and to guarantee to his family the possession of their properties, while in exchange the Colonna promised to evacuate Anagni and withdraw their troops to the kingdom of Naples.

Feeling safe, and despite warnings to the contrary, in an effort to save money Clement cut Rome's garrison to about five hundred men. This was the opportunity that Cardinal Pompeo and Moncada had been waiting for, and on the morning of September 20, the Colonna attacked Rome in force, putting the Vatican and other areas to the sack, lording it over the city for the next two days, and departing with an estimated 300,000 ducats in booty. Besieged in Castel Sant'Angelo and with few provisions, Clement could do nothing but accept Moncada's conditions: a four-month truce with the emperor, the withdrawal of his military forces from Lombardy, and a general pardon for all the Colonna; in addition, he would have to turn over Filippo Strozzi and one of Jacopo Salviati's sons as sureties for the agreement.

Once the news of the accord reached the allied camp, everyone started leaving the theater of operations, headed by the Duke of Urbino, just when an Imperial army several thousand strong had started to gather, concentrating in Bozen. Machiavelli remained a few days longer, using his time to write a detailed analysis of the situation. For him, della Rovere and the pope were the main culprits of the failed enterprise. Clement, in particular, had found himself stripped of cash for refusing to raise money in the manner of his predecessors (i.e., selling cardinals' hats for hefty sums) and then allowing himself to be caught in Rome "like a child." Machiavelli's glum conclusion was that "this whole matter is so messed up than not even Christ could put it straight."

On his way back to Florence Niccolò spent a few days in Piacenza with Francesco Guicciardini, who sent him to Borgo San Donnino (the present-day Fidenza) near Modena on some mission, although, as commissioner, Machiavelli would have liked to follow the Florentine troops sent to Rome to protect the pope (who, incidentally, had no intention of honoring the deal with the Colonna and had decided to exact his revenge against them at the right moment). Niccolò's stay in northern Italy meant that, eventually, someone else had to be chosen to replace him, much to Clement's regret, since he had told Guicciardini that he would have loved for Machiavelli to come to Rome.

Niccolò, however, had another task to accomplish, namely, to smoothe ruffled feathers. When in San Donnino he had gotten on the wrong side of the local commissioner, one Filicciafo, by constantly calling him *podestà* (roughly, governor, but also bailiff) instead of his proper title—"something which he resented, believing that you were pulling his leg in order to diminish his standing; and in truth he is very angry indeed," as an irked, if amused, Guicciardini would write to Machiavelli on October 30. Niccolò's love for deflating windbags once again had gotten the better of him, but these were the sort of people unlikely to take Machiavelli's jokes with good grace.

The extent of Filicciafo's rage can be glimpsed in a letter sent by Filippo de' Nerli, the governor of Modena, to Machiavelli on November 1. Nerli, who should not have been too surprised about Machiavelli's behavior, had received a full blast of the commissioner's—and for some reason Guicciardini's—anger, and he did not hesitate to describe his friends as "dangerous," "worse than charcoal," and people "better kept out of one's house." Filippo then asked Niccolò to send him, as promised, the first two books of the *Histories*. He also told him to relay his greetings to the "fogies," and in particular to Donato dal Corno, "who could be a man of quality, provided this winter he does not allow you to take up place in his shop next to the brazier and does not listen to your farts."

Before returning to Florence, Machiavelli paid a visit to Modena, and from there he wrote a letter to Guicciardini for the sake of appeasing Filicciafo. He also met Nerli, who greeted him with the words: "Is it ever possible for me to do something right?" Machiavelli had been prepared for this and replied laughing:

> My lord governor, do not be surprised, for it is not your fault but of this year; for nobody has managed to do things properly, and nothing has gone the right way. The Emperor could not have behaved worse by refusing to send any aid to his people, while he could have done so easily; the Spanish could have created serious problems for us, and have been incapable of doing so; we could have won, and have been unable; the pope believed that greater protection lay in the stroke of a pen than in a thousand infantrymen; only the Sienese have behaved well, so one should not be surprised if in these crazy times the crazy give a good account of themselves.* Thus, my lord governor, it would have been worse if you had performed well, rather than badly.

---

* The Sienese had a long-standing reputation for being utterly nuts, a feature believed to derive from drinking the waters of Fonte Gaia in the city's main square.

A somewhat calmer Nerli answered that if this indeed was the case, he would stop worrying. Soon after this exchange, Count Guido Rangoni— one of the commanders of the papal army and also the target of Guicciardini's rage—arrived. He gingerly inquired if the lieutenant general was still angry, to which Machiavelli quipped: "No, since the source of his wrath has been removed." The two spent some time together discussing Guicciardini's bad mood, and Rangoni flatly stated that he would prefer to go into exile in Egypt than to serve again under Francesco. Machiavelli rose to Guicciardini's defense and eventually managed to convince everyone that his friend's presence in the field had done more good than harm. Guicciardini had not been wrong to put his trust in Niccolò.

Machiavelli returned to Florence at the beginning of November, but his stay did not last long. At the end of the month he received a commission from the Otto di Pratica to go to Modena and confer with Guicciardini about how to protect Florence in the present circumstances. The Florentine government understood perfectly well that once the truce between the pope and the Imperialists expired, it would be absolutely necessary to pin down the enemy troops in northern Italy, lest they should decide to descend into Tuscany, a possibility that would no doubt have disastrous results. The Otto wanted an exact appraisal of the military situation, and in particular an estimation of what the Venetians, the duke of Ferrara, the Spanish, and everyone else intended to do next. The government showed particular concern for the thousands of German troops, the famous Landsknechts, encamped in the vicinity of Firenzuola d'Adda under their redoubtable commander Georg von Frundsberg.*

---

* According to a story often repeated, the "Lutheran" Frundsberg traveled with a golden noose with which he intended to hang the pope, and a number of ropes of crimson silk to do the same with the cardinals. In reality these "pious" intentions were held by one of his deputies. It should also be remembered that at the time Lutheranism was not perceived by many as a particularly revolutionary phenomenon, but simply another movement poised to reform clerical corruption. In any case, the Italians had little to learn in the field of violence against ecclesiastics; the Florentines, for example, had hanged the archbishop of Pisa at the time of the Pazzi Conspiracy.

The Florentine authorities had good reasons to be concerned, since Venetian intelligence had discovered that Bourbon intended to move south sometime in late December or January with Florence as its objective. The only credible force left to counter the Imperial advance was Giovanni de' Medici's *Bande Nere* (Black Bands), ostensibly in the service of the French. Unfortunately, Medici died on November 30 from a wound received during a skirmish with the Imperial troops as he tried to stop them from moving south. The Landsknecht had managed to cross the river Po a few days before, thanks to the treachery of the marquis of Mantua, officially one of Clement's allies, who was all too happy to let someone else taste the food of war.

Machiavelli wrote to the Otto on December 2, giving a bleak account of the situation. The Germans had moved south and at any moment could join forces with the Spanish coming down from Milan. The duke of Urbino had been doing nothing, and one could not trust the Venetians. Although the league had some 20,000 soldiers in the area, unless they were properly paid and brought together nothing could be accomplished. If peace was to be sought, then it would be better to negotiate with Don Ugo de Moncada, who had recently landed with a sizable army near Porto Santo Stefano in southern Tuscany. In the postscript of the letter, Niccolò noted the death of Giovanni de' Medici, "whose demise has been mourned by all." In another missive written the following day, he informed the government that certain signals made him believe that the duke of Ferrara had decided to throw in his lot with the emperor and that the Germans were moving toward Piacenza. Guicciardini had ridden off in that direction, and so Machiavelli announced his intention to return home.

The gloomy international situation and the inclement weather had sapped his good humor, while the weight of the years and the many efforts had started to take a toll on his health. Sometime before that, to help his digestion, he had started to use pills made from a mixture of aloe, cardamom, saffron, myrrh, betony, pimpernel, and Armenian bole. "They have brought me back to life," he had once written to Guicciardini, adding two dozen tablets to his missive for him to try. "Start taking one after dinner," he said. "Should it cause movement, stop there; if there is no effect, take two, three or five at most. On my part, I have never ingested more than two, and only once a week, or when I feel heaviness in my stomach or head." It would appear, however, that he had started using the pills as a panacea, possibly due to increasing bowel problems made worse by his love of good food. With age and ailments he had also developed a more meditative side of his character, increased by the political problems he loved to examine, but for which he now could see no feasible solution.

It is possible that it was when he was back in Florence, being then the time of Advent, that he composed one of his most controversial works—at least for some people. There is no doubt that the *Esortazione alla Penitenza* (Exhortation to Contrition) is an unusual piece of writing in Machiavelli's canon, its very Christian message producing much head-scratching among scholars—with different conclusions according to individual beliefs or ideology. Giuliano de' Ricci, Niccolò's grandson, informs us that Machiavelli belonged to a number of religious confraternities dedicated to prayer and good works—a normal thing for Florentines, who, due to their innate individualism and dislike for impositions, have never paid much attention to parish life. Machiavelli had been requested by the ruling board of one unspecified confraternity to give an allocution on penance, and Niccolò delivered the goods in a remarkable manner.

The examples he used to illustrate God's mercy concerned Saint Peter's triple denial of Christ and the forgiveness shown to a contrite David, despite his sins of adultery and murder. It may sound strange to hear the derisive author of *The Mandrake* using the words *"Miserere mei Domine"* (God have mercy of me) in one of his writings, yet one should not be too surprised, considering that Florentines can be simultaneously irreverent and reverent, toward the divine as well as the human. However, the last phrase of this pious lecture is revealing of Machiavelli's state of mind at the time, nearly the premonition of impending doom: "Be ashamed and repent of all the evil done, and clearly understand that what the world likes is but a brief dream." Niccolò, in his own way, had always been a dreamer: He had envisioned and theorized the perfect polity, the best military organization, the freedom of Italy's states, and the idea that men could shape their own destinies, despite Fortune's schemes. Now, after years of shattered illusions and disappointments, he had woken up to reality.

The real world was catching up to the theorist, as the Imperial troops in northern Italy waited for the truce between Clement and Charles to expire. The pope had half a mind to renew the treaty, even at the cost of 200,000 ducats, the amount demanded by the Imperial viceroy of Naples, Charles de Lannoy. With typical inconsistency, the news of a papal victory at Frosinone against the Spanish expeditionary force made him change his mind, and he announced that he would not abide by such harsh terms. However, negotiations for the truce's renewal continued, Lannoy wishing to extract as much money as possible from the pontiff, and maybe lull him into a false sense of confidence, while the pope believed time and the elements to be on his side. Many observers maintained that the Imperial forces could not resist much longer in the battle against the weather, hunger, and disease.

At the beginning of February 1527, the Germans were still near Fiorenzuola d'Arda, south of Piacenza, with the Spanish encamped to their west, while to the north stood a polyglot force some 8,000 strong, made up mostly of Italians, many of whom had, until a few months before, militated under the papal banner. Inclement weather had until then stopped them in their tracks, but hardship combined with lack of pay and victuals had created a volatile situation. Despite the truce, the soldiers had been pillaging the countryside without restraint. The duke of Urbino had approached within striking distance of the Imperial forces, but, displaying his usual prudence, had refrained from taking any significant action. He had reasons to be careful, since the duke of Ferrara had thrown in his lot with Charles, and the marquis of Mantua could not be trusted.

Strategically placed across the route linking northern with southern Italy, the Imperial forces could strike in any direction they chose, but most people believed that they eventually would move toward Florence or Rome. On February 3, a deeply worried Otto di Pratica sent Machiavelli to Parma to convince the allied commanders to place their troops so as to obstruct the Imperialists' advance. Niccolò arrived in Piacenza on the 7th, "due to enemy activity," conferring immediately with Guicciardini and the duke of Urbino. The latter agreed about stopping the Imperialists' march, but, typically, had no desire to make the first move. Given della Rovere's obstinacy, in the following weeks Machiavelli could do little more than keep the government informed about the enemies' situation, speculating about their possible movements. Nevertheless, he displayed cautious optimism—at least at the beginning—about possible developments as he examined the Imperialists' predicament:

> What they will do, God only knows, because there is a chance they don't know it themselves: If they did, they would have acted upon it, having already united their forces some time ago. It is believed they can't last long in this situation, providing our own ineptitude does not help them. And all those here who are experts in warfare believe we shall win, provided we don't lose for lack of money or good counsel. But the forces available are such that we could remedy these defects: first by adequate planning, and second, His Holiness must be committed.

But there were too many variables, and most of them unpredictable, in particular the pope's commitment. In truth, Machiavelli was as much in the dark as anyone else even as he tried to give rational answers to a very irrational situation.

The Imperialists were faring badly. Around the end of February they had united their forces and moved south, bypassing Parma before being stopped in San Giovanni in Persiceto, fourteen miles northwest of Bologna, by snow and rain. Starving, penniless, cold, and drenched, on March 16 the troops mutinied, demanding their pay. Frundsberg had a stroke while trying to calm down his Landsknechts, while Bourbon's quarters were ransacked by the rebellious soldiery. The situation only worsened when an envoy from Lannoy arrived with the news that the pope had agreed to a renewal of the truce, at the cost of a mere 60,000 ducats.

The soldiery, spurred on by dreams of plunder, rejected it outright, and Bourbon could only write to Clement that his army would be moving on toward Florence or even Rome—maybe, added the Imperial commander, this could be forestalled if His Holiness could send 150,000 ducats by April 15. The pope felt cheated, suspecting the request to be nothing but a ruse to extort money from him without any sort of guarantee that the bargain would be honored. Clement had correctly perceived that Bourbon could not control his troops; but as much as this thought depressed him, his indecisive nature did not allow him to move to confront the Imperial threat.

The danger became very real when on March 31 Bourbon started his advance south, in the face of token opposition from the league's forces and leaving a trail of destruction in his wake. Machiavelli had initially suggested that the Florentines buy time with money, "for he who has time, has life," but warned the government to prepare for Florence's defense, since it would be useless to try to bribe the enemy: Once Bourbon had his hands on the money, his troops would most likely clamor for more and then have an excuse to attack anyway if the requested cash was not given to them. Guicciardini still believed the Imperialists to be bribable, however, and wrote a note to that effect to his brother Luigi, recently installed as gonfalonier.

Yet, Guicciardini understood that without adequate troops, Florence would be at the enemy's mercy. Francesco Maria della Rovere commanded the only sizable military force available, but until then had shown no inclination to use it to the league's advantage; indeed, concerned with the safety of his own domains he had dispatched several thousand soldiers to protect them. The duke of Urbino has been accused of deliberate inertia, but it should be remembered that—his dislike for the Medici aside—he owed his allegiance firstly to Venice and could not afford to risk his employer's army.

This said, he certainly had every interest in keeping the pope on his toes and trying to squeeze out as much as possible from the situation. Guicciardini understood that some sort of enticement would be necessary to get della Rovere to move. The strategically and nearly impregnable fortress of San Leo had remained in papal hands after the Medici had lost possession of the duchy of Urbino, and Guicciardini had been trying to convince Clement to return it to Francesco Maria. Albeit unwillingly, the pope consented, and della Rovere finally started to move south.

Machiavelli had been observing the unfolding of events with increasing alarm, as attested by the tone of his letters to Francesco Vettori. By the beginning of April he had started to despair that something concrete would be done to stop the Imperialists' advance, dreading ever more that their objective might be undefended Florence. By now his confidence in Clement had disappeared completely; he could only watch with dismay as the pope made one political blunder after another. On April 5, he wrote to Vettori that after Bourbon's rejection of the truce, Guicciardini had suggested three possible options to the pontiff: The first was to continue the war, so as to allay the fears of the French and the Venetians about Rome attempting to negotiate a separate peace; should Clement reject this option, then he should try to pursue peace at any cost "and leave himself to be governed by Fortune"; but should this option also be rejected by the wavering pope, then one possibility remained—"which does not matter, and we should not talk about it"—namely, for Clement to flee Rome. The pope had chosen the second option, putting his trust in Lannoy: a risky decision, according to Niccolò, since the Imperial army, if adequately opposed, "could not conquer an oven."

Maybe Machiavelli had not yet received the news that the pope, after agreeing to the truce with the viceroy, had dismissed most of his remaining troops in order to save money. Machiavelli's gloom only increased ten days later when he told Vettori that the treaty needed to be consolidated by a show of arms, lest ruin should befall Florence. On the 16th he again wrote to his friend about the uncertainty of the situation and the options left for peace and war. Alarm, however, can be detected in the last paragraph of the letter: "I love Messer Francesco Guicciardini and my native city [more than my soul].* And I tell you from sixty years of experience, that never have there been such difficult times, where peace is necessary, and yet war cannot be abandoned, and being in the hands of a prince [Clement VII] who can barely meet the needs of peace alone or war alone." Machiavelli feared what the advancing soldiery could do to his family and property and had written home with instructions to take everything of value he had in the country into Florence or to the nearby fortress of San Casciano.

On the 18th he wrote again to Vettori, begging him, "for the love of God," to convince those in authority to break off all negotiations, since no treaty could be possible at this point: Discussing without concluding would be disastrous, and if anyone should say otherwise he was a "prick." Niccolò doubted that it would be possible to stop the Imperialists from entering Tuscany, or to eject them without a fight; Florence would have to carry the burden of two armies, "the friendly one being more insufferable than the enemy." He longed to be back in Florence, and on April 2 had written to his son Guido to that effect, also announcing to him that he had made a new friend in Cardinal Innocenzo Cybo (Cardinal Salviati's first cousin), "so great that I still marvel about it, and which will

---

* This is the usual rendering, since the original text is mutilated at this point. The only letters that can be detected are a "p" and an "st," which has led Giorgio Inglese and other commentators to speculate that Machiavelli may have used the word "Christ" instead of "soul"—something that Giuliano de' Ricci, bent on restoring Machiavelli's reputation, may have considered expedient to eliminate. Even if Inglese is correct—and to be honest, he says that the "st" can be imagined with "a lot of good will" (*molta buona volontà*), to Florentine ears Machiavelli's reference to the second person of the Holy Trinity does not appear particularly scandalous or unusual. In Florence one hears expressions such as *Ti garba fare il Cristo* ("You like to be Christ," to someone puffed up by his self-importance); *Non c'é Cristi* ("No Christ can change this," about an irreversible situation); and *Battere un Cristo* ("To hit a Christ," that is, to fall down spread-eagled on one's face).

bring you benefit." Like his Uncle Totto, Guido would eventually become a clergyman, and up to the very end Niccolò would try to feather his children's nests by creating a network of powerful connections.

Francesco Guicciardini had other worries. Realizing that no help would come from Rome, he badgered the duke of Urbino to take his army to Florence. Francesco Maria della Rovere did so unwillingly, and only after trying to extort 200,000 ducats from the city as surety that the Florentines would not strike a separate deal with the Imperialists. Guicciardini and Machiavelli arrived in Florence on the 22nd to find a situation of utter turmoil. The Florentines had been roped into an unpopular and costly war, and resentment against the Medici regime had grown by the day. On April 26, in the face of the approaching Imperialists, a revolt broke out, with droves of people rushing to the government square demanding weapons and a regime change. Order was restored only by the timely appearance of the duke of Urbino's troops and the promise of a general amnesty for those involved in the uprising.

Guicciardini fumed at Cardinal Passerini's incompetence for allowing the situation to deteriorate in the first place. In any case, della Rovere had arrived at the eleventh hour, for the Imperialists had entered Florentine territory on April 20; repulsed in their attempt to take the fortress of Pieve S. Stefano, they had continued their march south, two days later arriving in the vicinity of Arezzo and within striking distance of Florence. Lannoy had managed to reach Bourbon's camp and arrived in Florence with the Imperialists' demands: 300,000 ducats to be paid immediately in exchange for their retreat.

Luckily for the Florentines, the presence of Urbino's army and the recent upgrading of their walls made Bourbon reconsider his objectives; thus, after a few desultory attempts against the towns of Anghiari and Borgo Sansepolcro, the Imperial forces took a route southwest toward Siena. There they left their artillery in order to move more rapidly before taking the Cassian road, with only one objective in mind: Rome. Francesco Maria della Rovere followed, but always at a distance, and making little effort to hamper the Imperialists' progress. As a matter of fact, the duke of Urbino's strategy had its logic, since few people believed that such a rag-tag army devoid of artillery could actually manage to take a city like Rome. But the Imperialists were about to confirm Machiavelli's old axiom about Fortune favoring the daring.

Bourbon arrived at the gates of Rome on May 4, asking for a free passage through the city in order to move on to Naples. One of the reasons Francis I had not bothered to send troops, despite milking the pope for funds in every possible way, had to do with his plan to retake southern Italy. No matter what the outcome, Bourbon's campaign could only benefit the king of France: Should the Habsburg army suffer a defeat or disperse, he would have one less force to deal with; should Rome fall, the Imperialists would be too busy enjoying their booty to consider further fighting.

Clement had been abandoned by everyone, for the simple reason that his wavering attitude had only managed to create the deepest mistrust among his allies. To make matters worse, the pope had ignored an old maxim: *Si vis pacem para bellum* (If you desire peace prepare for war). Having declined to raise money in the same way as his predecessors, he had refused to sell cardinalates only to find himself penniless. With no soldiers and less funds, as the Imperialists approached Rome in a panic he hastily raised what troops he could, many being local levies; appealed unsuccessfully to the rich for cash; and sold three cardinal's hats for 40,000 ducats each.

It was a case of too little, too late. Having been refused passage through the city, on the morning of May 6 the Imperialists launched their attack. Bourbon was killed in the first assault, but his soldiers poured over the walls. Clement managed to rush to the safety of Castel Sant'Angelo, while his Swiss guards died to a man fighting a fateful rearguard action. What followed can be only described as utter nightmare, as the now leaderless Imperialists engaged in an orgy of rape, pillage, and murder. Nothing and nobody got spared. Women of every age and condition, including nuns dragged out of their convents and monasteries, were forced to cater to the soldiery's lust; men were tortured to make them reveal hidden treasure or just for the sake of sadistic pleasure. Those who attempted to resist were slain on the spot: Countless bodies lay strewn on the ground, among scattered relics, documents, and chattels.

Guicciardini calculated that about 4,000 people died during the assault and in the first hours after the taking of Rome. Religion and political allegiances mattered little to the adrenaline-maddened troops, Catholic Spaniards and Italians together with German Lutherans sacking churches and the houses of Habsburg followers indiscriminately; what remained fell into the hands of the Colonna peasantry. Indeed, it was said at the time that "the Germans were bad, the Italians worse, the Spaniards the worst of all."

The total booty amounted to a million ducats, excluding ransoms and extortions—even the Colonna palace, in which thousands had taken refuge, was spared, not so much because it was heavily defended, but due instead to those inside agreeing to pay huge sums of protection money. Together with the lucky ones who had managed to get inside Castel Sant'Angelo—more than a few hurled up in wicker baskets—from the ramparts Clement beheld the carnage below, having abandoned all hope of relief. The duke of Urbino—who had delayed his advance in order to force a regime change in Perugia—arrived at the outskirts of Rome a few days later, but, after a half-hearted attempt to liberate the pope, considering that nothing could be done to save the city, prudently decided to retire north.

Machiavelli had gone ahead of the league's forces to select billets for the soldiers and thus did not witness the events that followed in Florence when the news of the sack of Rome arrived in the city on May 11. Cardinal Passerini had the necessary forces to keep the city under control, but he found himself abandoned even by those who had until then been Medici supporters. The hatred for Clement had grown to fever pitch among the Florentines, who were tired of being treated like Rome's subjects and resentful of the 600,000 ducats they had been forced to pay for the pope's war.

On the 16th, a pratica recommended the restoration of the old Republican constitution, allowing the Medici to remain as private citizens. Passerini, however, considered it prudent to leave, together with Ippolito and Alessandro de' Medici, the youngsters' departure speeded up by their kinswoman Clarice Strozzi, who berated them, or at least people believed so at the time, for having turned her paternal house into a "mule's stable"—a barbed reference to their illegitimate birth. Isolated in his fortress, Clement ignored what was happening in his native city, but he knew all too well that without papal support the Medici regime could not last. He somehow managed to inform the Florentines, through Francesco Guicciardini, that he wished them to choose the form of government they preferred "for the city's benefit," an action Machiavelli would ridicule by saying that the pope gave away what belonged to him no more.

Niccolò's whereabouts at that time are unknown, but on May 8 he appears to have been in Viterbo, where, as Guicciardini would report, he had managed to capture an enemy messenger carrying letters for Lannoy. On May 22, Machiavelli wrote to Guicciardini from the port of Civitavecchia about organizing a relief expedition to free the pope, something he had discussed with the Genoese admiral Andrea Doria. Doria had expressed reservations about the plan, although in theory he approved of it. However, the Genoese had his own interest to look after and later would refuse to cede Civitavecchia to the Imperialists unless the pope paid in full the pay arrears Doria claimed were due to him.

By now Machiavelli had learned what had happened in Florence, for Doria commented that had the pontiff taken a similar decision a year earlier—that is, to restore the Republican liberties—he would not have found himself in the present predicament. Niccolò made his way back north together with the apostolic protonotary Piero Carnesecchi (who later would be executed for heresy), and during the voyage Machiavelli was heard to sigh many a time, having heard the city to be free. Giovanni Battista Busini, who provided this piece of information, believed that Machiavelli's despondency had to do with his regret for having served Clement, "for he utterly loved liberty." Maybe. But one is tempted to think that more than anything he lamented the works of Fortune: As had happened with Piero Soderini, his life had been overturned by someone in which he had placed his hopes, Clement VII, but who had proven unequal to Niccolò's trust.

Once back in Florence, he found a hostile climate toward those who had been close to the Medici. Most individuals who had favored the previous regime had either turned their coat in time (including Filippo Strozzi) or were keeping a very low profile. Yet he attempted to find employment with the new government, thinking that his recent experience in the field of fortifications, in particular, would be valuable. The Dieci di Balìa was revived on June 10, and Niccolò hoped to resume his old office of secretary. But despite the support of his friends Zanobi Buondelmonti and Luigi Alamanni, both recently returned from their exile, the Savonarolans who held sway over the city would have nothing of it. Instead, the place went to Francesco Tarugi, who until then had held the position of secretary of the Otto di Pratica.

For Machiavelli it was the final blow, aggravated by the fact that now even the ancients had betrayed him: Nothing like the sack of Rome could be found in antique sources; only cities in decline had suffered similar outrages.* Already ailing, Machiavelli took to his bed on June 20, suffering from fierce pains in the lower stomach. An attempt to cure himself with his famous pills did nothing to improve the situation; in fact, his condition worsened by the hour, and soon it became clear that he had little time to live.

Machiavelli's last moments have been the subject of fierce debates among scholars, divided between those who maintain that he died "godless," to use Paolo Giovio's expression, and their opponents, who wish to believe that he enjoyed the last rites of the Catholic faith. Giovanni Battista Busini, who admittedly disliked Niccolò, said that "he started to take those pills, so he grew weaker while the illness increased. He then recounted his famous dream to Filippo [Strozzi], Francesco del Nero, Iacopo Nardi, and others; thus he died very unhappily, joking all along."

---

* This same sense of bewilderment can also be found in the writings of Luigi Guicciardini and Francesco Vettori on the above-mentioned sack.

The laxative pills, on which Niccolò swore, were probably not the best medicine given the circumstances.

Feeling his life disappear fast, Niccolò called his friends and relatives to his deathbed, and, quite in character, related a recent dream. Supposedly he had seen a group of run-down, gaunt, ragged and poor individuals, whom he was told were the souls of Paradise, since "Blessed are the poor, for theirs is the kingdom of Heaven." He had then beheld another group, this time made up of noble-looking people dressed in regal or official attire, among which he recognized Plato, Plutarch, Terence, and other great writers of antiquity, all intent on discussing statecraft. He was told that these were the damned, because "the knowledge of this world is an enemy to God." Having been asked which group he wished to join, he answered that he preferred to be in Hell with the noble spirits to discuss politics, rather than in Heaven with the ragged.

Shocking as this may appear to some, Machiavelli was once again displaying a typical paradoxically Florentine sense of humor, enlarging on a pun he had already used in *The Mandrake*, and also poking fun at his own habit of donning curial clothes when writing his treatises. Yet, he had shown in his last years a greater respect for religion, while still remaining an inveterate anticlerical, and it is probable that he did call for a confessor as he felt death approaching.* He passed away between the 21st and 22nd of June, and was buried in the family vault at the Church of Santa Croce, spared the hardships that would soon hit his beloved Florence.

---

* We have this information from a letter allegedly written by his son Piero to his relative Francesco Nelli. The authenticity of the missive has been doubted by some scholars—mainly on graphological grounds. Even if written by some other hand than Piero Machiavelli's, the letter rings true because of the final paragraph, where it is said that Niccolò left his family "in utter poverty." It should be added that those who see a contrast between Machiavelli's religious irreverence and his ultimate religiosity ignore how widespread this attitude still is in Florence.

~

NAME-CALLING

To some perhaps my name is odious;
But such as love me, guard me from their tongues,
And let them know that I am Machiavel,
And weigh not men, and therefore not men's words.
Admir'd I am of those that hate me most.
　　　　　　　—CHRISTOPHER MARLOWE,
　　　　PROLOGUE TO *THE JEW OF MALTA*

No eulogy is worthy of such a name
　　　—INSCRIPTION ON MACHIAVELLI'S
　　　　MONUMENT IN THE CHURCH
　　　　OF SANTA CROCE, FLORENCE

The Florentine Republic that Machiavelli witnessed in his last days lasted for three years, the already highly politicized situation being swiftly hijacked by extremists. Moderates who wished to make

some sort of agreement with the emperor were pushed aside by the republican diehards, who held a semi-mythical belief in an alliance with
Francis I and were opposed to any sort of accord with the pope. When
the French suffered a reverse at Naples, and Clement managed to strike
a deal with Charles V, it was only a matter of time before the united forces
of the empire and the papacy would settle scores with Florence.

The city defended itself bravely during the ten-month siege that
lasted from October 1529 to August 1530, thanks to improved fortifications—partly Machiavelli's work—and the revived militia, albeit greatly
stiffened by a substantial number of professional troops. Florence eventually surrendered on terms, after its main field army had been destroyed
at Gavinana (August 3, 1530) and its commander in chief, Malatesta
Baglioni, turned his coat, thus sparing the Florentines from the same
horrors of the sack of Rome. By now most citizens had become disillu-
sioned with the fanaticism of the Republic's leadership that had brought
them nothing but war, famine, pestilence, and crippling taxation. After
the end of the siege, the pro-Medici forces, despite the surrender agreement, brought many of their opponents to justice, while taking steps to
ensure that the Republic would never again return.

Thus, in the two years following the end of the siege, the *balìa* that
was established in its aftermath enacted radical constitutional reforms.
The old executive institutions were abolished, with the exception of the
Twelve Buonomini, and the same happened to the councils of old. A new
council of two hundred people and a Senate of forty-eight individuals,
nominated for life, were established (among the senators figured some of
Niccolò's old friends, such as Francesco Vettori and Francesco Guicciardini). Finally, the *balìa* elected Alessandro de' Medici as chief executive,
with the title of "Duke of the Florentine Republic." Years of constitutional debate, political division, war, and hardship had caused the Florentines to end up with a *governo* far more *stretto* than they could have
ever imagined, and one that would last for another two hundred years.

The accession of Cosimo I de' Medici in 1537 consolidated the Florentine principate even more, after a final outburst of republicanism that
had among its supporters old Mediceans such as Filippo Strozzi. Cosimo

concentrated a lot of the power in his own hands, propping it with Habsburg support and a reformed militia, in the process much reducing the
role of the two new councils. The Medici were there to stay, and over
the years the dukes of Florence—and, later, the grand dukes of Tuscany—managed to develop a system of consensus and control that eventually brought them the respect of their subjects and allowed them to
reign peacefully, to an extent, until the extinction of the princely branch
of the family in 1737.

We may speculate about what Machiavelli may have thought of these
developments, had he lived long enough to see the return of the Medici.
Would he have thrown in his lot with the Republic, or kept a low profile?
His concern about *honore et utile* could lead us to envision a Niccolò writing opinions about the best way to defend Florence and also treatises in
the Republic's favor—after all, a lot of his pro-Medici friends had sided
with the new regime. Yet, his involvement with Clement VII would have
made him suspicious in the eyes of the extreme Republicans, and he may
well have ended up, like Francesco Guicciardini, in voluntary exile at his
country estate, writing, like him, a *Defensoria* and an *Accusatoria*.

During the siege, would he have escaped to the Imperialist headquar-
ters, or remained in the city to share the hardships of war with his fellow
Florentines? Would he have made it to the rank of senator after the constitutional reforms of 1530–1532? Giving even a tentative answer is not
easy, given the contradictory nature of Niccolò Machiavelli. For one
thing, partly thanks to misfortune, he had demonstrated throughout his
life an uncanny ability to back the wrong political horse, and so maybe
his untimely death spared him further humiliations. Indeed, the fact that
he had died in the Medici's good graces would eventually benefit his children—with the exception of Lodovico, fallen in battle during the siege
of Florence.

Bernardo chose to become an administrator, ending up as papal treasurer in Umbria; Cosimo I valued him, and once refused him a profes-
sorship in Pisa only because his application arrived when the academic
year had nearly started. Guido, a bookish individual, led a quiet life as a
clergyman. The fourth son, Piero, showed a rather more adventurous

spirit, after 1530 joining the Imperial forces to fight the Ottomans and from then onward traveling as a soldier all over Europe, ending up numerous times a prisoner of various Muslim foes. In 1556 he entered the service of Duke Cosimo I, rapidly making a career in the Medici navy and ending with the rank of lieutenant general of the galleys. One of the first knights of the military and naval *Order of Saint Stephen, Pope and Martyr*, founded by Cosimo in 1561, Piero Machiavelli had previously provided his master with a blueprint for Florence's future maritime strategy in a report, written around 1559, entitled *Disegno al Duca Cosimo de' Medici per Cacciar di Toscana Francesi e Spagnuoli e per Instituire una Armata Toscana* (A Proposal to Duke Cosimo de' Medici for the Eviction of the French and Spanish from Tuscany and for the Institution of a Tuscan Fleet). Piero had inherited some of his father's ability for hatching schemes, but, unlike him, had a sound grasp of the practical side.

The final tribute to Niccolò's memory, which also helps in no small way to blacken it, came from his friends and relatives, who after his death sponsored the publication of *The Prince*. The printer Antonio Blado issued an edition of the work in 1532, with papal permission, and added a dedicatory letter that he wrote himself to Filippo Strozzi. The letter praised Machiavelli for his political insights in describing the ways that a "new prince" should handle power. Another edition came out later that year in Florence as well.

The printing of *The Prince* made it available to a wide public at a time when many cultivated individuals in Europe understood Italian. However, since most people knew nothing of the circumstances surrounding the book's creation, Machiavelli's lack of any apparent morality in his approach to political reality turned him quickly into a devilish figure, responsible for every possible heinous deed committed by rulers from then onward. The French Calvinist Innocent Gentillet in his *Discours contre Machiavel*, published in 1576, would squarely blame *The Prince* for inspiring the actions of the Valois sovereigns, including the massacre of Protestants in Paris on the night of August 24, 1572: Queen Caterina de' Medici, after all, was a Florentine. From the Catholics Machiavelli received equally rough treatment, with the Jesuits Antonio Possevino (basing himself entirely on Gentillet) and Pedro de Ribadeneyra writing stinging refutations of Machiavelli's work.

By now any deceitful and cunning person or action had acquired the sobriquet of "Machiavellian," the byword of calculated evil. "Am I politic? Am I subtle? Am I a Machiavel?" utters one of the characters in Shakespeare's *The Merry Wives of Windsor*. Ben Jonson in *The Magnetic Lady* describes the arch-schemer Bias as "cut from the quar of Machiavel." In Christopher Marlowe's play *The Jew of Malta*, the prologue is delivered by Machiavelli's fiendish soul, who, among other things, states: "I count religion but a childish toy / And hold there is no sin but ignorance." In the English-speaking world, Niccolò had become "Old Nick"—the Devil himself. A few years ago, Avalon Hill published a board game about Italian Renaissance politics, significantly called *Machiavelli*, in which practically every dirty trick could be performed in order to win; in fact, given the title, the product's main limitation appears to have been the inclusion of game rules.

Machiavelli probably would not have been amused by the negative fame brought to him by *The Prince* (although he certainly would have appreciated the royalty checks associated with it), and, as already mentioned, even during his lifetime he had attempted to deflect some of the criticism by concocting a story about the work really being intended as a manual against tyrants. When someone chided him about the book's views on despots, he waspishly retorted: "I have taught princes how to be tyrants, but also their subjects how to get rid of them." In reality, however, it is more than likely that such a thought never entered Niccolò's mind while he was writing his "pamphlet." Probably Machiavelli, focused as he was on his "long experience in current affairs and the constant lessons of the ancient ones," did not think about the consequences likely to be produced by the absence of any sort of moral message—after all, the Italian rulers had a long tradition of being "Machiavellian" even before Machiavelli.

It is also true that Niccolò appears to have become more traditionally religious in his last years, and at the time of writing *The Prince* still displayed a degree of skepticism in metaphysical matters, influenced in this by his reading of classical authors—Lucretius in particular. He proved to be somewhat successful in spreading the message that his most famous work contained a covert Republican message, a fiction that lasted until his letter to Francesco Vettori of December 10, 1513, became available in print at the end of the eighteenth century. The difficulty in understanding Machiavelli's true motives—indeed, the difficulty in understanding Niccolò himself—stemmed also from the fact that after 1558 all his works were placed by the papacy on the Index Librorum Prohibitorum (Index of Forbidden Books), and reading them without incurring religious censure could be done only with the approval of the ecclesiastical authorities. Niccolò's evil fame had become such that even getting permission to consult the *Florentine Histories* was not an easy task. The attempts by Machiavelli's grandson, Giuliano de' Ricci, to rehabilitate his ancestor proved fruitless, and until the lifting of the ban in the mid–eighteenth century Niccolò's works could be found only in editions printed outside of Catholic Europe. Nevertheless, because of the belief that with *The Prince* he had intended to hammer despots, Machiavelli continued to have his readers and admirers, many of the latter in Protestant countries. Henry, Prince of Wales and son of King James I of England, once told the Florentine ambassador that he considered Machiavelli one of the highest authorities in politics.

The question of whether Niccolò can really be considered a Republican or not remains. Certainly, most of his writings would seem to point to an affirmative answer, but on closer examination one may get the opposite result. While he was secretary of the Ten, Machiavelli proved himself to be more than just a loyal follower of the government that employed him, but his willingness to serve the Medici after their return to power in 1512 shows that his main allegiance lay in the *honore et utile* that the new regime could provide. And yet, Machiavelli—and also Francesco Guicciardini, for that matter—held the belief that a Republican constitution of sorts suited Florence better than a principate, a rather traditional concept of Florentine politics.

History always conditioned Niccolò, and there is no doubt that he fell victim to his readings of ancient texts, developing the conviction that the lessons of the past could be applied verbatim to the present. For example, while his militia project was certainly sound, Machiavelli failed miserably by believing that unrewarded military service would automatically produce civic virtue. It would be up to the Medici rulers after 1530 to expand on Niccolò's project, creating a reliable conscript force recruited with guarantees of fiscal, judicial, and political privileges to those who chose to enlist, and operated via an efficient system of civilian control over the military. Still, the fact that the *Bande*, as the Tuscan militia came to be known, lasted until the second half of the eighteenth century is proof of the basic feasibility of Machiavelli's idea, once stripped of its archaeological burden. It is rather peculiar that Niccolò, who was of the opinion that humans move for selfish reasons, should have had such faith in the mechanical creation of a patriotic sense among unpaid and unmotivated militiamen. But then, as we have seen, Machiavelli was a very contradictory character.

The rediscovery of Machiavelli, starting with the mid-eighteenth century, has revealed his multifaceted personality, yet most of those who have studied Niccolò—detractors and apologists alike—have tried to find in his writings a consistency of thought that could be used to justify a partisan interpretation. On one side, Frederick II of Prussia—whose anti-Machiavellian polemic did much to rekindle interest in Machiavelli himself—considered *The Prince* utter poison, though sometimes, and unfortunately, accurate; on the other, Jean-Jacques Rousseau repeated the old canard about the book being an indictment against despots. (Both, however, praised Niccolò's aversion to the Catholic Church.)

The first attempt to put Machiavelli's complete works into print—and at the same time salvage Niccolò's character—happened in Florence in the years 1782–1783 in an edition sponsored by figures such as Pope Pius VI and the reformist grand duke of Tuscany Peter Leopold of Habsburg-Lothringen. Machiavelli had been turned into a man of the Enlightenment, and the next century would place on him the cloak of an *ante-litteram* positivist and Italian nationalist. Scholars such as Oreste Tommasini and Pasquale Villari, both authors of monumental biographies of Machiavelli, would depict him in such a manner, although we should be grateful to them for digging up and publishing an incredible amount of evidence, even if their commentary was often off the mark (of the two, Tommasini was the better researcher and Villari the better historian), and thus their contextualization of Niccolò's writings had a very anachronistic ring.

This trend continued, despite the fact that the availability, since the second half of the eighteenth century, of Niccolò's *opera omnia*—including private and public correspondence, diplomatic papers, and literary works—should have made clear that any attempt to pin Machiavelli down was like trying to dish out water with a pitchfork. In the twentieth century Niccolò became a precursor of Hegelian-style political systems. Benedetto Croce believed that with *The Prince* Machiavelli had been the first to separate politics from ethics, despite the fact that Niccolò had stated time and time again the need for a civic religion and set of mores—maybe ancient Roman and pagan in their structure, but not for the amoral.

The Italian dictator Benito Mussolini and the Italian Communist leader Antonio Gramsci both built on Croce's notion: the first perceiving Niccolò's idea of ruler as the embodiment of "the State," and the second seeing him as a forerunner of the Communist Party. The fact that *The Prince* could be a manual for totalitarianism triggered the criticism of scholars such as Leo Strauss and some of his followers, and still today the pendulum swings incessantly among political scientists about the correct interpretation of Machiavelli's works. To give the Devil his due, one cannot but admire the Machiavellianism of many such authors, in the sense that they use Niccolò's writings, and especially *The Prince*, to justify an anachronistic vision of the past in the same way that Machiavelli used classical antiquity as a yardstick to measure contemporary events. The pupils have bested their teacher at his own game.

The most important attempt to put Niccolò back in his proper place came from the pen of Roberto Ridolfi. A Florentine, an aristocrat, a descendant of Machiavelli, and a painstaking researcher, he understood better than others the personal and psychological dynamics that had helped to shape Niccolò's life and writings. The main problem was not that he personally liked Machiavelli—he adored him, and therefore set out on a semi-crusade to rehabilitate his name, engaging in polemics with his predecessors (Tommasini being a particular bête noir of his) and his contemporaries as he defended his vision of the "real" Machiavelli, a mission that often caused him to gloss over certain facts he considered detrimental to Niccolò's reputation. Besides, being a man of faith, Ridolfi fought tooth and nail to prove that the Florentine secretary—far from being an atheist—had actually been a good Christian for his whole life, despite his many vices. (Machiavelli's opposition to Savonarola, another of Ridolfi's heroes, was dismissed as the result of a lack of full intellectual maturity.)

The main strength of Ridolfi's work, the uncovering of new evidence aside, lies in his understanding that Machiavelli possessed that peculiar brand of spirit shared by Florentines to this day, Niccolò's grin being not so much an expression of his own but of his native city's cynicism. Now Machiavelli had at last become human, even if Ridolfi still considered him a genius; yet myths die slowly and not without a struggle, and every now and then a new edition of *The Prince* appears with an old and stale commentary. But given the Pavlovian effect of Machiavelli's name, it is only understandable that authors and publishers should wish to make a few pennies off Old Nick's back with the least effort possible.

Despite its fame—which is more telling of us than of Machiavelli—*The Prince* is in no way the foremost of Niccolò's works, that place being reserved instead to his theatrical production. *The Mandrake* and *La Clizia* can also be taken as examples of Machiavelli's evolving ideas and vision of life, which went over the course of many years from a substantially pessimistic to a rather more hopeful concept of mankind. Yet one should not forget that both plays were written with a Florentine audience in mind, and Machiavelli's writings are always eminently Florence-centered.

Indeed, Niccolò could be fiercely, if somewhat parochially, patriotic when aroused, as demonstrated by his work of uncertain date *Discorso o dialogo sulla nostra lingua* (*Discourse or Dialogue on Our Language*), in which, among other matters, he took the thirteenth-century Florentine poet Dante Alighieri to task, in an imaginary conversation, for the mistreatment of his fellow citizens. The dialogue served to reaffirm the primacy of the Florentine language, in particular the "salt" of everyday speech in contrast to the more formal, Tuscan-style speech of literary men. In the same vein, on one occasion he responded tartly to a Venetian's question about the learned Pietro Bembo attempting to teach Tuscan to the Florentines, saying: "I answer you in the same way you would if a Florentine attempted to teach the Venetian language to a Venetian."

His Florentine background and classical reading meant that Machiavelli's unquestionably sharp eye for people and situations often got waylaid by a rather provincial and at the same time abstract vision of reality. In addition, his high opinion of his own talents, united with a rather abrasive manner of delivering his opinions, managed to get him into trouble more than once. After his ousting from office in 1512, the conviction that his knowledge and experience alone would suffice to recommend him to the new regime would bring him to embrace, in turn, a despotic and a *soit-disant* democratic solution to Florence's political problems; in fact, *The Prince* and *The Discourses* were composed for a very specific readership—something one should take into account to explain the inconsistencies present in Machiavelli's thinking. Especially after the return of the Medici, Niccolò appears to have developed a tendency to tailor his thoughts and writings to what people wanted, or what he believed they wanted, to hear, always for the sake of *honore et utile*.

Unfortunately, he did not prove very good at this game, and he managed to return to politics only because of powerful patrons who not only enjoyed his company and witticisms but also appreciated his other talents. More than later writers, they understood and tolerated Machiavelli's weaknesses and flaws, sometimes being shocked or miffed, other times laughing at his escapades, and considering him first and foremost not a political or literary genius, but, more simply, an intelligent, cultivated, hilariously amusing person, and a Florentine to the core.

SOURCE NOTES

For reasons of space I have opted to reduce the reference apparatus to a minimum, including only those citations not clearly identifiable by consulting Machiavelli's works in a chronological order. Niccolò's writings are available in print—indeed, there is no lack of critical editions—and I have relied mostly on published versions of his texts. In some cases, in particular when in doubt or for those documents not specifically related to Machiavelli, I have checked the archival source in person, and in these cases I have provided the appropriate repository indications.

For Machiavelli's political and diplomatic correspondence, the most up-to-date edition is: N. Machiavelli, *Legazioni, Commissarie, Scritti di governo*, 5 vols., J. J. Marchand, D. Fachard, E. Cutinelli-Rèndina, A. Guidi, and M. Melera-Morettini, eds. (Rome: Salerno Editrice, 2002–2009). Since this edition covers, so far, only the years up to 1507, one should also consult: N. Machiavelli, *Legazioni e Commissarie*, 3 vols., S. Bertelli, ed. (Milano: Feltrinelli, 1964). Dated to an extent, but still useful, are vols. 3–6 of: N. Machiavelli, *Le opere*, 6 vols., L. Passerini, P. Fanfani, and L. Milanesi, eds. (Florence: Tipografia Cenniniana, 1873–1877). Somewhat imprecise, but nonetheless handy as a survey of Niccolò's military writings, is: N. Machiavelli, *Scritti inediti di Niccolo' Machiavelli riguardanti la storia e la milizia (1499–1512), tratti dal carteggio officiale da esso tenuto come segretario dei Dieci, ed illustrati da Giuseppe Canestrini* (Florence: Barbera and Bianchi, 1857).

For Machiavelli's literary and political works, see: N. Machiavelli, *Il Principe*, M. Martelli, ed. (Rome: Salerno Editrice, 2006); N. Machiavelli, *De Principatibus*, G. Inglese, ed. (Rome: Istituto Storico Italiano per il Medio Evo, 1994); N. Machiavelli, *Discorsi sopra la prima Deca di Tito Livio*, 2 vols., F. Bausi, ed. (Rome: Salerno Editrice, 2001); N. Machiavelli, *L'arte della guerra. Scritti politici minori*, D. Fachard, G. Masi, and J. J. Marchand, eds. (Rome: Salerno Editrice, 2001); N. Machiavelli, *Arte della guerra e scritti politici minori*, S. Bertelli, ed. (Milan: Feltrinelli, 1961); N. Machiavelli, *Mandragola*, G. Inglese, ed. (Bologna: Il Mulino, 1997); N. Machiavelli, *Clizia*, G. Davico Bonino, ed. (Turin: Einaudi, 1978); N. Machiavelli, *Scritti letterari*, L. Blasucci, ed. (Turin: UTET, 1989).

Machiavelli's personal correspondence can be found in: N. Machiavelli, *Lettere*, F. Gaeta, ed. (Turin: UTET, 1984); N. Machiavelli, *Opere*, vol. 2, C. Vivanti, ed. (Turin: Einaudi, 1999). Niccolò's private letters, and all his other works, are available in a single volume: N. Machiavelli, *Tutte le opere*, M. Martelli, ed. (Florence: Sansoni Editore, 1971). For Machiavelli's correspondence with Francesco Vettori and Francesco Guicciardini, see the excellent: N. Machiavelli, *Lettere a Francesco Vettori e a Francesco Guicciardini*, G. Inglese, ed. (Milan: B.U.R. Rizzoli, 1989). The English edition of Niccolò's personal missives is the solid: N. Machiavelli, *Machiavelli and His Friends: Their Personal Correspondence*, trans. and ed. J. B. Atkinson and D. Sices (Dekalb: Northern Illinois University Press, 1996). I should add, however, that, with a few exceptions, I have preferred to rely on my own translations of Machiavelli's writings and the other texts quoted in this volume. Web versions of Machiavelli's writings, in Italian, can be found at the following sites: www.liberliber.it/biblioteca/m/machiavelli/ (2/25/2010), and http://www.classicitaliani.it/index090.htm (2/25/2010), the latter containing most of the known private correspondence from and to Niccolò.

Machiavelli's personal papers are mostly in the Biblioteca Nazionale of Florence, under the listing *Autografi Palatini, Autografo Machiavelli* (or more simply *Carte Machiavelli*), the *Ginori-Conti* collection, and the file 985 of the *Nuovi Acquisti* series. In the Archivio di Stato of Florence the bulk of Niccolò's official documents is preserved, in particular in the collections *Dieci di Balìa, Signori, Signori Dieci di Balìa Otto di Pratica, Signori e Collegi*, plus a few other documents in the *Carte Strozziane*, first series, and the files 397 and 398 of the *Acquisti e Doni*. A comprehensive listing of the Machiavelli documentation, with the exclusion of some later additions, can be found in: N. Machiavelli, *Opere di Niccolò Machiavelli*, vol. 10: *Bibliografia*, S. Bertelli and P. Innocenti, eds. (Verona: Valdonega, 1979). The bibliography on Machiavelli himself is vast and increasing by the year. For an extensive, if incomplete, list up to the end of the 1980s, one can consult: S. Ruffo Fiore, *Niccolò Machiavelli: An Annotated Bibliography of Modern Criticism and Scholarship* (Santa Barbara, CA: Greenwood Press, 1990). Individual works used as references in this book are cited from time to time in the chapter-by-chapter notes that follow.

Machiavelli's standard biographies, fountains from which everyone—despite criticisms—drinks, are: O. Tommasini, *La vita e gli scritti di Niccolò Machiavelli nella loro relazione col machiavellismo,* 3 vols. (Rome: Loescher, 1883–1911); P. Villari, *Niccolò Machiavelli e i suoi tempi, illustrati con nuovi documenti,* 2nd ed., 3 vols. (Milan: Hoepli, 1894), 3rd ed., 3 vols. (Milan: Hoepli, 1911–1914), and 4th ed., 2 vols. (Milan: Hoepli, 1927); and R. Ridolfi, *Vita di Niccolò Machiavelli,* 7th ed. (Florence: Sansoni, 1978). A more recent treatment of Niccolò's life, incorporating some of the more recent findings, is: M. Viroli, *Il sorriso di Niccolò: storia di Machiavelli* (Rome: GLF editori Laterza, 1998). And one must not forget the oblique biographical approach found in: G. Sasso, *Niccolò Machiavelli,* 2 vols. (Bologna: Il Mulino, 1993).

For a chronological treatment of Florentine political history during Machiavelli's adulthood, see: H. C. Butters, *Governors and Government in Early Sixteenth-Century Florence, 1502–1519* (New York: Oxford University Press, 1985); J. N. Stephens, *The Fall of the Florentine Republic, 1512–1530* (Oxford: Clarendon Press; New York: Oxford University Press, 1983). Still fundamental for understanding the ideological and political milieu of the period is: R.v. Albertini, *Das florentinische Staatsbewusstsein im ubergang von der Republik zum Prinzipat* (Berne: Francke, 1955); in the Italian edition (Turin: Einaudi, 1970), the documents included are rendered in the language of origin. For historical accounts contemporary to Machiavelli, see: B. Buonaccorsi, *Diario de' successi più importanti seguiti in Italia, & particolarmente in Fiorenza dall'anno 1498 in sino all'anno 1512 raccolto da Biagio Buonaccorsi in que' tempi coadiutore in segreteria de magnifici signori dieci della guerra della città di Fiorenza* (Florence: Giunti, 1568); B. Cerretani, *Storia Fiorentina,* G. Berti, ed. (Florence: Olschki, 1994); F. Guicciardini, *Storie fiorentine dal 1378 al 1509,* A. Montevecchi, ed. (Milan: B.U.R. Rizzoli, 1998); F. Guicciardini, *Storia d'Italia,* 3 vols., E. Mazzanti, ed. (Milan: Garzanti, 1988); L. Landucci, *Diario fiorentino dal 1450 al 1516,* I. del Badia, ed. (Florence: Sansoni, 1883); J. Nardi, *Istorie della città di Firenze,* 2. vols., A. Gelli, ed. (Florence: Le Monnier, 1988); F. de' Nerli, *Commentari dei fatti civili occorsi dentro la città di Firenze dal 1215 al 1537,* 2 vols. (Trieste: Coen, 1859); P. Parenti, *Storia fiorentina,* 2 vols., A. Matucci, ed. (Florence: Olschki, 1994); J. Pitti, *Istoria fiorentina,* in ASI, 1, n. 1 (1842); B. Segni, *Storie fiorentine di messer Bernardo Segni, gentiluomo fiorentino, dal 1527 al 1555,* 3 vols. (Livorno: G. Masi, 1830); B. Varchi, *Storia fiorentina,* 3 vols., G. Milanesi, ed. (Florence: Le Monnier, 1858); F. Vettori, *Sommario della Istoria d'Italia, 1511–1527,* in F. Vettori, *Scritti storici e politici,* E. Niccolini, ed. (Bari: Laterza, 1972).

Archival holdings and other works frequently cited in the following notes can be identified by the following abbreviations:

ACRF: Archivio Capponi alle Rovinate, Firenze
ASF: Archivio di Stato di Firenze
ASI: Archivio Storico Italiano
BMLF: Biblioteca Medica Laurenziana, Firenze
BNCF: Biblioteca Nazionale Centrale, Firenze
BRF: Biblioteca Riccardiana, Firenze
CM: Carte Machiavelli
CR: Corrispondenza, Responsive
CS, Ia: Carte Strozziane, prima serie
GSAT: Giornale Storico degli Archivi Toscani
JMH: Journal of Military History
MAP: Mediceo avanti il Principato
MP: Mediceo del Principato
n.: number
p.: page
RSI: Rivista Storica Italiana
XB: Dieci di Balìa

PROLOGUE

The citation by Cristina Campo comes from: "Ville Fiorentine," *Il Giornale d'Italia*, June 16, 1966, p. 3.

The comment by Geoffrey Parker is in: G. Parker, *The Military Revolution: Military Innovation and the Rise of the West, 1500–1800* (Cambridge: Cambridge University Press, 1996), pp. 15–17.

On the matter of Niccolò's supposed activities as a banker in Rome during the 1480s, see: D. Maffei, *Il giovane Machiavelli banchiere con Berto Berti a Roma* (Florence: Giunti, Barbera, 1973), and the debunking of the above in: M. Martelli, *L'altro Niccolò di Bernardo Machiavelli* (Florence: Sansoni, 1975).

1. GRASPING, ENVIOUS, AND PROUD

The citation by Dante Alighieri is in: D. Alighieri, *La Divina Commedia*, Inferno, Canto 15, verses 67–68.

Genealogical and heraldic information on the Machiavelli can be found in: ASF, *Ceramelli-Papiani*, 2864; ASF, *Sebregondi*, 1845; P. Litta, *I Machiavelli di Firenze* (Milano: Bassadonna, 1838); BNCF, *Priorista Ricci, Quartiere di S. Spirito*, vol. 1. The anecdote about Boninsegna Angiolini is from: F. Sacchetti, *Il Trecentonovelle*, E. Faccioli, ed. (Turin: Einaudi, 1970), novella 90.

Piero di Giovanni Capponi's statement is in: ASF, MAP, 28, n. 393 (August 10, 1472). Piero Vespucci's letter is in: ASF, MAP, 88, n. 247 (January 12, 1479 [1480]).

For Bernardo Machiavelli's *ricordi*, see: B. Machiavelli, *Libro di ricordi*, C. Olschki, ed. (Florence: Olschki, 2007); C. Atkinson, *Debts, Dowries, Donkeys: The Diary of Niccolo Machiavelli's Father, Messer Bernardo, in Quattrocento Florence* (Bern: Peter Lang, 2002), which also includes the data on Ser Bernardo's *catasto* declaration. Niccolò di Buoninsegna Machiavelli's 1427 *catasto* entry is in ASF, *Catasto 1427, campioni*, vol. 65, f. 81.

For personal fortunes in Florence, see: R. Goldthwaite, *Private Wealth in Renaissance Florence: A Study of Four Families* (Princeton: Princeton University Press, 1968). The comment about 70 florins providing a dignified lifestyle come from: A. Mainardi, *Motti e facezie del Piovano Arlotto*, G. Folena, ed. (Milan: Ricciardi, 1953), n. 113. For the dialogue between Barlomeo Scala and Bernardo Machiavelli, see: B. Scala, *De legibus et iudiciis dialogus*, L. Borghi, ed., *La Bibliofilia*, 42 (1949), pp. 256–282.

Machiavelli's transcription of Lucretius's *De Rerum Natura* is described in: C. E. Finch, "Machiavelli's Copy of Lucretius," *Classical Journal* 56 (1960), pp. 29–32. The anecdote about canon Niccolò Machiavelli is in: BNCF, *Priorista Ricci, Quartiere di S. Spirito*, vol. 1, f. 160v.

Gino Capponi's aphorisms are in: ACRF, 34, *Notizie genealogiche della famiglia Capponi*, "Questi sono certi Ricordi, fatti da Gino di Neri Capponi, i quali fece in sua vecchiezza, quando stava in casa infermo del male, del quale si morì: e fu nell'anno 1420."

For the evolution of the Florentine power system in the fifteenth century, see: N. Rubinstein, *The Government of Florence Under the Medici (1434 to 1494)*, 2nd ed. (New York: Oxford University Press, 1997); R. Fubini, *Italia quattrocentesca: politica e diplomazia nell'eta` di Lorenzo il Magnifico* (Milan: Franco Angeli, 1994). For the anti-Medici conspiracy of 1466, see: M. A. Ganz, "Perceived Insults and Their Consequences. Acciaioli, Neroni and Medici Relationships in the 1460s," in *Society and Individual in Renaissance Florence*, W. J. Connell, ed. (Berkeley: University of California Press, 2002), pp. 155–172. For the Pazzi conspiracy itself, see: L. Martines, *April Blood: Florence and the Plot Against the Medici* (London: Jonathan Cape, 2003).

2. WORSE THAN A CRIME

Joseph Fouché's remark is in: J. Fouché, *Memoirs de Joseph Fouché, Duc d'Otrante, ministre de la police générale* (Paris: La Rouge, 1824), vol. 1, p. 310.

For Savonarola's life, see: R. Ridolfi, *Vita di Girolamo Savonarola*, 4th ed. (Florence: Sansoni, 1974); L. Martines, *Fire in the City: Savonarola and the Struggle for Renaissance Florence* (New York: Oxford University Press, 2006). For Savonarola's legacy, see: L. Polizzotto, *The Elect Nation: The Savonarolan Movement in Florence, 1494–1545* (New York: Oxford University Press, 1994).

For Machiavelli's comment on the aftermath of the del Nero conspiracy, see: Machiavelli, *Opere*, Passerini, ed., vol. 2, p. 134. For the controversy surrounding the plotters' execution, see: M. Jurdjevic, *Guardians of Republicanism: The Valori Family in the Florentine Renaissance* (New York: Oxford University Press, 2008), pp. 89–92.

For Guicciardini's remarks on Savonarola, see: *Storie Fiorentine*, p. 181. For Gino Capponi's comment, see: ACRF, 34, *Notizie genealogiche della famiglia Capponi*, "Ricordi, fatti da Gino di Neri Capponi." For Francesco Guicciardini's opinion on the clergy, see: F. Guicciardini, *Opere Inedite*, A. Canestrini, ed., vol. 1 (Florence: Barbera e Bianchi, 1857), p. 97. For Giorgio Ginori's ruthlessness, see: A. Poliziano, *Detti piacevoli* (Montepulciano: Il Grifo, 1985), n. 35.

For Luigi Guicciardini's opinion of Machiavelli, see: ASF, CS, Iª, 100, f. 59r (Luigi Guicciardini to Francesco Guicciardini, May 30, 1533). For Leo X's comment, see: E. Albéri, ed., *Relazioni degli ambasciatori veneti al Senato*, vol. 3, ser. 2 (Florence: Società Editrice Fiorentina, 1846), p. 51. For Giovio's opinion of Machiavelli's religious attitudes, see: P. Giovio, *Elogia doctorum virorum ab avorum memoria publicatis ingenii monumentis illustrium* (Basel: 1571), p. 206. For Giuliano de' Ricci's quote, see: BNCF, *Priorista Ricci, Quartiere di S. Spirito*, vol. 1, f. 161r. For contrasting views of Machiavelli's religiosity, see: E. Cutinelli-Rèndina, *Chiesa e religione in Machiavelli* (Pisa: Istituti editoriali e poligrafici internazionali, 1998); S. de Grazia, *Machiavelli in Hell* (New York: Vintage Books, 1994).

3. WARFARE AND STATECRAFT

Quotes by Machiavelli are from: *Il Principe*, chap. 3, 14; chap. 17, 16.

On Caterina Sforza, see: P. D. Pasolini, *Caterina Sforza*, 4 vols. (Rome: ELA, 1968). For military operations at Pisa, see: B. Buonaccorsi, *Impresa fatta dai Signori Fiorentini l'anno 1500 con le genti Francesi, per espugnare la città di Pisa, capitano monsignor di Belmonte*, F. Polidori, ed., ASI 4, n. 2 (1853), pp. 403–421.

"Do what is necessary": *Scritti inediti*, p. 100; "Should not proceed in fairness": quoted in F. Gilbert, *Machiavelli and Guicciardini: Politics and History in Sixteenth-Century Florence* (New York: Norton, 1984), p. 43, n. 65.

For Cesare Borgia, see: S. Bradford, *Cesare Borgia: His Life and Times* (London: Phoenix, 2001). For Machiavelli's criticism about refusing Pisa's surrender, see: *Discorsi*, bk. I, chap. 38.

4. TWO FUNERALS AND A WEDDING

Machiavelli's quote is from *Belfagor*: Machiavelli, *Scritti letterari*, p. 244.

On Primavera Machiavelli's marriage, see: B. Machiavelli, *Libro di ricordi*, passim. On Alessandra Macinghi-Strozzi's remark, see: A. Strozzi, *Lettere di una gentildonna fiorentina ai figliuoli esuli*, C. Guasti, ed. (Florence: Sansoni, 1877), p. 395. On the dowry fund in Florence, see: A. Molho and J. Kirshner, "Il Monte delle Doti a Firenze dalla sua fondazione nel 1425 alla metà del Sedicesimo secolo. Abbozzo di una ricerca," *Ricerche Storiche* 10, n. 1 (1980), pp. 21–48. For Alberti's comment, see: L. B. Alberti, *I libri della famiglia*, R. Romano and A. Tenemti, eds. (Turin: Einaudi, 1969), p. 135. For Kirshner's quote, see: J. Kirshner, "*Li Emergenti Bisogni Matrimoniali* in Renaissance Florence," in Connell, ed., *Society and the Individual*, p. 82. *Society and the Individual*, p. 82. On Niccolò Machiavelli's marriage with Marietta Corsini, and her dowry (nearly eight hundred "broad" florins), see: J. Kirshner, A. Molho, "Niccolò Machiavelli's Marriage," *Rinascimento*, vol. 18 (1978), pp. 293–295.

"An artisan": Strozzi, *Lettere di una gentildonna fiorentina*, pp. 470–471. On Marietta Corsini's family, see: L. Passerini, *Genealogia e storia della famiglia Corsini* (Florence: Cellini, 1858). "The defunct": letter by Barbera Salutati to Lorenzo Ridolfi, July 5, 1544, from Rome, in R. Ridolfi, "Machiavelli e una lettera della Barbera," *Rivista Storica degli Archivi Toscani*, vol. 1 (1929), pp. 202–203. On Machiavelli and the horrendous prostitute, see: ASF, CS, Iᵃ, 139, f. 216rv (Niccolò Machiavelli to Luigi Guicciardini, December 8, 1509).

On tutors corrupting youths, see: BMLF, *Ashburnham*, 1698, "Governo della casa e famiglia, et al generare et nutrire e figluoli," ff. 19v–31v. (I thank Dr. Catherine De Luca for drawing my attention to this document). For homosexuality in Florence in Machiavelli's times, see: M. Rocke, *Forbidden Friendships: Homosexuality and Male Culture in Renaissance Florence* (New York: Oxford University Press, 1996). On Machiavelli's "anal sex" with "La Riccia," see: J. N. Stephens and H. C. Butters, "New Light on Machiavelli," *English Historical Review* 97 (1982), p. 60.

5. BE MY VALENTINE

For Machiavelli on Cesare Borgia's cruelty, see: *Il Principe*, chap. 17.

"The weakness of our contemporaries": *Discorsi*, bk. 3, chap. 27. On Pistoia's civil war, see: W. J. Connell, *La città dei crucci: fazioni e clientele in uno stato repubblicano del 400* (Florence: Nuova Toscana Editrice, 2000). On military conventions for Florence and Cesare Borgia, see: G. Canestrini, ed., *Documenti per servire alla storia della milizia italiana dal secolo XIII al XVI*, ASI 15 (1850), pp. 269–271; "De rebus pistoriensibus," BNCF, CM, 1, n. 11. "According to what

Niccolò Machiavelli has told us": *Opere*, Passerini, ed., vol. 3, p. 345. "To heal a divided city": *Discorsi*, bk. 3, chap. 27. For the Insurrection of Arezzo and Borgia's involvement, see: U. Ademollo, *Vitellozzo Vitelli e la ribellione d'Arezzo del 1502* (Rome: E. Voghera, 1502). "This lord": ASF, XB, CR, 66, n. 369 (Francesco Soderini and Niccolò Machiavelli to the Signoria, June 26, 1502). On Antonio Giacomini-Tebalducci, see: J. Pitti, *Vita di Antonio Giacomini Tebalducci*, in ASI, n.s. 4 (1853), pp. 103–270.

6. HOLLOW WORDS

"The natural hatred": Machiavelli to the Ten, November 4, 1503, from Rome, in Machiavelli, *Opere*, Passerini, ed., vol. 4, p. 327.

For Piero Soderini's election and political attitude, see: R. Pesman Cooper, "L'elezione di Pier Soderini a gonfaloniere a vita. Note storiche," ASI 125 (1967), pp. 145–185; R. Pesman Cooper, "Piero Soderini: Aspiring Prince or Civic Leader?" *Studies in Medieval and Renaissance History*, new ser. 1 (1978), pp. 69–126.

"Devoured piecemeal": Machiavelli, *Opere*, Passerini, ed., vol. 4, p. 94. On Cesare Borgia's "militia," see: J. Larner, "Cesare Borgia, Machiavelli and the Romagnol militia," *Studi Romagnoli* 17 (1966), pp. 253–268. "Your judgement": BNCF, CM, 3, n. 12 (Niccolò Valori to Niccolò Machiavelli, October 11, 1502).

For Machiavelli's description of the Senigallia events, see: *Descrizione del modo tenuto dal Duca Valentino nello ammazzare Vitellozzo Vitelli, Oliverotto da Fermo, il signor Pagolo e il duca di Gravina Orsini.*

"Laws may exist": Alighieri, *Divina Commedia*, Inferno, Canto 16, verse 97.

On Cardinal Francesco Soderini, see: K. J. P. Lowe, *Church and Politics in Renaissance Italy: The Life and Career of Cardinal Francesco Soderini, 1453–1524* (Cambridge: Cambridge University Press, 1993). For the events following the death of Alexander VI, see: L. von Pastor, *The History of the Popes, from the Close of the Middle Ages: Drawn from the Secret Archives of the Vatican and Other Original Sources*, vol. 6 (London: Kegan Paul, 1901), pp. 185–215.

"Tucci is beside himself": BNCF, CM, 3, n. 26 (Biagio Buonaccorsi to Machiavelli, December 4, 1503). "Prudent and descreet": cited in Connell, *La città dei crucci*, p. 235. Machiavelli's gift for rubbing people the wrong way has been analyzed in: J. Najemy, "The Controversy Surrounding Machiavelli's Service to the Republic," in G. Bock, Q. Skinner, and M. Viroli, eds., *Machiavelli and Republicanism* (Cambridge: Cambridge University Press, 1990), pp. 101–117.

7. A MOST BEAUTIFUL THING

Quote by Luca Landucci is from: Landucci, *Diario fiorentino*, p. 273.

"Will not provide": quoted in Villari, *Niccolò Machiavelli*, 3rd ed., p. 468. "Your lordships shall see": Canestrini, *Milizia italiana*, p. 270. Machiavelli's letter to Giacomini of August 20, 1504 is printed in: Villari, *Niccolò Machiavelli*, 3rd ed., pp. 609–610. "These clear and faultless": BNCF, CM, 6, n. 78 (Report by Biagio Buonaccorsi, c. 1506). See also: Buonaccorsi, *Diario de' successi*, pp. 92–93.

"These people like the idea": ASF, XB, CR, 80, f. 8r (Machiavelli to the Ten, January 2, 1506). "In disorder and with little food": ASF, XB, CR, 80, f. 241r (Machiavelli to the Ten, February 5, 1506). "Equipped with breastplates": Landucci, *Diario fiorentino*, p. 273. "Some inflexible and strict official": BNCF, CM, 4, n. 13 (Cardinal Soderini to Gonfalonier Soderini, March 4, 1505). For the question regarding the roots and structure of the Florentine militia, see: G. Sasso, "Machiavelli, Cesare Borgia, Don Micheletto e la questione della milizia," in G. Sasso, *Machiavelli e gli antichi e altri saggi*, vol. 2 (Milan: Ricciardi, 1988), pp. 57–117; R. Pesman Cooper, "Machiavelli, Francesco Soderini and Don Michelotto," *Nuova rivista storica* 66 (1982), pp. 342–357.

"I shall ignore": BNCF, CM, 1, n. 78 (Machiavelli's report on Florence's militia, 1506). "And in any case": BNCF, CM, 1, n. 63 (Machiavelli's report on the handling of the Florentine militia, 1506). "The soldiers' behavior or some commander's prowess": quoted in P. Giovio, *Le Vite di dicenove huomini illustri* (Venice: Giovan Maria Bonelli, 1561), p. 293v.

8. THE ARMED PROPHET

Quote by Machiavelli: *Il Principe*, chap. 6, 6.

"An action worthy of eternal fame": *Discorsi*, bk. I, chap. 27.

"Under the guise of invented names": BNCF, *Priorista Ricci, Quartiere di S. Spirito*, vol. 1, f. 161r.

Francesco Vettori's mission to the Imperial court is examined in detail in: R. Devonshire Jones, *Francesco Vettori: Florentine Citizen and Medici Servant* (London: Athlone Press, 1972), pp. 17–33.

The Strozzi-Medici marriage is treated in detail in: M. M. Bullard, *Filippo Strozzi and the Medici: Favor and Finance in Sixteenth-Century Florence and Rome* (Cambridge: Cambridge University Press, 1980), pp. 45–60. For Machiavelli's involvement, see: L. Strozzi, *Le vite degli uomini illustri di casa Strozzi* (Florence: Landi, 1892), pp. 96–97.

9. COUNCIL AND CONCILIATION

For Machiavelli's quote, see: Machiavelli, *Opere*, Passerini, ed., vol. 6, p. 57.

For the League of Cambrai, see: A. Pinetti, *Dalla Lega di Cambrai alla pace di Noyon (1508–1516). Cronistoria martinenghese da documenti inediti* (Bergamo:

Istituto Arti Grafiche, 1916); E. Musatti, *La lega di Cambrai e la difesa di Padova* (Padova: Gallina, 1911).

For Machiavelli's letter to Alamanno Salviati, see: M. Luzzati and M. Sbrilli, "Massimiliano d'Asburgo e la politica di Firenze in una lettera inedita di Niccolò Machiavelli ad Alamanno Salviati (28 Settembre 1509)," *Annali della Scuola Normale Superiore di Pisa*, Classe di Lettere e Filosofia, serie 3, vol. 16, n. 3 (1986), pp. 825–854. The original text is available online at: http://download.sns.it/normalenews/archiviomachiavelli.pdf (2/25/2010).

10. THE NIGHT PIER SODERINI DIED

For Machiavelli's doggerel to Soderini, see: BNCF, *Magliabechiano*, 7, 271, f. 115r.

On Prinzivalle della Stufa's conspiracy, see: ASF, *Otto di Guardia e Balia, Repubblica*, 148, ff. 266v–267r, 272rv; Cerretani, *Storia fiorentina*, pp. 309–402.

For the "Gallican" council and its consequences, see: K. M. Setton, *The Papacy and the Levant, 1204–1571*, vol. 3, *The Sixteenth Century* (Philadelphia: American Philosophical Society, 1984), pp. 110–115.

"For passionate reasons": Guicciardini, *Opere inedite*, vol. 6, p. 93 (Francesco Guicciardini to Luigi Guicciardini, August 22, 1512).

"Very dark times ahead": Villari, *Niccolò Machiavelli*, 3rd ed., p. 166.

For the sack of Prato and the events preceding it, see: C. Guasti, *Il sacco di Prato e il ritorno dei Medici a Firenze nel 1512*, 2 vols. (Bologna: Romagnoli, 1880), plus the three contemporary narratives of the sack published in ASI 1, n. 1 (1842). Guasti's book contains Baldassarre Carducci's and Pierfrancesco Tosinghi's correspondence on the matter.

"Thus one can say for certain": Vettori, *Sommario*, f. 10v.

11. SATAN'S PROGENY

Reginald Pole's comment on Machiavelli is from: R. Pole, *Apologia ad Carolum Quintum*, trans N. Webb, in *Cambridge Translations of Renaissance Philosophical Texts*, vol. 2, *Political Philosophy*, J. Kraye, ed. (Cambridge: Cambridge University Press, 1997), p. 275.

For the Boscoli-Capponi plot, see: L. della Robbia, *Recitazione del caso di Pietro Paolo Boscoli e di Agostino Capponi (1513), scritta da Luca della Robbia*, in ASI 1, n. 1 (1842), pp. 283–309.

"In wars than the city": Stephens and Butters, *New Light on Machiavelli*, p. 67.

For Machiavelli's correspondence with Francesco Vettori between 1513 and 1515, see: J. Najemy, *Between Friends: Discourses of Power and Desire in the*

Machiavelli-Vettori Letters of 1513–1515 (Princeton: Princeton University Press, 1993).

For Sanudo's comment on Julius II's death, see: M. Sanudo, *I Diari di Marino Sanuto*, 58 vols., R. Furin, F. Stefani, N. Barozzi, and G. Berchet, eds. (Venice: Visentini, 1879–1903), vol. 15 (1887), p. 561.

"Behave with a thousand cautions": Vettori, *Sommario*, f. 15r. For Leo X's advice to Lorenzo de' Medici, see: *Instructione al Magnifico Lorenzo*, T. Gar, ed., in ASI, app. 1 (1842–1843), pp. 300–305.

On Machiavelli allegedly being part of the Medici circle before 1494, see: M. Martelli, "Preistoria (medicea) di Machiavelli," *Studi di filologia italiana* 29 (1971), pp. 377–405. On Machiavelli's relationship with Biagio Buonaccorsi, see: G. Sasso, "Biagio Buonaccorsi e Niccolò Machiavelli," *La Cultura* 18 (1980), pp. 195–222.

"One should keep them active": ASF, CS, Iª, 136, f. 221r (Francesco Vettori to Paolo Vettori, February 17, 1513).

For the English translation of *The Thrushes*, see: N. Machiavelli, *Lust and Liberty: The Poems of Machiavelli*, trans. J. Tusiani (New York: Obolensky, 1963), p. 46.

"Should Lorenzo try to force me": Tommasini, *La vita e gli scritti*, II, part 2, pp. 977–978.

For the *Ghiribizzi d'Ordinanza*, see: J. J. Marchand, "I *Ghiribizzi d'ordinanza* del Machiavelli," *Bibliofilia* 73 (1971), pp. 135–150.

Cardinal Giulio de' Medici's letter to Pietro Ardinghelli appears in: C. Guasti, *I manoscritti Torrigiani donati al R. Archivio di Stato di Firenze: descrizione e saggio* (Florence: Cellini, 1878), p. 67.

For Riccardo Riccardi's anecdote about Lorenzo de' Medici snubbing *The Prince*, see: BRF, MS 785, *Zibaldone di Riccardo Riccardi*, f. 56r.; trans. in N. Machiavelli, *The Prince, with Related Documents*, W. J. Connell, ed. and trans. (Boston: Bedford/St. Martin's, 2005), p. 142. Professor Connell's edition of Machiavelli's work is possibly the best available in English—or any language— to date.

For Biagio Buonaccorsi's information on *The Prince*, see: Machiavelli, *De Principatibus*, p. 47. For Niccolò Guicciardini's letter to his father, Luigi, see: Stephens and Butters, *New Light*, pp. 68–69. The translation of Reginald Pole's testimony on Machiavelli's intentions regarding *The Prince* can be found in: Machiavelli, *The Prince, with Related Documents*, p. 165.

For Giovanni Battista Busini's damning criticism of Machiavelli, see: G. B. Busini, *Lettere di Giovanbattista Busini a Benedetto Varchi sopra l'assedio di Firenze*, G. Milanesi, ed. (Florence: Le Monnier, 1860), p. 85.

Machiavelli's involvement in Agostino Nifo's rewriting of *The Prince* is argued plausibly in: S. Bertelli, "Machiavelli riproposto in tutte le sue opere," ASI 157 (1999), pp. 789–800.

12. THE BYSTANDER'S GRIN

"And the only hope for a reward": Machiavelli, *La Mandragola*, Prologue, verses 57–59.

For Lorenzo de' Medici's military force, see: ASF, MAP, vol. 137, n. 1022 (1515); n. 1042 (no date, but 1515).

For Leo X's triumphant entry into Florence, see: I. Ciseri, *L'ingresso trionfale di Leone X in Firenze nel 1515* (Florence: Olschki, 1990).

For the Rucellai Garden group, see: F. Gilbert, "Bernardo Rucellai and the Orti Oricellari: A Study on the Origin of Modern Political Thought," *Journal of the Warburg and Courtauld Institutes* 12 (1949), pp. 101–131; C. Dionisotti, "Machiavellerie (V): la testimonianza del Brucioli," RSI 91 (1979), pp. 26–51; L. Passerini, *Degli Orti Oricellari, memorie storiche* (Florence: Cellini, 1854).

On Francesco Guicciardini's criticism of the *Discourses*, see: F. Guicciardini, *Considerazioni intorno ai discorsi del Machiavelli sopra la prima Deca di Tito Livio*, in Guicciardini, *Opere inedite*, vol. 1, pp. 3–79.

"The body sins, not the mind": T. Livius, *Ab Urbe condita*, bk. I, chap. 58.

13. A HISTORY OF LIES

For Machiavelli quote, see: Machiavelli's letter to Guicciardini, May 17, 1521.

"I am pleased to know": Filippo Strozzi to Lorenzo Strozzi, March 19, 1519 [1520], in Tommasini, *La vita e gli scritti*, vol. 2, part 2, p. 1081.

For Alessandro de' Pazzi's rejoinder to Machiavelli's project for constitutional reform, see: "Discorso di Alessandro de' Pazzi al Cardinale Giulio de' Medici— anno 1522," ASI 1, n. 1 (1842), pp. 420–432, esp. p. 429. There is some evidence that in 1522 Cardinal de' Medici intended to implement at least part of Machiavelli's scheme, as stated in: J. Pitti, *Apologia de' Cappucci*, in ASI 4, n. 2 (1853), p. 326. The supposed draft of a decree, in Machiavelli's handwriting, exists in: BNCF, CM, 1, n. 79.

For Bandello's anecdote about Machiavelli making a royal mess of Giovanni de' Medici's company, see: M. Bandello, *Tutte le opere*, F. Flora, ed. (Milan: Mondadori, 1966), p. 464. For the establishment of a Florentine military tradition in the Renaissance, see: N. Capponi, "I ceti dirigenti fiorentini e l'arte della Guerra (1494–1537)," in *I ceti dirigenti in Firenze dal gonfalonierato di giustizia*

a vita all'avvento del ducato: atti del VII Convegno, Firenze 19–20 settembre 1997,
E. Insabato, ed. (Lecce: Conte, 1999), pp. 203–212. For attempts to make sense
of Machiavelli's military thinking, see: B. Cassidy, "Machiavelli and the Ideology
of the Offensive: Gunpowder Weapons in *The Art of War*," JMH 67, n. 2 (2003),
pp. 381–404; M. L. Colish, "Machiavelli's Art of War: A Reconsideration," *Renaissance Quarterly*, 51, 4, (1998), pp. 1151–1168; T. R. W. Kubik, "Is Machiavelli's Canon Spiked? Practical Reading in Military History," JMH 61, n. 1
(1997), pp. 7–30; T. J. Lukes, "Marshalling Machiavelli: Reassessing the Military
Reflections," *Journal of Politics* 66, n. 4 (2004), pp. 1089–1108.

For Scipione Ammirato's opinion of Machiavelli as a historian, see: S. Ammirato, *Istorie Fiorentine*, vol. 5, F. Ranalli, ed. (Florence: Batelli, 1848), p.
169.

For Donato Giannotti's testimony on Machiavelli's historical method, see:
D. Giannotti, "Lettere inedite di Donato Giannotti," L. A. Ferrai, ed., *Atti del R.
Istituto Veneto di Scienze, Lettere ed Arti*, ser. 6, n. 3 (1884–1885), 1570–1571
(Donato Giannotti to Marcantonio Micheli, June 30, 1533).

14. FORTUNE'S FICKLENESS

For Francesco Gucciardini's aphorism, see: Guicciardini, *Opere Inedite*, vol.
1, pp. 207–208.

For the 1522 conspiracy, see: C. Guasti, "Documenti della congiura fatta
contro il cardinale Giulio de' Medici nel 1522," GSAT 3 (1859), pp. 120–150,
185–213, 239–267. For Jacopo Nardi on Machiavelli's involvement, see: Nardi,
Istorie, vol. 2, p. 72. For Filippo de' Nerli's comment, see: Nerli, *Commentarii*,
vol. 2, p. 12. Jacopo Pitti would remark that the *Discourses* were "the voices of
the Rucellai Gardens' chamber music, and he [Machiavelli] the trumpet." See
Pitti, *Apologia de' Cappucci*, p. 294.

"I believe far better": ASF, CS, I[a], 136, c. 236rv (Francesco Vettori to
Francesco del Nero, February 5, 1524). Filippo de' Nerli's letter to Francesco
del Nero is published in Villari, *Niccolò Machiavelli*, 3rd ed., pp. 433–434.

15. LOST OPPORTUNITIES

"You know how many opportunities": Niccolò Machiavelli to Francesco
Guicciardini, May 17, 1526.

For the events concerning the sack of Rome, see: J. Hook, *The Sack of Rome*
(New York: Palgrave Macmillan, 2004); A. Chastel, *Le sac de Rome, 1527* (Paris:
Gallimard, 1984); C. Milanesi, ed., *Il sacco di Roma del 1527. Narrazioni di contemporanei* (Florence: Barbera, 1867). For the intellectual crisis caused by the

Sack of Rome, see: K. Gouwens, *Remembering the Renaissance: Humanist Narratives of the Sack of Rome* (Leiden: Brill, 1998).

"He started to take those pills": Busini, *Lettere di Giovanbattista Busini*, p. 85.

Machiavelli's dream was first recorded in: E. Binet, *Du salut d'Origène* (Paris: Sebastien Cramoisy, 1629).

The controversial letter by Piero Machiavelli to Francesco Nelli, concerning Niccolò's death, is in: BNCF, CM, 1, n. 84.

EPILOGUE: NAME-CALLING

"To some perhaps my name is odious": C. Marlowe, *The Jew of Malta*: Prologue, verses 5–9.

For Cosimo I de' Medici on Bernardo Machiavelli, see: ASF, MP, 6, f. 263r (Cosimo I de' Medici to Alessandro del Caccia, September 30, 1545).

For Piero Machiavelli's report, see: G. Lesca, "Piero di Niccolò Machiavelli. Gloria d'una marineria italiana," *La Rinascita* 4, n. 20 (1941), pp. 583–602, esp. pp. 586–596.

For the various interpretations of Machiavelli up to the twentieth century, see: Machiavelli, *The Prince, with Related Documents*, pp. 22–31, 166–189. "Am I politic": W. Shakespeare, *The Merry Wives of Windsor*, Act III, scene 1. "Cut from the quar": B. Jonson, *The Magnetic Lady*, Act I, scene 7.

"I have taught princes how to be tyrants": "Vita di Niccolò Machiavelli," in N. Machiavelli, *Le Opere di Niccolò Machiavelli*, vol. 1 (Florence: Cambiagi, 1782), p. xiii.

For the opinion of Henry, Prince of Wales, on Machiavelli, see: ASF, MP, 78, non-n. f. (Ottaviano Lotti to Belisario Vinta, July 13, 1611).

For a discussion of Machiavelli's republicanism, see: H. C. Butters, "Political Allegiances and Political Structures in the Writings of Niccolò Machiavelli and Francesco Guicciardini," in C. Shaw, ed., *Italy and the European Powers: The Impact of War, 1500–1530* (Leiden: Brill, 2006) pp. 91–106. About Machiavelli writing for a select audience, see: E. L. King, *Rolling a stone for the Medici: Machiavelli's pedagogical service to the Medici family*, Ph.D., dissertation, University of California, Berkeley, 2005.

"I answer you in the same way you would": "Vita di Niccolò Machiavelli," pp. xiii–xiv.

INDEX

NOTE

The case—cited in the preface—of the scholar mixing up Niccolò Machiavelli with his cousin and namesake, underscores a very real problem when compiling an index related to Renaissance Florence. At one time during our Niccolò Machiavelli's life they were at least four members of his family carrying his same name, and two had fathers called Bernardo. Florentines most commonly employed the patronymic, even going back a few generations, to distinguish one namesake from an other, but would also employ personal nicknames (eg. Niccolò di Giovanni Machiavelli known as *il Chiurli*—the Curlew), ones connected to some feature typical of a certain lineage (eg. Capponi *di banco*—of the bank), or related to geographical provenance (e.g., Ricasoli "della Trappola"—from the feudal holding in the upper Valdarno connected with a particular branch of that family). For the sake of clarity, when necessary I have followed the above conventions.

Because of the Florentine custom of married women never losing their maiden names (for example, one may find in documents entries of this tone: "Lucrezia di Lorenzo di Piero de' Medici, wife [*donna*] of Jacopo di Giovanni Salviati"), I have opted to list all female characters under their original family (for instance: Corsini, Marietta and not Machiavelli, Marietta).

Sovereigns invariably come under their family name, followed by their title: Valois, Charles VIII of, King of France. Ferdinand II of Aragon figures under Trastámara; as in the text, I have listed Spain as a country, although, strictly speaking, in reality it was a union of separate polities under a single ruler. I have also tried to keep all names in the language of origin, except in those cases where an accepted English usage exists.